tear here

Top Ten Secrets to Managing Your Money in the '90s

1. **Knowing how your credit applications are scored will help you get credit.** This is one of the biggest secrets of the personal finance world. You will learn in this book the types of credit applicants who make the grade on the basis of certain criteria—and how you can make the grade, too.

2. **Fatten your retirement nest egg by investing your money in a tax-deferred account.** By sheltering your investments (and hopefully profits!) from Uncle Sam until you retire, you can earn more in a tax-deferred account than a taxable account. You have a number of options available to you that you'll learn about in this book.

3. **Don't get tricked by low-ball interest rates advertised by financial institutions.** When you are shopping for a loan—whether a home equity loan, auto loan, or mortgage loan—don't be dazzled by gimmick rates and freebies. You must consider the total cost of the loan, based on how much you borrow, plus the up-front fees and closing costs, where applicable.

4. **Treat yourself like a bill, and pay yourself first.** Write yourself out a check or have an amount electronically withdrawn from your bank account into an investment (you'll learn where in this book). It's a great way to build your wealth.

5. **Pay your insurance premiums annually.** It sounds like a simple strategy, but most folks don't do this. If you were to pay your car insurance or homeowner's insurance on an annual basis, you could save up to 20 percent more than if you were to pay monthly or even semi-annual premiums.

6. **When you buy a new car, avoid dealer financing.** Want to save 1 to 2 percent on your auto loan right off the bat? Avoid dealer financing altogether. Forget an independent finance company, too, where the rates are even higher. Go to a bank, thrift, or credit union, obtain a pre-approved loan for the amount you plan to finance—and save money!

7. **Dollar-cost average your way to wealth.** Dollar-cost averaging is simply investing a fixed amount of money on a regular basis into an investment, such as a mutual fund or dividend reinvestment program. By investing with this self-disciplined financial strategy, you can slowly reach your long-term financial goals.

8. **Home equity loans can be dangerous if you're not careful.** Taking out a home equity loan or home equity line of credit can explode in your face if you're not careful. The bottom line? If you don't make your payments, they could take your most valuable asset—your home!

9. **Shop around for a bank account that doesn't nickel-and-dime you to the poor house.** It's no secret that banks and thrifts are slapping fees on everything from talking to a teller on the phone to making a transaction at a rival ATM machine. But not *all* banks and thrifts do so, and others have fees that are much lower. So shop around and save money!

10. **Do your homework.** It's amazing how many people spend so much time researching a potential vacation hot-spot, yet they won't do their homework for any of their personal finance decisions. The steps in this book will help you along your way.

alpha
books

The Money Questions That America Asks Most

Answers to the most commonly asked questions about personal finance: bank CDs, stocks, bonds, mutual funds, credit cards, college planning, retirement, insurance, mortgages... you name it!

Everyone has his or her own personal money problem. While you're reading all the valuable information and money tips in this book, you'll probably say to yourself, "I have a *very special* personal financial question I'd like an answer to." Chances are that the authors, Robert K. Heady and his daughter Christy Heady, have the answer. They write a nationally syndicated weekly newspaper column titled "Money Answers," in which they answer thousands of reader questions.

To help you strengthen your financial position even more, the authors have compiled the most-frequently asked questions they've come across from real people just like yourself. The answers are yours FREE OF CHARGE—without obligation—just for being a reader of *The Complete Idiot's Guide to Managing Your Money*.

These are some of the typical questions you'll see answered in your free Money Answers report:

"I've just been turned down for a loan. Are credit inquiries a negative factor on my credit report?"

"My husband, 72, is on a pension and gets Social Security. He had an accident a few months ago and can't get around—and the huge medical bills aren't all covered by Medicare. Our mortgage is paid, thank goodness. Any advice?"

"I've got $20,000 in cash. Should I split my investments between bank CDs and mutual funds, or put all my money in a federally-insured account? Which funds are safest?"

"I've got lots of debts and can't seem to get out from under them. I'm thinking of taking out a home equity line of credit and consolidating my debts. Is this a good move?"

"I have a Treasury bond that's down almost 10 percent in value. Should I sell it and put the money back into my bank savings account?"

"My kids are going to college in a few years. My wife's working, but we need help planning for our children's tuition bill. What can we do?"

"I got a call from our insurance agent about switching life insurance policies because we're getting older. Is this a wise thing to do?"

"A friend who's a stockbroker advised me to invest in a load growth stock mutual fund. I've never invested in a mutual fund before. I have $5,000 to invest. Should I do it?"

"My parents don't have a will, a trust, or any type of estate plan. What could happen if they don't do anything?"

"We found the new house we like, and we've been sitting on the fence waiting for mortgage rates to bottom out before we lock in. Any tips?"

Here's how to get your free Money Answers to the most commonly asked questions:

1. From the following, select any **ONE** money category you think you need help on the most, and note this on a piece of paper.

   _____Bank savings and investing

   _____Debt rebuilding

   _____Auto loans

   _____Retirement planning

   _____Insurance

   _____Estate planning

   _____Credit cards

   _____Mortgages and refinancing

   _____Home equity loans and lines of credit

   _____Saving for college

   _____Stocks, bonds, mutual funds (investments)

   _____Senior money strategies

2. On the same piece of paper, jot down your most important money question that comes to mind.

3. Mail that, along with a *stamped, self-addressed envelope* to:

   Money Answers
   P.O. Box 14875
   North Palm Beach, FL 33408

4. Your copy of the most frequently asked money questions on the category you selected (with the answers) will be mailed to you in the stamped, addressed envelope you provided. Allow three weeks for delivery.

   P.S. In your note, feel free to comment on any aspect of *The Complete Idiot's Guide to Managing Your Money*. This is *your* book, and we want to help your pocketbook in every way we can—every day of the year!

The COMPLETE

IDIOT'S
GUIDE TO
Managing Your Money

by Christy Heady and Robert Heady

A Division of Macmillan Computer Publishing
A Prentice Hall Macmillan Company
201 W. 103rd Street, Indianapolis, IN 46290 USA

This book is dedicated to Gretchen, our beloved mother and grandmother, who devotedly taught the children of this world and ensured her place in heaven by always putting the other person first.

©1995 Alpha Books

International Standard Book Number: 1-56761-530-9
Library of Congress Catalog Card Number: 93-56761-168-0

98   8

Interpretation of the printing code: the rightmost double-digit number is the year of the book's first printing; the rightmost single-digit number is the number of the book's printing. For example, a printing code of 95-1 shows that this copy of the book was printed during the first printing of the book in 1995.

This publication contains the opinions and ideas of its authors and is designed to provide useful advice in regard to the subject matter covered. The authors and publisher are not engaged in rendering legal, accounting, or other professional services in this publication. Laws vary from state to state, as do the facts and circumstances of various investment opportunities, and this publication is not intended to provide a basis for action in particular circumstances without consideration by a competent professional.

The authors and publisher expressly disclaim any responsibility for any liability, loss, or risk, personal or otherwise, which is incurred as a consequence, directly or indirectly, of the use and application of any of the contents of this book.

Printed in the United States of America

Publisher
Marie Butler-Knight

Managing Editor
Elizabeth Keaffaber

Acquisitions Manager
Tom Godfrey

Development Editor
Heather Stith

Production Editor
Kelly Oliver

Manuscript Editor
Barry Childs-Helton

Imprint Manager
Kelly D. Dobbs

Designer
Barbara Kordesh

Cover Designer
Karen Ruggles

Illustrator
Judd Winick

Indexer
Brad Herriman

Production Team
*Gary Adair, Angela Calvert, Brad Chin, Kim Cofer,
Lisa Daugherty, Jennifer Eberhardt, David Garratt, Mike Henry,
Joe Millay, Erika Millen, Beth Rago, Karen Walsh, Robert Wolf*

*Special thanks to Alan Lavine and Gail Liberman
for ensuring the accuracy of this book.*

iii

Contents at a Glance

Contents

Introduction

No matter who you are—an ordinary family that's head-over-heels in debt, a senior citizen confused by investment choices, or a college freshman starting to build your credit—there's something valuable here for you. You need practical, down-to-earth help written in plain English... no "blue sky theories"—even that's a confusing subject!

So we're putting the language of money into basic, everyday street language instead of the commonly seen financial mumbo-jumbo that only an accountant can figure out. We want *you* to understand it and to make heads or tails of your personal financial situation.

This is a book written from the trenches, not from an ivory tower. We don't live there, and neither do you. The world of personal finance has become too darn complicated for the average Joe and Jane to understand. Meanwhile, the glut of financial information keeps growing faster than a barrel full of sea monkeys.

So the two of us, father and daughter, are doing this for *you*. We have been inside banks and brokerage firms, the mortgage companies, car dealerships, and the credit bureaus. We've answered thousands of questions from consumers who desperately needed help. We'll show you, chapter by chapter, the most important basics you should know. We'll arm you with tips that will immediately strengthen your personal money situation.

Sure, the cards are stacked against you because of the complex way the money jungle works. But by learning the inside tricks that you'll never read in a newspaper or magazine article (or hear in a 20-second sound bite on TV), you're going to come out dollars ahead. And what else? We're going to take the "I" out of "idiot" for you by telling it like it is. Just the bare facts, and some tips and tricks to help you along your way.

The book will help you:

➤ Avoid costly mistakes and save a bundle.

➤ Earn more when you invest.

➤ Save more when you borrow.

➤ Cut through the muck before you get trapped in the wrong deal.

➤ Rebuild your credit if it's been injured.

But most importantly, this book will help you *relax* with better financial peace of mind.

If you are looking for a no-nonsense book that will finally help you manage your hard-earned cash, you've come to the right place. Here's how it works.

Part 1, "You and Your Money," establishes some basic information about getting started in managing your money. This section will help you learn how to make that first big decision—getting started! Plus, you'll learn secrets about getting out of debt—and how to stay out. You'll also find secrets to cutting costs on everything you buy—from groceries to airline tickets to long-distance telephone service. Chapter 2 tells you how to make effective personal financial planning decisions by learning what to read, what to watch, and who to believe.

Part 2, "Banking Fundamentals," is a section that will surprise many of you with its revealing Chapter 5, "Ten Money-Making Secrets Your Friendly Banker Won't Tell You." The entire section is devoted to how banks make tons of money from your bank accounts, whether you have $25 or $2,500 sitting in them. But it doesn't stop there. You'll learn how to stop being nickeled-and-dimed to death with bank fees, find out the secrets of CD shopping (and who pays the top rate), and how to spot the key warning signals when it's time to move your account.

Part 3, "Interest Rates: How to Ride the Roller Coaster," gives you the easiest crash course in interest-rate math you'll ever find. Those interest-rate numbers are confusing, so this section breaks the topsy-turvy world of interest rates into a language *everyone* can understand. Plus, once you learn how interest-rate cycles work, you'll be able to make better, educated decisions in your personal financial planning and investments.

Part 4, "Credit and Loans—Getting Money When You Need It," is for everyone who has ever tried to get credit (and didn't), or attempted to cut credit card costs but didn't know how. Additionally, you'll find secrets to car shopping and mortgage shopping, and the biggest tip of all in the credit world: how credit agencies really "score" your application—and what you can do to make the grade.

Part 5, "Simple Investment Strategies," explains basic information about the world of investing. You'll learn how to set up investment objectives, which types of investments work best for you and your tolerance for risk, and ten smart money moves that will enable you to reach your financial goals. Plus, there's specific investment information just for seniors—and those who one day will be—which is *all* of us!

Part 6, "Money Issues You Don't Have to Deal with Every Day," discusses various issues that are imperative to understand in financial planning. You may not come across them often... but when you do, boy, are some of them doozies. This section will show you how to squeeze more out of your paycheck, how to cover your assets and protect your wealth through money-saving insurance strategies, and how to make Uncle Sam your friend by learning up-to-date tips on taxes.

Part 7, "Getting Ready for the Year 2000," is a definite must-read for anyone preparing for the inevitable: the information superhighway, sending your children to college (and paying for it without going broke), and estate planning. You'll discover how to make your personal computer work for you in your financial planning decisions—a task for computer geeks *and* neophytes.

Paying for your children's college education will be the second largest expense you'll tackle, so a chapter is dedicated to making the process a bit easier on your wallet. And finally, estate-planning strategies are given in the last chapter, which every person should read. This chapter can help your grandparents, your parents, and especially *you*.

Extras

We know you don't own a secret decoder ring to help you in the confusing world of financial planning—and you shouldn't have to. This book has a few easy-to-recognize signposts that offer tips, tricks, and tidbits to help you along your way. Look for these elements in this book that will point you in the right direction:

Want a better and less costly way of managing your money? These tips are some of the biggest secrets you'll ever learn in the personal financial planning world.

Watch your wallet, folks. Sometimes making the wrong decision when you manage your money can add up to trouble—and a lot of bucks. Take heed of these warning boxes to help save you some dough.

The world of financial planning is often confusing, mysterious, and just plain puzzling. Not anymore. These boxes will put you in the know, so you *know* what you are doing.

REALLY?

These little boxes contain extremely useful information that you definitely need to help you make educated decisions in your personal money management. Read them!

Acknowledgments

We sincerely acknowledge the following people and companies who provided research and assistance for this book:

Bank Rate Monitor; *The 100 Highest Yields*; Fran Lyons of Scoring Solutions, Inc.; Karen Harrragan of Auremmia Consulting Group; TRW, Inc.; Consumer Resource Institute, Inc.; Ruth Susswein of Bankcard Holders of America; Peter Roberts of the College Savings Bank; Chuck Carlson of the *DRIP Investor*; Fritz Elmendorf of Consumer Bankers Association; Rosemary Knutson-Gonzalez of the Social Security Office—Chicago; The Investment Company Institute; Morningstar, Inc.; the American Association of Retired Persons; John Lee; Oscar Woodall; Larry Sanborn; and Henry M. Lucking.

Many thanks to a financial dynamic duo, Alan Lavine and Gail Liberman, who devoted (and toiled) an enormous amount of time critiquing and editing this book. Thank you for all of your help, your suggestions, and your support! Our research assistant Lisa Scumaci was also an invaluable help digging for the latest information in the personal finance world. Laura Breitenreiter of Coldwell Banker explained the home-buying process in easy-street language—thank you! Special thanks go to Mark Enochs, Audra Gable, and Phil Kitchel for their diligent last-minute editing.

Christy Heady would like to personally acknowledge her husband, John A. Pavela—thank you for all your support through the development of *another* book. Your love and encouragement enabled me to reach another milestone (and deadline!) in my career.

Above all, Robert K. Heady would like to honor the memory of the late James Vincent O'Gara, executive editor of *Advertising Age*. In the beginning, long ago, he made this book possible by taking a chance on a wet-behind-the-ears reporter and teaching him the accuracy, integrity, and care that makes for good journalism.

Foreword

If you've picked up this book, chances are it's not because you *really* think of yourself as a complete idiot. More likely, you've had trouble managing your money because it seems too complex, too confusing, and just too time-consuming. On the other hand:

➤ You're tired of banks that charge higher and higher fees for your checking account, but offer you lower and lower interest on your savings.

➤ Your credit card bills keep mounting, even though you keep making payments every month.

➤ You know you need insurance, but you're not sure how much you need or how much it should cost.

➤ You're intrigued by investing and by the promise of wealth you read in the ads for brokerage firms and mutual funds, but you can't seem to get enough money together to make ends meet.

➤ Most of all, there are things you want out of life—a home, college education for your children, a secure retirement—that you may be afraid you'll never achieve.

Sound like you? It certainly sounds like the readers of the magazine I work for. From the letters we receive, I know that many people are concerned about how to get out of credit problems, how to cut banking and investment costs, how to get the best loans for cars and homes—the basic knowledge they need to make the most of what they have. And they don't want to spend a lot of time worrying about money. After all, money is a tool—one that should help you enjoy life now and provide you with the resources to live out your long-term dreams.

If you're like my readers, *The Complete Idiot's Guide to Managing Your Money* is for you. The daughter-and-father team of Christy and Robert Heady has put together the kind of basic information you need to take control of your finances. For example, they answer such questions as:

➤ How can I cut my banking costs?

➤ How can I get the highest savings rates?

➤ What can I do about my credit-card debt?

➤ Should I buy a house or rent?

➤ How much home can I afford—and what's the best loan for me?

➤ How can I start investing when I only have a small amount of money left over each month?

➤ How can I cut my insurance costs?

➤ Which kinds of insurance do I need? And which kinds don't I need at all?

➤ How can I keep more of my money from Uncle Sam—*legally*?

The Complete Idiot's Guide to Managing Your Money is easy to understand, entertaining, and—most of all—authoritative. The authors are regular contributors to *Your Money* magazine. As publisher of *Bank Rate Monitor* and *100 Highest Yields*, Robert Heady combines an insider's knowledge of the savings and borrowing industry with a consumer's desire to get the best deal from banks and other institutions. Christy Heady writes about all facets of personal finance and investing.

You don't have to be a genius to take control of your finances. *The Complete Idiot's Guide to Managing Your Money* is a practical, easy-to-read guide that can put you on the road to financial security.

Tom Siedell

Managing Editor, *Your Money*

Part 1
You and Your Money

Money affects everything we do. It gives us freedom to travel, shop, and live extravagantly. It also determines whether or not we can do these things. And when we plan wisely, money gives us a sense of accomplishment, like that feeling you get when you pay all the bills and have some money left over!

The most important reason to manage your money is to get control. It goes beyond you and your pocketbook or your wallet. Acquiring control over your personal finances can change your future. But in order to get control, you must make the first big decision—getting started!

Once you make the decision to manage your money, this section teaches you how to stop falling behind and get ahead in the world of personal finance (fondly known by many as a "money jungle"). This section gives you secrets of cutting costs on everything you buy, what to read, what to watch, and who to believe. Knowing these secrets will help you *and* your *pocketbook.*

Chapter 1

Grab Good Financial Planning by the Tail

In This Chapter

➤ Financial planning won't bite you

➤ How scare tactics *trick* you into *not* planning for your future

➤ How the five biggest secrets of financial planning have nothing to do with money

Do you know what the hardest thing about managing your money is? *Making the decision to do it.*

You wouldn't think it would be difficult. We make decisions every day of our lives: what to wear to work, what to eat for lunch, which video to rent for the children. Those decisions are easy. It's when the word "money" is brought up that your palms start to sweat and your brains turn to oatmeal.

It shouldn't be that way. We have access to more information about managing our finances than anyone in the world. Just go to your local bookstore and browse through the business section for proof. Titles that promise "NO MORE MONEY PROBLEMS—GUARANTEED!" grace the shelves. So if we have all of these resources, *why* do we still have problems managing our money?

Two reasons. First, no one has taught us how to make the decision to manage our money—a crucial first step in financial planning. Second, none of the books, magazines, newspapers, TV or radio programs have offered a secret decoder ring to help us decipher all of the financial gobbledygook they report. Yet, you cannot pick up a newspaper without reading about the rise and fall of mortgage rates, the increase in fees at your local bank, or the topsy-turvy action on Wall Street. What does this all have to do with you? Plenty.

The decisions you make about you and your money are affected by all of these factors and more. Think about it. If you are in the market to buy a home and mortgage rates go up, you may not be able to afford the home of your dreams. End result? Your decision about which home to buy changes. Perhaps your bank charges you a buck every time you use an ATM machine. You need to decide if you still want to bank at Friendly Federal.

You don't need a superhero to begin. This chapter will help you learn how to make the decision to manage your money and teach you simple steps to create financial security.

REALLY?

Here's a list of some freebies that can help you manage your money; they can also reduce the hassle of searching for a credit card and reaching your financial goals.

➤ Free information is available if you call the Consumer Counseling Credit Services at (800) 338-CCCS.

➤ "Nine Tax Tips for Mutual Fund Investors" is a free pamphlet that helps clear up the confusion about the tax effects of buying and selling mutual fund shares. Call (800) 336-3063.

➤ Investment Company Institute is one trade group for mutual funds; it offers many free pamphlets, including "Money Market Mutual Funds: Part of Every Financial Plan." Call (202) 293-7700.

➤ The Federal Reserve System, which regulates the U.S. banking system, offers booklets that cover a wide range of subjects. These include "The ABCs of Figuring Interest," "Buying Treasury Securities," and "Making Deposits: When Will Your Money Be Available?" Call (202) 898-6947.

➤ The National Association of Life Underwriters will send you a free booklet titled "Shaping Your Financial Fitness," and many other brochures about insurance products. Call (202) 331-6000.

➤ Pension Benefit Guaranty Corporation offers free pamphlets, including "Your Pension: Things You Should Know About Your Pension Plan." Call them at (202) 778-8000.

➤ The National Council of Senior Citizens publishes many free brochures, including "For a Good Retirement: Some Things You Should Know." Call them at (202) 347-8800.

➤ T. Rowe Price offers a helpful, free kit on retirement planning. Call (800) 638-5660.

➤ Fidelity Investments publishes "A Step-by-Step Guide to Planning Your Retirement." Call (800) 544-888.

➤ The United States Department of Education, through its Federal Student Aid Program, offers many publications about educational and financial planning. Call (800) 433-3243.

➤ To receive brochures about various insurance products, contact the Insurance Information Institute at (800) 942-4242.

➤ The Federal Trade Commission offers a myriad of pamphlets about credit-card-related issues. Contact them at (202) 326-3650.

Don't Let the Scare Tactics Trick You

The next time you're in a bookstore, look at the first chapter of five other financial planning books. You'll find a common theme: scare tactics from scary statistics—except the authors call them "motivational information." Who do they think they're kidding?

Although the information they report is accurate, it's far from motivating. Sure, it's true that by the year 2010 it will cost nearly $122,000 to get a four-year education at a public university. It's also a fact that if you make a $2,000 purchase on your VISA with 19.8 percent interest and only meet the minimum payments, it will take you more than 30 years to pay off that purchase. And we've all seen the projections that if you currently make $26,000 a year you should only expect to receive about $420 a month in Social Security benefits when you retire—that is, if Social Security is still around.

While all of that information is correct, are these scare tactics working? Do they make you get off your duff and start managing your finances? After hearing from thousands of Americans who still have money problems, we didn't think so.

No Matter How Much You Make, You CAN Do It

A friend of ours (let's call her Melba) makes $24,000 a year. She is 32 years old and supports herself and her daughter on her salary as a receptionist for a law firm in Chicago. She works hard to make ends meet, often skimping on luxuries in exchange for day-to-day necessities.

Melba doesn't live beyond her means but rather *within* her means. She carries only one major credit card with no annual fee and the lowest interest rate in the country (she demanded her interest rate be reduced; the credit card company obliged). She keeps a daily record of her pocket money and contributes the maximum amount to her company's retirement program. In fact, she has accumulated more than $7,500 in her company's 401(k) retirement program and still pays the bills. What's Melba's secret? Motivation.

We all make excuses to get out of managing our money (no time, not enough extra cash, or retirement is far, far away). One big reason we avoid planning is because of fear. Many people think that if they take a bare-bones look at their finances, they'll have to accept that they're in debt or don't have enough money to pay for their child's college education. Then they may think that they'll wind up old and impoverished. Goodness, why worry about that now? Others simply think managing their money is B-O-R-I-N-G. Save for the future? D-U-L-L. No instant gratification. Why put that extra $100 bucks in a savings account to earn 23 cents?

REALLY?

The statistics on how we relate to managing our money to save for our futures are not encouraging. A Merrill Lynch study concludes that if Americans continue to save at the rate they do now, they may end up with only 36 percent of the money they'll need to maintain their current standard of living. Meaning: they will have only 36 percent of what they need if *they continue to save at their current rate*, independent of Social Security.

Why have we developed such a nonchalant attitude toward the future, anyway? During our childhood, many of our parents gave us a piggy bank and a few pennies and taught us to "save for a rainy day." But few explained *why* we were supposed to do it.

Planning for your future doesn't mean you're expecting something terrible to happen. Buying a life insurance policy doesn't mean you're going to die, does it? Much of your fear will quickly disappear once you realize how easy it is to make your savings grow for retirement. It's never too early to learn—or to start. The whole idea of managing your money is to save a dollar here and there and then take that dollar and build it into two. Believe it or not, it's a concept that you can practice—and you don't need to be a money whiz to do it, either.

Begin Without Even Thinking About Money

No matter how much money you make, there are investment products available to you—even $25 a month can get you started. And no matter if your expenses seem out-of-sight, you can learn how to cut back on some expenses to help save and meet your financial goals. It's easy once you learn how—and you will when you read this book!

Are you ready? Put away your wallets and your pocketbooks because getting started in financial planning has nothing to do with money. Zip. Nada. It has to do with you and how you make decisions.

Achieving success is really the result of making good decisions, and achieving your success is based on a long-term focus. That's all. A bad decision results in a learned experience, but it's still a decision.

What happens when you don't make any decisions? Someone else makes them for you. Do you want someone else making the decisions about building your financial security? Think of this as something you've been putting off; ask yourself the following:

➤ Why have I been putting it off?

➤ What do I have to fear by not doing it?

➤ What type of pleasure do I receive by indulging in procrastination?

➤ What will it cost me if I don't do it now?

Take this information and apply it to the following simple steps toward getting started in financial planning:

➤ **Make the decision to *make a decision.*** Sounds silly, huh? Making a decision is often the hardest step. But if you break it up into simple little steps, you'll find decision-making easy and far from intimidating. Just say "okay," and you've done it.

➤ **Make decisions often.** Let's use an analogy. Every year without fail during the first week of January, memberships and the line for the Stairmaster at your local health club increase. The New Year's diet is in full swing, and every gym rat in the nation has made the decision to do something about his health, his image, and his weight. But this doesn't last very long because these people only make a decision once; they don't decide on a daily basis "I'm going to go the gym today." If these people made decisions often, perhaps they would reach their fitness goals. If you make the decision to create a personal financial plan, are you going to stick with it just once?

➤ **Be flexible.** You don't live in just a black and white environment. You need to allow for some gray areas—which often disguise themselves as mistakes. Remember, although mistakes come from making the wrong decision, they create experiences you learn from, which might help you make the *right* decision next time!

➤ **Enjoy making decisions.** Making decisions can be a blast! For example, if your mistakes help you learn to make better decisions, and the next time you make a decision it turns out to be a great opportunity, wouldn't you have enjoyed making that decision? You'll enjoy it more when you create more great opportunities!

➤ **Create short-term and long-term goals.** Many people plan for their financial futures by working so hard today that by the time they reach their long-term goals, they're exhausted and have forgotten why they worked so hard to get there. Long-term goals are important, but so are short-term goals. If you create and meet short-term goals, you won't have to wait 30 years to feel a sense of accomplishment or satisfaction.

➤ **Do your homework.** It'll be more fun than studying for that geometry test you prepared so hard for in high school! Doing your homework in the money world will allow you to make your money work as hard for you as you do for it.

When you work through these secrets, you are shaping your financial destiny, and it all starts with a simple decision!

And Now for the Money Part

It's time to take step number two in the lessons of financial planning: setting some goals.

If your goal is to win Saturday night's lottery, forget it. Winning the lottery is a great way to create instant wealth, but playing it is not. And if you do win the lottery, you'll have enough financial planning burdens to make you go berserk. So let's talk about setting some more practical goals.

Setting goals isn't difficult. It's figuring out how to reach them that gives you a run for your money (no pun intended). You know that you need short-term and long-term goals, so take out two pieces of paper and let's get started. On the first piece of paper, write down any short-term goals you want to accomplish. These may include but are not limited to creating an emergency fund and paying off your credit cards and student loans.

Divide the next piece of paper into four time frames: five years, ten years, twenty years, and thirty years. Write down what you want to accomplish in each. For example, in five years you may want to buy a house. Ten years from now you may want to take a vacation to Europe. Twenty years from now you'll have to send the kids to college. And thirty years from now you plan to retire.

pieces of paper, write down how much money each goal
quire. Be honest with yourself; the amount of money
meet each goal may surprise you. You may have already
e of the money that you'll need. If so, good for you.
have or not, most of you are going to have to learn how
ur money to be able to achieve your goals.

Now total up how much money you're going to need to meet
all of your goals. The numbers are astounding, aren't they? But that
doesn't mean you have to change your goals. In fact, you can keep
those goals and accomplish many of them by following the concepts
in this book! This book is designed specifically to help you meet the
short-term and long-term goals that you have set for yourself and for
your family—and save money in the process.

All it takes is a little knowledge and some self-discipline. Most
folks say that knowledge is power. But we disagree. Knowledge is power
if—and only if—you put it to use!

The Least You Need to Know

➤ The first step toward managing your money is making
the decision to start planning for your financial future.

➤ Don't let mistakes keep you from making more decisions. Think of a mistake as something that will help
you make a better decision the next time.

➤ Write down your short-term and long-term financial
goals and how much money you need to achieve
them. Then read the rest of this book for information
on how to reach those goals.

➤ Grabbing good financial planning requires you to do
your homework, and you've already learned the first
part of homework and research: you are studying this
book!

➤ When you're looking for free pamphlets don't rule out
mutual fund companies. Often they offer a number of
investment and personal financial planning kits.

Chapter 2

Managing the Debt Monster

> **In This Chapter**
>
> ➤ Top secrets to help break those bad money habits
>
> ➤ Learn how to be a debt-buster
>
> ➤ Tips on getting—and *remaining*—out of debt
>
> ➤ Filing for bankruptcy—the last resort

It's Sunday afternoon and you're perusing the classified ads. You come across an ad that reads, "For only $159.95, the Bills 'n Thrills Company can reveal the secret to reducing your debt! No more ugly credit card bills!" In fact, it guarantees to get rid of any bad marks on your credit report.

Only $159.95. You mull it over. "Gee, I'm tired of paying those finance charges on my VISA," you say. "And I don't want to talk to my creditors anymore."

"Don't worry—we'll call your creditors and arrange a payment schedule," says this promising advertisement. Sounds like a deal, huh? No way.

Unfortunately, many Americans have fallen prey to swindlers who promise to get rid of your ugly bills or pledge a squeaky-clean credit report. These scam artists only cause more harm than good. If you are trying to tackle the debt monster, a swindler won't help you—but this chapter will. You'll learn top-notch secrets to reduce your debt, measure your financial health, and reduce your expenses.

Are You in Debt Trouble?

To determine whether you are having problems managing your debts, indicate whether the following statements are true or false:

___ You use credit cards where you used to pay cash, such as at the grocery store and restaurants.

___ You have depleted your savings—or worse, used cash advances from credit cards—to pay old past-due bills.

___ You have lost track of how much you owe.

___ You put off paying your telephone and utility bills in order to pay high credit card bills and other debts.

___ You regularly receive letters from collection agencies.

If most of your answers are true, you have a debt problem. Read on to find out what you can do about it.

Measuring Your Financial Health

Checking in with a financial doctor rates right up there with having your teeth cleaned. Painful—and the taste of rubber gloves is not pleasant—but if you want pearly whites, you've got to go through the torture.

In managing your money, your goal is to get out of debt, right? Once you meet that goal, what do you want to accomplish financially? Do you want to...

Buy a car? (See Chapter 14.)

Buy a house? (See Chapter 15.)

Send the kids to college? (See Chapter 26.)

Retire comfortably? (See Chapter 27.)

Before you reach those goals, you must figure out how bad the problem is. To do that, you must do three things to measure your financial health. First, compare your assets to your liabilities by completing the worksheets in this chapter. Second, determine what your expenses are. Third, create a budget and trim the financial fat. The best way to begin is to…

Add Up the Pluses and Minuses

There's no greater mess to clean up than unorganized, mismanaged financial affairs—which is why so many people stick to organizing their financial records about as long as they do a New Year's diet. Determining your *assets* (what you own) and *liabilities* (what you owe) gives you a clear picture of what you're worth.

Begin with organized records. These may include, but are not limited to, checkbook registers, recent bank and brokerage statements, copies of your income tax returns (keep these for at least three years), and paycheck stubs. Forget the shoebox theory—keep these and all of your financial records in a well-organized file cabinet for your personal finances.

Once you have all of your information intact, you can fill in the first of three worksheets (taken from *The Complete Idiot's Guide to Making Money on Wall Street*), which is a financial property assets worksheet and includes all the money in your bank accounts, brokerage accounts, and other investments.

Financial Property	Date Purchased	How Much Did You Pay?	Today's Date	What's It Worth Today?
Bonds (type)				
Bond mutual funds (type)				
Certificate of deposit				
Checking accounts				
Coin collections				
Money market accounts				
Pensions & profit sharing plans				
Savings accounts				
Savings bonds				
Stocks				
Stock mutual funds				
Treasury securities				
Other				
Total Financial Property				

A financial property assets worksheet.

Next, by completing your personal property worksheet—which is also an asset—you'll assess how much your physical property is worth. For example, your home is probably the largest (in physical size and financial size) asset you own. Write in when you bought your home, what the price was, and how much it's worth today. If you're not sure—and want to make more than an educated guess—contact an appraiser to be certain.

Personal Property	Date Purchased	How Much Did You Pay?	What's It Worth Today?
Appliances (washer & dryer, etc.)			
Automobiles			
Boats, campers			
Computers			
Furniture			
Fur coats			
Home			
Home furnishings			
—curtains			
—rugs			
—tableware (glasses, dishes)			
—blankets			
—lamps			
—silverware			
Jewelry			
Paintings			
Stereos			
Televisions			
Miscellaneous			
Total Personal Property			

A personal property assets worksheet.

Finally, calculate your *liabilities*—all the things you owe. The main thrust of this worksheet deals with loans, such as auto loans, student loans, and your mortgage, but remember to put down ALL of your outstanding credit card balances (yes, ALL of them). Your liabilities show how much debt you carry.

What You Owe	To Whom	Interest Rate %	When Is It Due?	How Much Do You Owe?
Bills, bills, bills				
—electric				
—gas				
—retail stores				
—telephone				
—other				
Loans to family				
Loans to friends				
Automobile loans				
Bank loans				
Credit cards				
—credit card #1				
—credit card #2				
—credit card #3				
Furniture loans				
Student loans				
Mortgage				
Home equity loans				
Miscellaneous				
Total Liabilities				

A liabilities worksheet.

Two kinds of debt traditionally exist, although we're going to add a third: good debt, bad debt, and you-just-have-to-pay-it-to-live debt. This last type of debt would include electric bills, gas bills, and telephone bills. More often, they're referred to as expenses, although they are "owed" debts.

The single largest component of good debt would be your mortgage loan because your mortgage is for your house, which is an *asset* (hopefully an appreciating one!). You must report your mortgage loan on your liabilities worksheet.

Bad debt makes up the bulk of the liabilities worksheet. It is what siphons most consumers' paychecks.

Americans have long been battling a war to reduce bad debt. Bad debt is what you still owe on your car, your credit cards, your unsecured personal loans, and even your student loans. Obviously, the name of the game is to have as few "bad-debt" liabilities as possible and to increase your wealth substantially.

Bad debt works *against* you, although Americans are too happy living moment to moment to realize this. They relish in the ability to "buy now and pay later." Credit cards, the biggest enticers, have lured many consumers into vulnerability—about $178 billion worth. Boy are they seductive—costly, too!

Chapter 13 is chock-full of credit card tips and tricks. It's a must read for anyone who wants (or needs) to know how to get the best deal on a credit card and how to avoid nasty fees and finance charges.

As an example, suppose you buy a leather couch for $1,500 and put it on your MasterCard. You can't pay the entire bill this month, but that's no problem! You only have to make a minimum payment to remain in the issuer's good graces. However, as other debts start adding up, you only meet the minimum payment for the next year or so, or at least until you get out of the hole with your other bills. Then, one year later, a friend drops her cigarette on the couch. Now it's torched, and you need a new couch. You get rid of the couch, but you're still paying for it on your credit card. "Surely I've paid it off by now," you think. Well, think again.

How long does it take to pay off such a debt? If you *only* meet the minimum monthly payments, and your credit card has an average annual percentage rate (APR) of, let's say, 19.8 percent interest, it will take you more than 22 years to pay off that $1,500 couch. This is a classic example of how bad debt can work against you. The more debt you are burdened with, the longer it will take to dig yourself out of a hole. Therefore, your first priority should be to eliminate non-productive debt.

Motivate Your Mind to Kick the Habit

There aren't any self-hypnotic tapes to help cure overspending (maybe there should be). However, your personal motivation and goal-setting can surely help. Picture this: You have no debt and an investment account worth $75,000. How does it feel? Many psychological experts urge consumers to use their imaginations instead of their wallets to help with their finances.

REALLY?

Here's a motivating statistic that might light a fire under your seat. If you're making 12 percent interest on your investments but are paying off a credit card balance of 19.8 percent on your $1,500 purchase, the money you make on your investments turns into a negative 7.8 percent. Wait—there's more! If your money is in a taxable account, you have to pay taxes on any income or capital gains; you can't even write off the credit card interest on your taxes.

Once you have the proper motivation, try the strategies discussed in the following sections to reduce your debt.

Use Your Savings

Before you use your savings to pay off the budgetary fat, determine your debt-to-equity ratio. Oooh, all those numbers sound intimidating, huh? It's simple! All you have to do is answer one question: How much of your paycheck goes to pay your debts? The smaller the percent of your monthly pay allocated to credit cards (as well as other loans and debt) is, the better.

You know you're in bad shape—completely overextended—if you're flirting with a debt-to-equity ratio of 75 percent debt to 25 percent equity. Even 50–50 isn't good. The rule of thumb is this: *current assets should be approximately two times greater than current liabilities.*

So lump together all of your assets (what you own) and your liabilities (what you owe). If you have socked away a ton of cash in your bank account and you have revolving debt on your credit cards, it's time to pay those off. Why not use your savings? It'll be in your best interest, since you won't be paying any more than you have to!

> If you're still swimming in debt and can't make ends meet by reducing your expenses, consider boosting your income—either through a part-time job or odd jobs you can do on weekends. Every little bit helps.

Go on a Money Diet

Is that extra ten dollars burning a hole in your pocket? Do you feel compelled to spend it? Even if you are deluged with pre-approved credit card offers in the mail, it doesn't mean you should take them. It is not wise to buy now and pay later.

Since there aren't any nutrition labels that warn consumers whether or not they're getting a good deal, it's up to you to spend your money wisely. You can look at where your money goes to see where you can trim the fat.

Here are 10 ways *not* to spend money... starting today:

➤ Never buy extended warranties or service contracts. Buy products that come with good warranties from retailers who stand behind what they sell. Since many service contracts generate high profits for businesses, some experts agree they're generally not a good deal for consumers.

➤ Are speed dialing and three-way calling really necessary? The services cost approximately $2 to $3 extra per month, but that adds up to hundreds of dollars over a few years. Stick with basic telephone coverage.

➤ If you're in the market for a new car, make sure you carefully read the tips and tricks offered in Chapter 14. Many consumers see a flashy new car as an investment, but it's not! When you drive a new car off the lot, it immediately loses a certain percentage of its value—typically 20 percent! If you do your homework, you can buy a used car that's next to new for a fraction of the original sticker price.

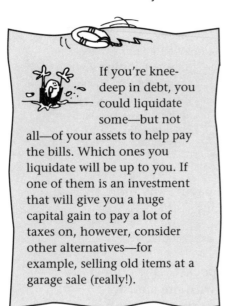

If you're knee-deep in debt, you could liquidate some—but not all—of your assets to help pay the bills. Which ones you liquidate will be up to you. If one of them is an investment that will give you a huge capital gain to pay a lot of taxes on, however, consider other alternatives—for example, selling old items at a garage sale (really!).

➤ One of the most superfluous items that Americans buy—and don't use—is new exercise equipment. If you sell the treadmill and exercise bike that are collecting dust, you probably could pay off one of your credit card bills.

➤ Never go shopping when you're bored, down in the dumps, or hungry. That's recreational shopping, and it can cost you plenty! You'll probably buy things you don't need and probably can't afford just to make yourself feel better. Think of an alternative: exercise, play with the dog, or make your spouse a romantic dinner.

➤ Most consumers don't realize that everything goes on sale eventually. Wait for the sale. (You'll learn more about shopping tricks in the next chapter.)

➤ The biggest mistake consumers make is carrying more than one credit card. The more plastic you own, the more chance you'll lose track of your spending. One major credit card is enough. (You'll find a list of the best credit card deals in Chapter 13.)

➤ Here's a great way to cut costs on expensive water-heating bills: reduce your water-heater temperature from 145° F to 120° F, and you'll save 10 to 15 percent on your next bill.

➤ Go to matinees instead of evening movies. They're often discounted. In some cities, matinee prices are as much as 50 percent less than regular evening prices. You can also buy movie theater "fun-pack" tickets at reduced prices.

➤ Better yet (for all you movie buffs out there), save the $7.75-per-movie charge and wait for the flick to come out on video. They always do, don't they?

These are specific examples of how you can immediately start saving on some of your expenses, which ultimately reduces your debt.

Get Outside Help

If you're having trouble implementing these strategies to resolve your debt crisis, it may be time to seek outside help. Contact your local credit counseling office through the national number (800) 338-CCCS. Another available resource is the National Center for Financial Education, P.O. Box 34070, San Diego, CA 92163, which provides support services for cardholders who need assistance managing credit.

It's a Budget to Your Rescue!

Unless we light a firecracker and place it under your chair, the only way we can motivate you to keep track of where your money goes is to scare you. So here goes. If you don't track where all your money goes, what will happen? Over time, the following things will happen: you'll wind up in the cold month of January wondering how the heck you spent $2,769 on Christmas presents for the family, you'll know your banker better than you'd like because you'll probably bounce checks all over town as a result of mismanaging your finances, and someday you'll live on a monthly Social Security benefit check of $455 (that's it!) because you piddled all your money down the drain when you were young. Does that scare you? It should!

Stay away from anyone who promises to help you with your debt trouble "for a small fee." These people work for places known as *recovery houses*, and they're preying on everybody—especially the elderly. Contact the FTC at (202) 326-3650 to report any wrongdoing. The best organization to help you manage your debt is your local Consumer Credit Counseling Service office. However, the only person who can get you *out* of debt is *you*!

"Budget" is a scary word; it's too constrictive for some folks. What you need to understand, however, is that everybody needs to have a daily record of where all their money goes. Accept it and motivate yourself toward the feeling of accomplishment. The true reward of having a budget is something all Americans want: control. Imagine having control over *all* of your finances. Once you do, you can reach your dreams and financial goals even faster!

What Do You Spend Money On?

First, you need to figure out where your money goes. Create your expense categories and fill in the amount you spend on a monthly basis for each category. To get a more accurate picture, you may want to check all your receipts from the past several months. Your categories can include but are not limited to:

➤ **Auto expenses:** Car payments, auto insurance, maintenance, gas (save your receipts!)

➤ **Clothing expenses:** Overgarments, undergarments (all your garments), shoes, and socks

➤ **Dental expenses:** Periodic cleaning, dental work, oral surgery, and so on (not covered by insurance)

➤ **Dining expenses:** Restaurant expenses, even if it's for fast food

➤ **Entertainment:** Movies, plays, concerts, the zoo, whatever

➤ **Education:** School supplies, tuition bills, and so on

➤ **Gifts:** Birthdays, holidays, weddings, Bar Mitzvahs

➤ **Groceries:** Separate into two categories—food and drugstore items—if possible.

➤ **Home-based business:** This should be broken down into smaller categories, including equipment, supplies, taxes, and so on.

➤ **Household items:** Plants, furniture, dog (just kidding)

➤ **Household expenses:** Items necessary for the upkeep of the house: paint, lawn maintenance, and so on

➤ **Insurance:** Separate your policies into categories, such as life, health, and homeowners.

➤ **Rent/Mortgage:** Your biggest expense (probably); important for tax return purposes

➤ **Taxes:** Real estate and income taxes paid (don't forget income tax refunds as a source of income)

➤ **Utilities:** Phone, electric, gas, water

➤ **Vacations:** Hotel stays, airplane tickets, new luggage, meals, sightseeing tours, souvenirs

There's probably more, but this list gets you started on the right foot.

Trim the Fat!

From the expense categories you create, pick a few expenses you can live without... for good. If the children are stuck on seeing a movie every Friday night, rent a video instead of going to the show.

As another example, set yourself a limit—such as to eat out only twice a month. The second largest component of "where your money goes" is dining out. That nasty habit costs the average American almost $4,200 a year. You could pay for Junior's tuition at some state universities with that dough. Keep the following tips in mind to help reduce some of your expenses and save money in the long run:

➤ Establish an emergency fund that equals about three month's worth of basic expenses. Then you won't have to turn to plastic for every unexpected bill.

➤ Lower your tax withholding. Why give the IRS a free loan while you're paying an average 16 percent interest on your debts?

➤ Increase the deductibles on your automobile insurance. Even bumping up a $100 deductible to a $500 deductible could lower your premiums on comprehensive insurance by 25 or 30 percent a year.

Battling Debt's Biggest Culprit

Americans have been able to *buy now and pay later* since the evolution of the plastic credit card. But this plastic has caused millions of Americans a problem: with enticing credit card offers promising generous credit lines, it has become impossible to climb out of debt.

That's why you should treat your credit card as a tool, not a cure-all. The rule of thumb: If you don't have the cash, don't use the card! A credit card should be used as a convenience for emergencies; it is nothing more than a tool. Having a credit card or two is a necessity, but becoming laden with $20,000 in credit card debt is a burden—and a very common one. Typical clients of Credit Counseling Centers of America are dual-income families with high incomes. However, they have fallen into the habit of overspending; they have no savings—and up to $20,000 in credit card debt.

To save a few hundred dollars a year on finance charges (and work at maintaining a squeaky-clean credit report), follow the tips listed in Chapter 13 on how to cut your credit card costs in half.

Be a Debt-Buster!

If there's one rule you remember from this chapter, let it be this one: *Pay your bills on time.* Almost all lenders will look at whether you're current or late with your bills. Most lenders are lenient, and will tolerate a maximum of 30 days late. If you are currently behind on your accounts, catch up before you apply. This is how you can make the grade to get credit. You have to fit the profile of the people who pay their bills on time.

Filing for B-A-N-K-R-U-P-T-C-Y

Financial troubles have led millions of Americans to file for bankruptcy, often using the process as an "alternative." How wrong. Filing for bankruptcy is the *last resort* to your financial woes, not a choice. If you are in debt and *need* to file, however, there are pitfalls you can avoid.

Most often, you don't have to file unless it's necessary—declaring yourself bankrupt is not an alternative, it's a necessary solution. One bankruptcy attorney in Chicago claims that he has yet to see a situation where the filing was not required.

If you are having difficulty meeting your rent or mortgage payments, you're completely extended beyond your credit limit, the collection agencies are uncooperative, and you need more than a credit counselor, you may need to file a *Chapter 7* or a *Chapter 13*.

There are two basic ways of filing for personal bankruptcy. Chapter 7 gets rid of all debts (except some taxes and maybe alimony payments); Chapter 13 allows people with steady income to pay off bills over a 36-to-60-month period.

The first thing you should do is seek the advice of an attorney, who will guide you into which bankruptcy proceeding you should file, according to your personal debt situation.

Here's how they work. When you file either Chapter 7 or Chapter 13, you are issued a restraining order by the court which will protect you from all further proceedings against you until all previous debts are cleared. The restraining order includes protection against wage garnishing, creditor harassment, and foreclosures without a court order.

Chapter 7 is used mainly if you have unsecured debts. For example, if you have furniture or appliances as unpaid collateral, you can return these without paying for them. But if you want to keep these things, you might be allowed a reaffirmation agreement with your creditors. Also, attorneys' fees are set so you can establish an installment plan.

Chapter 13, a wage-earner plan, brings immediate relief by letting you pay your bills rather than letting them go (unlike Chapter 7). You are eligible for an extension plan that allows you to pay back all your bills within a certain period of time, usually 36 to 60 months. Costs incurred by the attorney are added to the total of your other debts and are paid through your payments to the court trustee.

The bright side to filing for bankruptcy is immediate relief. The dark side is a black mark that remains on your credit record to haunt you for 10 years.

But all is not lost. It is still possible to potentially establish a "new" credit record and obtain a credit card: a *secured credit card*. Some companies that offer secured credit cards have guidelines that are a bit more flexible. If you've filed for bankruptcy and need information about applying for a secured credit card, read another kind of Chapter 13—the one in this book.

The Least You Need to Know

➤ To measure your financial health, add up the worth of everything you own and compare it to the cost of everything you owe. A financially healthy person should have twice as much in assets as he or she has in liabilities.

➤ To reduce debt, use some of your assets (such as your savings) and reduce expenses so that you can pay more towards the debt.

➤ If you need extra help dealing with your debt problems, contact your local credit counseling office through the national number (800) 338-CCCS.

➤ To keep your spending on track, you need to establish a budget. Budgeting basically involves recording how you currently spend your money and then figuring out how you can change your spending habits in order to achieve your financial goals.

➤ Filing for bankruptcy is not an "alternative" or a "choice." It should be looked upon as a last resort.

Chapter 3

Shop 'Til You Drop—It Really Pays Off!

In This Chapter

➤ Money-saving tips your folks never told you

➤ Warehouse clubs: Are they for you?

➤ How to choose a long-distance carrier

➤ Shopping from the easy chair: Does it really pay off?

There's a four-letter word that sends chills down the spines of millions of consumers:

SALE.

Americans have developed a voracious appetite for anything that's a bargain. People have discovered that they like to shop at discount stores and scout for bargains. They just want to save money. But the trend of saving money has gone beyond the old days of just clipping coupons on a Sunday afternoon. Today's smart shopper scans newspaper ads for bargains and looks for savings tips in newsletters. Face it, frugality is in.

However, you don't have to be cheap to be frugal. This focus on frugality has forced consumers to become better informed and make better choices. And it doesn't mean that you're a penny-pincher or a tightwad. You're just smart about your money (after all, you work very hard for that paycheck). This chapter will alert you to some pretty interesting money-saving strategies to help you save some dough.

What Supermarkets Don't Tell You

Next time you're at the grocery store, look at all the items on the shelf from top to bottom. Notice anything? Grocery stores usually place the most expensive items at eye level, where they are more likely to be selected on impulse. If you want to be a smart shopper, look at the entire group of products before you decide which to purchase (unless of course you prefer the more expensive brand!).

Don't fall prey to all of those "on sale" items at the front of the store. The company that distributes those items and products actually pays for the space to place the merchandise. You won't really find any bargains until you dig deep inside store aisles.

And finally, make sure you comparison shop. Although the generic brands usually save you money, some house and national brands can actually be *cheaper* than generic brands.

Well, if you're going shopping, get on out there. But don't forget your coupons!

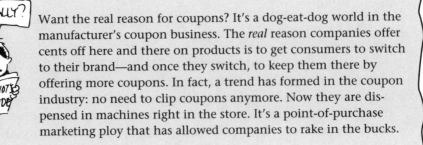

REALLY? Want the real reason for coupons? It's a dog-eat-dog world in the manufacturer's coupon business. The *real* reason companies offer cents off here and there on products is to get consumers to switch to their brand—and once they switch, to keep them there by offering more coupons. In fact, a trend has formed in the coupon industry: no need to clip coupons anymore. Now they are dispensed in machines right in the store. It's a point-of-purchase marketing ploy that has allowed companies to rake in the bucks.

Smart Shopping 101

Did you know that a pack of razor blades costs $6.80 in Tokyo but only $3.75 in Los Angeles? Lipstick that averages $5.00 a tube in the United States costs five times that much in Brazil. And in Tahiti, a can of ginger ale runs $4.00 and a bag of Doritos goes for $5.00. For those Americans who think U.S. prices are high, know that the average comparison of most selected goods and services costs less in the States than anywhere overseas. However, that doesn't mean we shouldn't practice smart shopping!

REALLY? Did you know that every time you use a "preferred-shopper" card to pay for groceries or drugstore items your grocer compiles personal information about you? Sure, you may be using the card for the three or four bucks it saves you right then, but it's actually saving you more than that. What you buy with that card is added to a computer file corresponding with your number. Then, when you receive coupons in the mail, you'll find coupons for similar products that you frequently shop for. If you don't mind having someone "watch" your shopping habits, those coupons can help save you money on your groceries in the long run!

If you make a concentrated effort to be a smart shopper, you can develop better spending habits and save money. Whenever you hit the mall or grocery store, keep these tips in mind:

➤ **Use cash—not plastic—if you are buying perishable or depreciating items.** Just because many national-chain grocery stores accept all major credit cards doesn't mean you should whip out your plastic at the check-out counter. Remember how long it takes to pay off that card when you make only minimum payments? Imagine paying off a gallon of milk, a bunch of bananas, two cans of New England clam chowder, and a box of Twinkies for three years.

➤ **Just because an item is on sale doesn't mean the price has hit rock-bottom.** Shopaholics love a sale, but often merchandise (especially clothing) isn't a bargain until it's at least 40 percent off the regular price. When a store takes 10 percent off an item, they're barely paying for your tax in some states; that's no deal.

➤ **Buy only what you can afford.** If you don't have the cash to buy something, don't use a credit card to make the purchase. Carrying a balance on a credit card only requires you to carry debt for months and months.

➤ **Bargain with the merchandiser.** You can't do this at a grocery store (unless the merchandise is damaged), but try it at privately owned stores. How? Above all, be discreet. A store owner will not reduce a price if she thinks your deal will become public information. Likewise, don't roughhouse the owner; instead be tactful with your approach. Come across as a serious shopper who intends to spend some cash (you'll lose your edge if you use plastic). Select a couple of the items you want to purchase, have the owner add up the entire bill, and then act uncertain. Ask the owner if this is the best price she can give you. It may not always work, but it's worth a shot.

➤ **Don't buy for convenience.** If you want to save money on groceries, don't shop for the convenient items, such as carrots that are already cut up or premixed pancake batter. Even if you have coupons for these items, you'll save more money in the long run if you cut up your own carrots and mix up your own pancake batter. If you do buy for the sake of convenience—for example, at that local 24-hour, all-night corner place with the gas pumps out front—understand that you'll pay extra for those chocolate-covered doughnuts and a gallon of milk. Sometimes you may *have* to pay "convenience store" prices for diapers, cough medicine, or toilet paper—but don't make a habit of it.

➤ Keep your receipts, and watch for ads featuring the merchandise you already bought. Some stores will honor your receipts and returns if you buy it at full price one week and it goes on sale the next.

Buying in Bulk

You can save 30, 40, even 50 percent on your next grocery bill if you buy in bulk—and borrow a friend's station wagon to haul it home. But it doesn't always work to your advantage.

The common misconception about buying your groceries in bulk (at a warehouse food club, for example) is that you have to buy the 10-gallon jar of peanut butter in order to get a deal. Not true—unless you *like* a lot of peanut butter. You may have to buy more volume of a certain item, but if you're going to buy that amount in smaller quantities over an extended period of time anyway, you're better off. If you do the math, you can see how much you save on some items.

For example, a three-gallon tub of laundry soap is $9 at your favorite warehouse supermarket. In your regular supermarket, a one-gallon tub of the same laundry soap is $5, and if you bought three gallons, you would pay $15. So you save six dollars by shopping at a warehouse supermarket. But that's for an item like laundry soap, which won't perish. A 10-pound bag of bananas is a different story.

Items such as sugar, flour, milk, eggs, laundry soap, and coffee filters tend to be less expensive at a warehouse supermarket, while other items such as meat tend to cost less at the grocery store. So what's the point? It pays to comparison shop.

One thing to consider is that it costs money to join a warehouse supermarket— the membership fee can be as high as $35 a year. Most of these warehouse clubs also require that you be a member of an organization or have an employee membership through your company. If you want to join a warehouse club, see if your church, company, or other organizations participate.

Once you shop one of these places, you'll find that warehouse clubs are fun. Where else can you buy a rack of lamb, a VCR, and a sweatsuit all under one roof? But be careful. That doesn't mean you have to buy one of everything. And remember to take your coupons to these warehouse supermarkets to see if they honor them; you could save even more!

Fiber-Optic Wars

Feeling bombarded by all of the telephone advertising wars? Not sure if you need "circles" or want "true savings?" The big three—AT&T, MCI, and Sprint—have armed themselves for combat. And it could sabotage your pocketbook if you're not careful.

What many consumers don't know is that since the deregulation of the telephone industry in 1984, there are a total of 400 other companies that provide long-distance service. *Four hundred?* Yep.

The bottom line is that there is very little difference in the standard rates charged by the big three phone carriers. Mind-boggling, huh? Well, it doesn't have to be if you follow these important steps:

➤ **Choose a plan based on YOU.** Even if all of your friends and your family have MCI, you're not guaranteed to save more money. You need to evaluate your calling patterns. Do you make most of your calls during the day? Are you a chatterbox only from 7:00 to 9:00 p.m. on weekends? Whatever the case, once you log your calling patterns, you'll be able to choose a program that suits your needs—and is easy on the wallet!

➤ **Make sure you choose some type of plan.** If you don't specifically request a certain plan, some companies will pick one for you. And, as you learned in Chapter 1, you can't grab good financial planning by the tail if you let someone else make your financial decisions. It's the plan—not the company—that's most important.

➤ **Even if you've picked a plan, re-evaluate your telephone patterns six months from now.** Yes, this gives you more homework, but you want to save money, don't you? If your calling plan has changed dramatically, you'll need to analyze your bills to make sure you're still saving as much as possible.

➤ **Rates shouldn't be the sole factor in your decision.** If one major carrier charges only 22 cents a minute for a long-distance call, and another carrier charges 24 cents a minute but offers you more perks (such as prepaid calling cards), choose the latter. Although you want the best price, you also want the best components.

➤ **If you're still befuddled, contact the Telecommunications Research & Action Center.** Known as TRAC, this organization will send you a copy of its complete Tele-Tips residential rates comparison chart for $3. Write to TRAC, P.O. Box 12038, Washington, DC 20005. Make sure you enclose a self-addressed, stamped envelope. The chart features costs for five-, 10-, 15-, 30-, 50- and 150-calls-per-month scenarios, as well as scenarios for heavy day use, average use, and heavy night and weekend use.

Flying the Friendly Skies on the Cheap

If you want to be a shrewd traveler, you're going to have to do more to save money than travel to vacation spots during the off-peak season. One way to save on traveling is to never ever accept the first fare quoted. Research indicates that half of the time, some other airline has a flight within the same time you want to leave but it has a special, less-expensive fare.

One of the best money-saving strategies for travelers is to change your eating habits. Eating every meal out can eat up (forgive the pun) all of your money. To control your food budget, try to eat only twice a day, and if possible, buy your food at a nearby supermarket and eat it in your hotel room. You can save hundreds of dollars by doing this. In fact, some smart travelers opt for a room with a kitchenette so they can cook their own meals—a wise decision.

Here's a tip you'll love—although it sounds too good to be true. For both foreign and domestic travelers, if you use International Travel Consultants (based in Asheville, North Carolina), you can possibly earn a refund. Individuals who spend anywhere between $1 and $20,000 can receive up to 25 percent of the agency's commission. This commission is paid by airlines, hotels, and so on, so the agency returns a portion of its commissions to travelers who use its services. Rebates are awarded on a quarterly basis. For more information, call (800) 467-5214, or write to P.O. Box 167, Asheville, NC 28802.

If your schedule allows you to, take a "bump" if it's offered. Typically this is when an airline will offer free tickets to volunteers who give up their seats in the event that the airlines overbooked the flight. Unless the airline can get you on another flight for the same destination within an hour, you'll get a free flight. However, if you're willing to take a bump, bring a good book.

Lazy Shopping

Suppose it's late at night, and you're flipping channels. All of a sudden you see it—the bargain of a lifetime. A genuine 14k gold bracelet with cubic zirconia diamonds interlaced with faux emeralds for only $79.95. "Only seven left!" screams the shopping channel host. Panic ensues as you pick up the phone and dial the number so you can buy your dream present. But alas, you're too late. All gone.

Tragedy? No. It would probably be the best thing that could happen to you.

Notice the "easy payment" schedule shopping channels offer. Instead of paying $79.95 right off the bat for your bracelet, you can make three easy payments of $29.95. Do the math. $29.95 multiplied by 3 is almost 90 bucks—a lot more than you would pay if you were to pay in full. It's their way of "financing." And here's another catch: Because these three easy payments are billed to your credit card, you can end up paying interest twice: once for their financing, and again for your credit card's financing if you don't pay the balance off each month.

Shopping channels entice millions of Americans to buy more unneeded merchandise than ever. How? Because they're very visual, provoking the "see-it-buy-it" habit. In fact, the most recent figures indicate that in 1993 QVC and the Home Shopping Network raked in more than $1 billion in revenue. Is this merchandise a bargain? No, not when you consider the mistakes people can make when they shop via TV.

For example, you can't send cash or write a check when you purchase an item from a shopping channel. Each time you make a purchase, you must use a credit card, which is a habit you're trying to cut back on. Plus, you have to pay for shipping charges, which often add $10 to $20, depending where you live.

And what happens if you receive defective merchandise? Good question. Sure, you can send it back, but it's often a troublesome process, and you're stuck with a gadget that looks like it belongs in a Star Trek mausoleum.

The Least You Need to Know

➤ It may be worth the price of joining a warehouse supermarket if you normally buy lots of nonperishable items (and have the room to store them).

➤ Getting the best deal on long distance is easy: match your calling habits to one of a company's plans. And remember, you don't have to stick with one of the big three.

➤ Buying stuff you see on TV is usually not a good idea. You have to buy it with a credit card, and it's difficult to return if something is wrong with it.

Chapter 4

The Quickest Route Through the Money Jungle

In This Chapter

➤ Why you can't believe "interest rate experts"

➤ How to map your money game plan

➤ Which investments are safe and which ones aren't

➤ How asking the right questions pays off

If one fact comes crashing through today's money-management jungle, it's that millions of average people are just as baffled, confused, and frustrated by investments as you are.

The guy with $20,000 in cash to stash somewhere doesn't have a guaranteed clue of where to put it or for how long or at what interest rate. He wonders who he should trust, whether his broker is telling it to him straight, and how safe his bank is.

Expert advice is hard to come by. Even top economic gurus goof when they try to call the shots on interest rates. This chapter is the first step toward carving your way through the jungle.

Watch Those Conflicting Reports!

Sure, you scan the newspaper, watch TV, subscribe to a financial newsletter or two, or chat with your banker, broker, or financial planner to try to keep up. You even perk up when the neighbor tells you she has a friend who has a friend who knows somebody named Mabel who's been living comfy off her investments. You have to sponge up every tip you can. But then you have to sort through the maze of information. Your gut says you still don't have the right information, and so much is happening so fast that the knowledge you went to bed with last night is outdated by the time you wake up.

For example, the stock market is super-sensitive to interest rates. When rates have gone down in recent years, stock prices have gone up; when rates rise, stocks prices drop. In early 1994, when everyone was positive that the Federal Reserve was going to boost rates, stockbrokers were dancing on Wall Street. New economic data showed the country's inflation rate was only 2.7 percent, the same as the year before, because consumer prices weren't moving up as fast as expected. As a result, stock prices jumped because experts believed that maybe the Fed wouldn't have to raise rates to head off inflation after all.

Only four days later more data came out, painting a whole different picture. Industrial prices on things like paper and steel had taken a big jump. Wham! The stock market tumbled because the experts said if manufacturers began charging more on their products, those higher prices would be passed on to consumers in a few months. Analysts did a quick flip-flop. Inflation was still a threat, they said, and the Fed would definitely raise interest rates.

The so-called economic experts and gurus who track the financial world have a terrible batting average when it comes to predicting anything.

One big problem is that news reporters often pick up wrong predictions from the "experts." For example, a TV financial reporter may warn that "higher rates are around the corner," and that they "will affect consumer mortgage payments and what you pay to buy a car and charge on credit cards." You're better off comparing many different news sources—especially the in-depth business pages of leading newspapers—because these will give you more of a balanced, general view of what's happening.

Where You Can Go for All the Good Stuff

You've already learned that many jungle guides (the economic and financial "experts") don't carry a compass. Some—but not all—people in the media don't really know their way, either. Even if some of them did, you couldn't learn everything you need to know from a 20-second sound bite.

So where can you go? Here's a rundown of the different sources of information available to you—and what you should be looking for from each one when you do your homework.

Newsworthy Newsletters

There are hundreds and hundreds of newsletters around, eagerly gobbled up by millions of novices and professional investors. *All* those little journals can't be right, can they?

No, not all of them can. Many simply give their opinions and theories without backing them up with good, solid data. Others make a killing by preaching gloom and doom, scaring the pants off readers in hopes they'll want to be better prepared before the world ends. All too often, the publishers who create these newsletters are self-serving—churning 'em out in the front room and taking in money to manage investment portfolios through the back door.

Don't waste your time or money on every single newsletter out there. Your subscription bill alone would be thousands of dollars before you invested one red cent! Instead, zero in on respected sources who know what they're talking about and who have the best track record of picking good investments, giving good advice, and providing the facts and figures to back it all up.

One way to cut through the muck is to follow *The Hulbert Financial Digest*. This is the newsletter of newsletters. For only $37.50 for a monthly, five-issue trial subscription, you have access to the ratings of the top 130 newsletters over a period of seven years. The *Digest* covers newsletter recommendations and performance based on three time periods: eleven years, five years, and from January 1987 to the most recent quarter.

Trying to track down the latest information in the banking industry? Need help locating an out-of-state bank that pays the highest interest rates on its CDs? Subscribe to *Bank Rate Monitor* (800/327-7717; $48 for an eight-week trial subscription) to chase the highest CD rates in the country and keep up with the latest interest rate trends and changes in the banking industry.

If you want thorough updates about the mutual fund industry, look into Sheldon Jacobs' *No-Load Fund Investor* or Morningstar's *5-Star Investor*. Both publications focus on performance information and highlight current events in the mutual fund industry. The *No-Load Fund Investor* (914/694-7420) is $109 for twelve monthly issues and Morningstar's *5-Star Investor* publication (800/876-5005) is $65 for a one-year subscription.

What's on the Boob Tube

Here's a quick rundown of the financial programs on television that report on latest financial market news and business industry changes. By learning the information provided in this book, you'll be able to determine how the stories and reports on these TV programs affect your wallet.

CNN's *Moneyline*, which airs Monday through Friday at 7:00 p.m. EST, is packed with nationwide and worldwide coverage of breaking business news, financial market stories, and straightforward economic reports from financial editor Myron Kandel. Their early 1995 launch of *Business Day*, which airs every morning at 6:00 a.m. EST, also covers newsworthy business reports. CNN's *Your Money*, which airs on Saturdays at 9:30 a.m. EST and 3:30 p.m. EST with host Stuart Varney, gives viewers information about the ins and outs of personal finance.

Nightly Business Report is a daily TV program that airs on PBS stations at 6:30 p.m. EST. Veteran financial journalist Paul Kangas hosts *NBR*, covers the action in the stock market, and interviews many investment experts. A sister program of *NBR*, *Morning Business Report*, airs daily at 6:00 a.m. EST and is hosted by Melissa Conti.

CNBC (Consumer News and Business Channel) covers the financial markets and business news round-the-clock. During the trading day, several stock market tickers crawl at the bottom of the screen. The channel offers many short, half-hour programs that deal with specific investments such as mutual funds, real estate, and technology stocks.

Wall Street Journal Report, hosted by Consuelo Mack, airs every Sunday morning at 6:00 a.m. EST. This program—considered the television version of the daily newspaper *The Wall Street Journal*—captures the key financial events of the week and interviews experts in the financial and business fields.

Reading All the Fine Print

One of the most consumer-friendly newspapers is *USA Today*, which offers a "Money" section. This section not only covers the most urgent stories of the day about the financial markets, but also gives information about the nation's top business happenings—and many personal finance stories that affect *you*.

Here's a list of others you may want to take a look at:

Money Magazine (800/633-9970) is a monthly publication that broadly covers areas of personal finance and money management, ranging from investment articles to feature stories. This long-established magazine also carries a special section on where to find high-yield CDs and good deals on credit cards.

Smart Money (800/444-4204) is a monthly magazine that also reports on a wide scope of personal finance matters. Its investigative articles show which investments will earn the reader top interest, which ones won't, and why.

Kiplinger's *Personal Finance* (202/887-6400) is also a monthly publication geared to the individual's personal financial needs. Articles have an educational tone and cover everything from financial planning to stocks and bonds and other investments.

Your Money Magazine (312/275-3590) is a bimonthly publication geared toward individual investors. This popular magazine gives a wealth of advice on personal finance issues. It also discusses investment products, insurance planning, and savings and borrowing rates. Many articles reveal how you can get more bang for your buck by discussing key strategies to saving money in the personal finance world.

Wall Street Journal (800/568-7625) is one of the most powerful daily business newspapers available. You learn about "Who's Who" and "What's What" in Wall Street. It covers virtually every type of financial market—nationwide and worldwide—and reports world events that have an impact on your money. It's most famous for its

"C-section," which lists the critically acclaimed column "Heard on the Street"—a great place to find out today what's going on tomorrow. Plus, if there's a new trend in CDs, stocks, or bond investing, odds are that *Journal*'s ace reporters will cover it.

Business Week gives readers no-holds-barred articles and reports about companies and specific company profiles. Additional stories include performance information, business strategies, personal investing, economic reports, and Wall Street's latest news. *Business Week* is also available online through America Online.

Investor's Business Daily is a daily financial newspaper that, once you cut through all of the gobbledygook, is a relevant source for the inside scoop on national and worldwide companies.

Understanding the Mumbo-Jumbo

If someone were to pull you off the street and ask you to explain the difference between *rate* and *yield*, what would you say? No need to feel at a loss for words anymore. After you learn what these terms mean, not only will you be able to tell what the difference is between rate and yield, but you could probably educate your banker or broker about the methods of compounding, too.

A **rate** is what you earn on a CD or savings account before compounding (don't worry—that's defined here too), or the interest you are charged on a loan.

A **yield** is the interest you earn after the rate has been compounded.

Compounding simply means more interest being added to the interest you've already earned.

APY stands for *Annual Percentage Yield*. It's the total amount of interest you earn on an account in one year.

APR stands for *Annual Percentage Rate*. Usually associated with loans, the APR is a complex mathematical formula that basically includes other charges on the loan, in addition to the interest rate.

An **index** is a well-known benchmark, such as the prime rate used by a financial institution to set its interest rates. The rate you earn or pay will move up or down according to changes in the index.

We've been tracking interest rates and bank, stock, bond, and mutual fund accounts for years—and answering thousands of questions from troubled average Joes and Janes. From these experiences, we've learned that you need to know the basic concepts outlined in the next sections to successfully make your way through the jungle.

What Kind of Investor Are You?

You do have a personal financial game plan, don't you? You should have a fairly good idea of what your cash position and costs might be in the early and distant future. (If you need a good review, go back to Chapter 2.)

So ask yourself: What does that picture look like—today, next month, or next year? Get a pencil and jot it down. How much have you set aside for investing? What are your short-term and long-term debts? What is your likely income over the next couple of years? Your job position? Your age? Your health?

It doesn't stop there. Are you living off a comfortable inheritance left to you by a rich uncle, or are you scraping along with monthly checks from investments that are indeed your lifeline? Are you saving for a little cottage by the sea? Will Junior need beaucoups of extra bucks if he decides to go for his master's degree? How much will you need to retire, excluding your Social Security and pension? What about unforeseen medical bills and other emergencies?

Before you set foot in the money jungle, estimate how much extra money you have to invest, how much more you're shooting for, and when you'll need it. This rule applies whether you're out to make just a few hundred bucks or are wheeling and dealing in the seven figures. Your number of investment choices is mind-boggling. So before you set out on your safari with machete in hand, go into a quiet corner and have an honest little chat with yourself to determine what kind of investor you are.

How Willing Are You to Take a Risk?

Are you the super-conservative type who can't—or doesn't want to—risk a penny? For example, do you need an extra-safe, regular fixed income to make ends meet? If so, your game plan should zero in on federally insured banks, savings and loans (also called *thrift* institutions), credit unions, and Treasury bonds and certificates.

41

If you're not extremely conservative, you have some money you'd like to speculate with (in case some tipsters told you the stock of New Electronic Widget Company will go through the roof), and you won't miss the money if you lose, you might want to dabble with a slightly more risky investment. You can dabble in the stock and bond markets or stash your cash in mutual funds if you're feeling a little adventurous.

However, if you're not at all conservative, and you like to fly by the seat of your pants, no-holds-barred, tinker in the commodities markets.

Whichever approach you decide is for you, keep in mind that your goal should be to obtain the greatest reward with the least amount of risk. Once you establish your risk tolerance, you'll be able to find your way through the money jungle a lot easier. Chapter 19 reviews the different types of investments available to you (no matter what your threshold of pain is), and Chapter 20 tells you smart money moves you should be making now based on your level of risk. For a complete review of how to successfully invest on Wall Street, pick up a copy of *The Complete Idiot's Guide to Making Money on Wall Street*.

Uncle Sam Offers the Best Safety Net

Deposits at banks, thrifts, and credit unions are backed by the full faith and credit of the federal government. That's not just idle talk. Even if you're over 60 and remember the Great Depression when the banks closed, consider this fact:

No one ever lost a dime in a federally insured bank, thrift, or credit union for up to the $100,000 insurance limit.

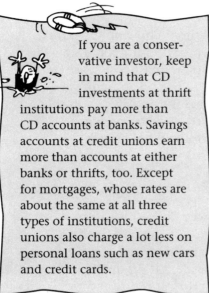

If you are a conservative investor, keep in mind that CD investments at thrift institutions pay more than CD accounts at banks. Savings accounts at credit unions earn more than accounts at either banks or thrifts, too. Except for mortgages, whose rates are about the same at all three types of institutions, credit unions also charge a lot less on personal loans such as new cars and credit cards.

That also takes into account the late 1980s when hundreds of sick outfits went belly-up. Today, institutions have rebounded like you wouldn't believe, and they're making record profits. So you can toss aside whatever outdated fears you might still hold. And if you're wondering just how safe Treasury securities are, they are backed by the full faith and credit of the U.S. government.

The Federal Deposit Insurance Corporation (FDIC) protects deposits at banks and thrifts for up to $100,000 per person, including principal and interest, at the same institution. The National Credit Union Administration (NCUA) provides essentially the same protection for depositors at credit unions. However, any amount above the $100,000 figure is not protected, so don't even think about depositing more than that into one account. If you have more than $100,000 to invest, consider opening multiple accounts.

It's possible to insure *more* than $100,000 by creating several different joint accounts and trust accounts, as Table 4.1 shows. You may never have a million bucks at your disposal, but here's how the wealthies beat the system by insuring as much as $1.4 million for a family of four at the same institution.

Table 4.1 A Family of Four with Over a Million Bucks

Account Type	Accounts		Amount
Individual	Husband		$100,000
	Wife		$100,000
	Child 1		$100,000
	Child 2		$100,000
Joint Accounts	Husband & Wife		$100,000
	Husband & Child 1		$100,000
	Wife & Child 2		$100,000
	Child 1 & Child 2		$100,000
Trust Accounts	Husband	Wife	$100,000
	Wife	Husband	$100,000
	Husband	Child 1	$100,000
	Husband	Child 2	$100,000
	Wife	Child 1	$100,000
	Wife	Child 2	$100,000
TOTAL			**$1,400,000**

How Much Money Can You Afford to Lose?

This question doesn't apply to federally insured banks, where you're protected; it only involves the gamble you take with uninsured investments. If, say, a federally insured bank offers you a yield of 8 percent on a one-year $10,000 CD, you're guaranteed to earn $800 in a year. You'll get back $10,800 on your $10,000 investment. You can't say that about speculative investments such as stocks and bonds, although the gamble may pay off with earnings higher than what you'll earn from a bank.

For example, if in 1924 you had invested $1,000 in the S&P 500 (a basket of 500 stocks that makes up the Standard & Poor's) and let it ride through the ups and downs of the stock market, you would have nearly $465,000 today! Does that mean the stock market isn't risky? No—because the stock market could average a negative 10 percent return one year, and a positive 10 percent return the next. It just means that the longer your money is invested and the more diversified your investments are, the more you reduce your risk.

Table 4.2 shows how different types of investments have performed against inflation over a 20-year period. Note, for example, that there has been less volatility between the maximum and minimum return on government bonds than there has been with stock investments.

Table 4.2 Investments Versus Inflation

	Maximum	Minimum
Common stocks	16.9%	3.1%
Long-term government bonds	9.0	0.7
Intermediate-term government bonds	9.4	1.6
Treasury bills	7.7	0.4
Inflation	6.4	0.1

How Long Can You Be Without the Money?

This is a critical decision lots of people skip over. If you're tempted to succumb to the razzle-dazzle of a stockbroker's pitch or some super-high rate in a bank ad, before you plunk down your cash, remember this: you might need the money sooner than you think.

A **liquid** account means that you may withdraw your money from the account at any time without paying a penalty.

If you need your cash six months or a year down the road for an emergency or something else you hadn't planned for, what are you going to do? What if the investment rate picture and other financial factors change and you want to move your money to a higher-earning instrument? What do you do then? If you withdraw your funds early, you'll probably be charged a stiff penalty.

Answering all of these questions helps you figure out what type of *liquidity* you are looking for in an investment. Table 4.3 shows how each investment product is ranked not only by risk but also by liquidity—and if there are any penalties for cashing in!

Table 4.3   Liquidity in the Money Jungle

	Investment Type	How Quickly Can I Get My Money?	Penalties?
LEAST RISKY:	Federally insured: Savings accounts	Immediately	No
	Checking accounts	Immediately	No
	Certificates of Deposit	At maturity	***
	Treasury bills	Five days after selling or wait until maturity	No
	U.S. Gov't money funds	Next day	No

*** If you liquidate your CD before maturity, you face a 10 percent early withdrawal penalty and an IRS penalty.

continues

Table 4.3 Continued

	Investment Type	How Quickly Can I Get My Money?	Penalties?
SMALL TO MODERATE RISK:	Savings bonds	Six months	Loss of interest
	Money Market mutual funds	Next day	No
	U.S. Gov't securities	Five days after selling or wait until maturity	No
	U.S. Federal Agency bond funds	Next day	No
MODERATE TO SLIGHTLY HIGHER RISK:	Mutual funds	Next day	No
	Municipal bonds	Five days after selling or wait until maturity	No
RISKY:	Blue-chip stocks	Five days after selling	No
	Closed-end mutual funds	Five days after selling	No
	Small cap stock mutual funds	Next day	No
	Small cap stocks	Five days after selling	No
	Corporate bonds	Five days after selling or wait until maturity	No
	Convertible bond funds	Next day	No
VERY RISKY:	Futures/commodities	Depends on contract	Varies
	Options	Next day	Varies
	Gold	Varies	N/A
	Sector funds	Next day	No
	Junk bonds	Five days after selling	No

Which Type of Investment Will Probably Earn Top Dollar?

We don't have a crystal ball, but we can explain how and where the laws of the jungle come into play.

The disadvantage of bank investments is that they usually pay less than you could earn with stocks, bonds, or mutual funds. How much you'll earn at the bank depends on current interest rates and where they'll be months or years from now. The advantage is that you won't lose your shirt.

Get out your telescope and look at the jungle through both ends. If you look at it from a narrow viewpoint—just one year, 1994—you'll see that bank CDs earned more. On a typical $1,000 investment in that year:

Common stocks earned $13.

Bonds lost $29.

A one-year bank CD earned $31.

A five-year bank CD earned $47.

But when you turn the telescope around and look at the big picture, stock investors made out better than bank CD customers in the 10-year period between 1984 and 1994.

Interest rates, especially bank rates, go up and down like a roller coaster. You must not only time your investment move just right, you must also know for how long (or short) a period you should invest, such as how long to lock up a CD rate. All these tricks are explained in Chapters 8 and 12.

Ask the Right Questions— Get the Right Answers!

Failing to ask the right questions is a mistake that goes to the top of the pile. It often separates the winners from the losers in investing. The time to pin down your banker or broker or even your financial planner is *before* you sign on the dotted line, not afterward. That sounds simple enough, right? Of course. Except very few people know which questions to ask! It's an art in itself, but you can do it.

On bank accounts, study the key questions in Chapters 6, 7, and 8. These cover buying CDs and basic savings accounts, opening a checking account, and figuring out which fees to avoid.

Never—I repeat, never—take the word of the average teller or account representative at a bank. They are honest and well-meaning folks, but often they haven't been clued in on the bank's latest interest rates or other changes in bank policies. Always ask to speak to an officer.

How bad can it get? One day when we were surveying bank CD rates in a Florida city, ten different employees at five different banks gave us twelve different interest rates on the same account! Believe us, checking and double-checking your information pays off—always. As they taught us in journalism school, "If your mother tells you she loves you, check it out."

If you're still confused by all the rates, yields, and gibberish, use the best machete of all. Ask the bank one simple question: "If I give you my money today, how much will I have in my account at the end of one year—in dollars and cents, not percent—after subtracting all fees and charges?" It works like a charm, and you'll probably see the bank rep's face turn twelve shades of purple. But don't stop there. Ask the same type of question when you borrow: "How much will my total cost of the loan be in dollars?"

If you're dealing with a full-service broker, tell him that you want discounts on your commissions. Ask him if he will meet with you every three months to review your account. Most brokers do business only by phone, rarely face-to-face.

Ask them the same question: "How many dollars will I have at the end of the year?" It may be difficult to pinpoint an answer since the financial markets fluctuate quite a bit, but if you can nail down the track record and performance history of this broker, you're ahead of the ballgame. Home run!

Lastly, make sure you watch those hidden fees. At first glance, it looks like there are only two big patches of trees in the jungle:

➤ The money you put in

➤ The money you take out

Not so. There's something else lurking out there. Hidden among the jungle's branches and vines are a million fees and charges that can whittle down your cash—without you even noticing it! (See Chapters 6, 7, and 8.)

The best way to protect yourself is to shop the fees at several outfits. You'll be amazed at the differences. For example, if you don't generate at least $100 in commissions at Smith Barney Shearson, your account will get slapped with a $50 inactivity fee.

Before you sign any document, ask for a copy of the bank's or broker's complete fee schedule. Take it home and study it. When you go back, ask for an explanation of every conceivable charge you could get hit with in the type of account you're opening. Just by following those tips alone, you'll probably get back many times your small investment in this book!

The Least You Need to Know

➤ Take any investment advice you get—whether it's from a neighbor, the paper, or a TV financial "expert"—with a grain of salt. Check out the sources and the facts for yourself before you put your money down.

➤ Before you invest a dime, know what your financial goals are, how much money you can play around with, and how much risk you can handle.

➤ Federally insured CDs and Treasury securities are the safest investments, but you can make more money in stocks, bonds, and mutual funds over the long haul. Check out Chapter 19 for more information.

➤ Don't be afraid to ask your banker or broker questions, especially if you don't understand something. Make sure you're aware of all the fees that could be involved when you do business with these people.

Part 2
Banking Fundamentals

Name one person you know who doesn't *have a bank account. It's pretty difficult, isn't it?*

When you learn about the mechanics of banking fundamentals, it goes beyond having your ATM machine swallow your ATM card. Many financial institutions are nickel-and-diming you to the poorhouse. Banks are making tons of money from all those bank accounts—no matter if you have $100 or $100,000 in them, they're raking it in. How do they do it? Fees, fees, fees.

By doing your homework in this section, you'll learn how to get the best deals on checking and how to beat those low-paying savings accounts by kicking the two-percent habit that millions of people fall into. But we don't stop at checking and savings accounts. We reveal who pays the top rates on CDs, how to check the real *bottom-line value in a "relationship package," and how to spot the warning signals that let you know it's time to kiss your banker goodbye.*

I KNOW HE TAKES IT A LITTLE SERIOUSLY, BUT HE'S THE BEST INVESTMENT BANKER AT THE COMPANY...

YOU GOTTA BE KIDDING?!
THIS IS A JOKE RIGHT?
WHO SENT YOU?

Chapter 5

Ten Money-Making Secrets Your Friendly Banker Won't Tell You

In This Chapter

➤ How banks make a bundle by nickel-and-diming you with fees and charges

➤ Why banks sometimes drag their feet in raising or lowering rates

➤ Why you're being pushed away from tellers and toward ATMs

➤ The tricks banks use to get your money

The average person knows zilch when it comes to understanding how and why banks operate the way they do. It's all a person can do to balance a checkbook and hunt for high savings rates and low borrowing rates. But banks have a strategy when they raise rates or lower them. There's a method to their madness when they lure you to automatic tellers and when they charge outrageous interest on credit cards and loans. And they know you probably won't complain when they pay you measly interest on your passbook and checking accounts.

Banks have to make money to stay alive. But you can keep more of that money in your pocket if you learn some of the banker's innermost secrets. This chapter explains some of the key ones in simple English.

How Banks Stay in the Black

Banks come out ahead when they rent your money (savings accounts and CDs) at one price, then peddle that same cash to someone else in the form of loans (credit cards, auto loans, and mortgages). Look at the bank as though it were a little one-room building with two doors—one in front, the other in the back. You deposit your savings at the front door, the bank marks it up, then lends the money to folks lined up at the back door to borrow.

One big reason many institutions went bust a few years ago was that they loaned money to home buyers at very low rates, such as six or seven percent. They got locked into those cheap loans for years and years. That was okay—as long as they only had to pay their savings customers five percent on savings. The banks pocketed the difference, which is called their "spread." But then, in the early '80s, the federal government started something called "deregulation," which permitted banks to pay whatever rate they wanted on savings accounts.

REALLY? Between 1985 and 1989, there were 848 banks that failed, according to the Federal Deposit Insurance Corporation. In that same period, the number of thrift institutions that failed was 647, according to the Office of Thrift Supervision. By 1994, however, the number of failures was dramatically reduced: only 13 banks and two thrifts.

In 1989, the thrift industry lost a total of $17.9 billion, while banks showed profits of $15.7 billion. By 1994, thrifts had rebounded into the black, posting a profit of $1.5 billion in the third quarter alone. Banks' profits, meanwhile, soared to a grand total of more than $40 billion for all of '94.

Boom! By mid-1984 CD rates shot up to 10 percent and higher. It suddenly cost banks more to get your money at the front door than what they were earning off those long-term loans at the back door. Banks began to lose their shirts! Economic wizards were predicting that it would cost taxpayers anywhere between $80 billion and $500 billion to bail out the sick industry.

As the country rolled into the 1990s, you heard less and less of that kind of talk. Why? Because bankers went to school, so to speak, on all those mistakes—and made darn sure they protected themselves against that situation. When interest rates began to plunge, banks cut their savings rates faster than they cut loan rates. That's called *managing the spread*. The result was their profits got bigger and bigger. In addition to financing the enormous banking bailout by paying more taxes, you picked up the tab by earning less on your savings and paying more when you borrowed.

Fees and Charges: The Other Money-Makers

Fees and charges have been growing like weeds. These ugly little demons keep taking more and more out of your wallet (see Chapters 6, 7, and 8). How do banks get away with it? Simple. Customers focus mostly on interest rates—not on fees. The bank slips in a higher fee here, a new little charge there, and you hardly notice it.

Fees have become so important to banks that they're now considered "profit centers" all by themselves. In fact, one banker stood up at a big convention a few years ago and proclaimed that his institution had suddenly discovered they were making money hand-over-fist from bounced-check charges.

One year it costs you 50 cents to use an automatic teller machine, the next year the fee has crept up to 75 cents. That might not sound like much, but multiply it by

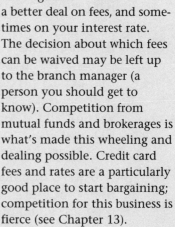

Banks don't advertise this fact, but you can negotiate a better deal on fees, and sometimes on your interest rate. The decision about which fees can be waived may be left up to the branch manager (a person you should get to know). Competition from mutual funds and brokerages is what's made this wheeling and dealing possible. Credit card fees and rates are a particularly good place to start bargaining; competition for this business is fierce (see Chapter 13).

millions of customers using their ATMs three or four times a month, and you get an idea of how much money is involved. The number of fees is increasing, too. For example, many banks now charge customers $25 an hour for helping to balance their statements, or for doing special research.

Bank-beater secret: Ask your bank for a copy of its fee disclosure statement. Match it against your banking behavior; switch to a low-fee outfit if necessary.

How Banks Work the Rates

This section explains some tricks that banks use to make the interest rates work to their advantage.

First, banks often push long-term CDs when interest rates are low, and short-term CDs when interest rates are high. Remember that little front-door/back-door example, how banks make sure they mark up your money to earn their profit spread? Well, there's another sly maneuver. Banks want to rent your savings money at the cheapest possible cost (see Chapter 8).

Let's say CD rates have been rising for several months. You're all excited to see a five-year account that used to earn 5 percent interest now paying 6 percent. That's a whole extra 1 percent, right? So you're tempted to grab the deal.

But suppose the bank believes that interest rates will continue to rise for another year. By then, the five-year CD will be paying maybe 7 percent. If you lock in at 6 percent now, you've bilked yourself out of that extra 1 percent. On a $10,000 five-year CD, you'll lose $500 by not waiting. Here's why: By opening the account now, you'll earn $600 a year for all five years, or a total of $3,000 in interest. But if you buy the CD next year instead, when the rate is up to 7 percent, you'll earn $3,500 on the same $10,000 investment. In other words, $500 more.

Keep in mind that the reverse is true when rates are falling. Banks then promote short-term CDs more heavily. If you lock up a long-term account, you'll protect yourself with a high yield for a longer stretch of time.

Bank-beater secret: Buy short-term CDs when rates are rising, go long only when rates are declining.

Second, banks drag their heels in raising savings rates after they increase their prime rate. The banks' prime goes up or down depending on how well the economy is doing. And the rate influences most of the bank's other interest rates, including savings and personal loans. In a perfect world, you'd expect that if the prime rate increases or decreases by, say, one-half of a percent, then your savings and loans would change by the same amount, right?

> **WHAT?**
>
> The **prime rate** is the bank's benchmark rate. Supposedly it's what banks charge their most favored business customers when they borrow. The little mom-and-pop store that doesn't have shiny credit will be charged a higher rate—such as 2 or 3 percent above the prime rate.

That's not how it works. What typically happens is this: When the prime jumps by a half-percent, banks boost your CD rates more slowly. It may take months for your CDs to increase by as much as the prime. That way, banks can increase their profit by lending at the higher rate for a while before increasing the amount they have to pay you in interest. Score one for the banks.

Bank-beater secret: When the prime rate goes up, take out the loans you need immediately. Go short with CDs until the prime goes down.

Third, banks pay you zip on interest checking, money market accounts, and passbook savings. For some strange reason, millions of Americans keep stashing more than $1 TRILLION in low-paying savings accounts and even lower-earning checking accounts. They could make a bundle more by shifting to CDs. Chalk that up to American savings habits (see Chapter 8).

Banks are euphoric over that idiotic consumer behavior. They're getting the cheapest money of all through the front door by peddling 2 and 3 percent savings accounts that cost them way less than CDs.

Here's how banks play the "spread." These are the differences in average rates some banks pay on savings and checking accounts versus loans and investments:

Bank	MMA	Interest Checking	New Car Loan	Credit Card
Chemical Bank, New York	3.30%	1.26%	11.50%	17.80%
Wells Fargo, Los Angeles	2.35%	1.00%	11.00%	19.80%
First Nat'l, Chicago	3.20%	1.75%	9.60%	n/a
Union Bank, San Francisco	2.38%	1.00%	9.75%	19.80%
Collective Bank, Philadelphia	2.60%	1.51%	8.25%	18.90%

Bank-beater secret: Don't keep a dime more than you need in low-rate MMAs and passbooks. Figure how much you won't have to touch for *X* length of time; put that money into higher-paying CDs for that period of time.

Why Banks Try to Steer You Toward ATMs

Gone are the days when your friendly teller handled all your transactions. It's not a conspiracy, exactly, because the whole world—including banks—is becoming more electronic. It helps efficiency and productivity. If some mechanical marvel can replace a human being, the bank saves money. And banks love it. Their tellers have to put up with fewer people acting like pests in front of a long teller line. Some outfits go so far as to charge customers $1 for a live teller transaction.

On special checking accounts for low-balance customers, banks will charge you more for your transactions if they are not through an ATM. You could be clipped with a higher charge if you make a simple balance inquiry through a person instead of a machine. When banks close their doors at 3:00 p.m., they know you'll have to conduct your late business electronically.

The upside of this trend is that you can get fast cash any time of the night from an ATM. Plus, as banking becomes more electronic, one day you won't even have to visit an ATM. You'll do your banking from your home computer, telephone, and La-Z-Boy chair.

The downside is that some banks charge you extra for the convenience. Here's a sample of what some banks charge for withdrawals, balance inquiries, or a transfer of funds—it'll leave you feeling nauseated!

Bank of America, San Francisco	$2.00
First Interstate Bank, Los Angeles	$2.00
NBD, Detroit	$1.50
Wachovia Bank, Winston-Salem, N.C.	$1.25

In other words, just finding out how much of *your* money you have left in their bank can cost you two bucks!

Do banks make money from ATM transactions? You bet. Look at it this way: It can cost a bank tens of thousands of dollars to equip just one branch with an ATM system. But consider how much they save in human labor by having *hundreds* of thousands of transactions handled by machines!

Bank-beater secret: Cut your number of ATM transactions to the bone. Check what each trip to a machine costs. Reduce fees by withdrawing more money all at once, instead of taking out small amounts several times.

The Truth About High Credit Card Rates

How come over the past decade, while your savings rates were jumping up and down like a Mexican bean, banks kept their credit card rates sky-high? On fixed-rate cards, for instance, the rate never went lower than 17.25 percent and was as high as 19 percent. At the same time, savings rates gyrated between 11 percent and a disgusting two percent. Wouldn't *you* like to borrow money at two percent and lend it out at 18 percent? You could live a nifty life with that scheme!

The banks' "official" explanation is that they need those high card rates to cover their operating costs, and nasty things like card fraud, counterfeiting, bad debt, and so forth. Horsefeathers. A more likely reason is that the banking lobbies fought hard for years to raise state usury laws—the maximum amount banks and other lenders in a state can charge on loans. They wound up getting three out of every four states to pass laws setting the usury ceiling at 18 percent.

Card issuers are now afraid that if they bring their rates down too low, the states might change their laws to something below 18 percent. And if they did, well heck, the banks might not get those high usury ceilings back again. Do you suppose that's why so many of the giant banks have transferred their credit card operations to states such as Delaware and South Dakota, which have *no* usury ceilings? Don't ever expect the banks to admit any of this to you. They won't.

> **Bank-beater secret:** Kiss those 18-percent cards goodbye. There are lots of cheaper cards out there (which you'll learn about in Chapter 13).

Loans Behind Closed Doors

Banks have many tricks when it comes to lending money. One trick they use to get your money in the first place is to promote low introductory rates on loans. The reason that this trick works is that a lot of Americans are just plain suckers for what looks like a cheap deal and they don't bother to read the fine print before they sign up at their bank.

Suppose that while other outfits peddle a variable-rate credit card at 15 percent, Megabuck Bank pushes a six percent rate. Sounds good—until you read the flyspeck footnote at the bottom of the ad. The rate is only good for six months, after which it rises to the banks' prime rate plus maybe six percentage points. If the prime is at nine percent, the card rate eventually goes to 15 percent.

In another example, Friendly Federal lures you into a home equity loan at four percent, which appears to be a lower interest rate than what other outfits offer. They're out to grab you before you decide to do business across the street. The same thing happens. The rate only applies for a few months, and then—bingo!—it jumps up like an antelope. In both situations, you probably could have found a better deal at a different bank. Don't get snookered. Remember that nothing is for nothing in this world.

Bank-beater secret: If the deal looks too good to be true, it probably is. Read the fine print before you sign the dotted line.

One strategy banks use to maximize the return they get on the money they lend out is *not* to lend you any money unless they think you *don't* need any. It happens over and over again. Two guys, Dick and Harry, apply to the same institution for a loan. Dick's family is strapped. They got behind in their debts after Dick lost his job, and they've been living off their credit cards and savings accounts, which are almost dry. The family rents a small house, and has no expensive jewels or other collateral to pledge against a loan. Dick and the family go to church every week, have never told a lie, and have a child ready for college. They need $5,000 to tide them over and maybe start a small lawn-maintenance service until Dick gets another regular job.

Harry's situation is different. The family has $120,000 equity in their home, owns another piece of property, has $20,000 in CDs, four credit cards, and a paid-off car. They want to borrow $50,000.

Question: Which loan application do you think will whistle through the bank, and which one will probably be rejected? If the bank does approve Dick's loan, which family would you guess will pay nearly 16 percent in interest on an unsecured, no-collateral loan—and which one will be able to borrow at perhaps only two percent above the prime rate?

Bank-beater secret: Dick should contact Consumer Credit Counseling Services (800-388-2227). Even though the contact will appear on his credit record, CCCS will (for little or no fee) help his family set up a payment plan with creditors. Second, Dick and his wife should write out a detailed business plan for their new business and present it to the bank. The plan should include a financial projection of revenues, costs, and profits. (Tips on how to strengthen your credit application appear in Chapter 17.)

Harry probably is A-okay, although nowadays the bank may want his shirt size, blood type, and a promise to name his first-born after the bank's loan officer to get the money!

The Least You Need to Know

> ➤ Banks earn much of their money by renting your money in savings, checking, and CDs at lower rates than they charge to lend it out.

> ➤ Another way banks make money is to charge customers fees (which are increasing all the time) to use their services.

> ➤ Banks often make interest rates work in their favor by pushing long-term CDs when interest rates are low and short-term CDs when interest rates are high, waiting a while to raise savings rates after they increase their prime rate, and paying you zip on interest checking, money market accounts, and passbook savings.

> ➤ To get you to take out a loan, banks may offer low introductory rates. They may be unwilling to give you any money, however, unless you appear to have money to spare.

Chapter 6

How to Get the Best Deal on a Checking Account

In This Chapter

➤ Which type of checking account will fit you like a glove

➤ How to avoid getting nickeled-and-dimed to death with fees

➤ The secrets to shrewd shopping

➤ The two biggest mistakes to avoid

➤ How to beat low-interest accounts

Suppose someone walked up to you and said, "Hey, here's a couple hundred extra bucks. Take it. It's yours." You'd think that person had a screw loose, right? Yet, that's how much money many people could put in their pockets every year if they only knew what their checking accounts are really costing them. Problem is, few bother to add up the almost invisible costs of using their checkbooks. Even fewer bother to shop for the best deal—and the deals are out there.

Checking accounts are the most take-it-for-granted accounts there are, which makes it easier for the banks to slip in fees and charges you don't notice. This chapter will show you how to get the most out of your checking account by explaining how banks manage these accounts, how to figure out what kind of account you need, how to shop for the best deal, and how to avoid those ugly fees.

Checking Account Basics

Banks want to get their hands on your checking account more than any other type of account. They refer to checking customers as their "core" accounts, because they figure if they've got your checking, they also have the best shot at landing your CD, personal loan, and mortgage business. And if you're a *high-balance* checking customer (instead of somebody whose balance consistently runs below $1,000), all the better for institutions. They have more money to lend out at a profit while they're paying you zip in interest.

To figure out how much your current checking account is costing you—and how you can get a better deal—you must know how banks manage such accounts. This section explains how to distinguish between the different types of checking accounts, how to figure out fees, and how banks calculate your checking account balance.

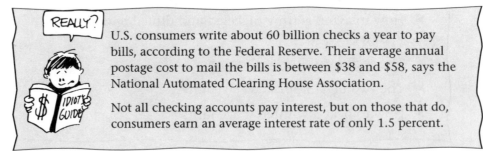

U.S. consumers write about 60 billion checks a year to pay bills, according to the Federal Reserve. Their average annual postage cost to mail the bills is between $38 and $58, says the National Automated Clearing House Association.

Not all checking accounts pay interest, but on those that do, consumers earn an average interest rate of only 1.5 percent.

Why You're Getting Nickeled-and-Dimed to Death

Guess what? While you've been looking the other way, your banker has been working behind the scenes, quietly jacking up his checking fees and charges.

He's getting away with murder because few checking customers scream or complain about the rising costs. To most folks, carrying a checkbook is as natural as getting up in the morning and brushing their teeth.

The fees creep in so quietly that you probably don't even notice them—fifty cents here, a dollar there. It's not until your monthly statement arrives that you discover strange, new little costs popping up like measles on your statement.

Plus, even if the bank pays you interest on your checking account, it probably isn't enough to pay for your cabfare across town.

Mistakes You Should Avoid... Beginning on Day One

Chances are that when you walked into a bank and told them you wanted to open a checking account, an account representative sat you down, filled out your application, then asked, "Would you like our Miserbuck Special where you only have to keep a $100 balance and pay a $10 a month 'maintenance' fee? Or our Royal Megabuck account where we waive the fee provided you keep a balance of $5,000?" Then came the emotional closer: "Do you prefer the blue checks with the whale art in the background, or the green ones with the daffodils and philodendrons?"

He or she then gave you a set of "starter" checks and a "Fee Disclosure" document on the bank's fees and charges (required by law) in small type. You probably didn't bother to read all that tiny mumbo-jumbo. That was mistake number one.

The account rep may not have reviewed with you your month-by-month checking behavior so that you could match it against the different kinds of fees on the types of accounts the bank has available. That was mistake number two. It would have helped you trim your checking costs.

The fact is, many people could put an extra $100 to $200 in their pockets every year if they only knew what their checking is really costing them. Problem is, few

Money Market Accounts (MMAs) aren't really l00-percent checking accounts at all. They're savings accounts that typically earn from two to four percent more interest than interest-bearing checking accounts pay. With an MMA, you are limited to writing only three checks per month to "cash" or parties other than yourself. If you're confused about whether an account you're considering is an MMA, ask this one simple question: "How many checks a month can I write on the account?" If they say "Three," you know it's an MMA. If the answer is "As many as you want," it's a genuine checking account.

bother to add up the almost-invisible costs of using their checkbooks. Even fewer bother to shop for the best deal—and the deals are out there.

The Different Types of Checking Accounts

Banks like to give their checking accounts weasel-worded names to distinguish one from the other, or to make you believe the account is something it's not. When you bump into names like "Master Checking," "Super Value Checking," "Special Checking" and "Regular Checking"—maybe even offered by the same bank—the result can be one big, mind-blowing maze. Even worse, some banks try to palm off higher-interest Money Market Accounts (MMAs) as checking accounts by giving them a weasel-worded name like "Money Market Checking" or "Money Fund Checking."

To cut through this confusion, just remember that most checking accounts generally fall into one of three broad categories:

➤ An account that charges lower fees but pays you no interest.

➤ An account that pays you a piddling interest rate but charges higher fees.

➤ A "basic checking" account for people with low income. These accounts don't pay any interest, but they have low-minimum balance requirements and low fees.

If you're a senior citizen or otherwise fall into the low-income group, there may be an extra-cheap checking account waiting for you. Responding to social pressure, more banks are offering *basic banking accounts*, sometimes called *lifeline accounts*. In at least seven states they are required by law: Illinois, Iowa, Massachusetts, Minnesota, New Jersey, New York, and Rhode Island.

Account-opening fees range from zero to $25. You're allowed up to 10 free withdrawals per month, and the maximum monthly service charge is $3. The minimum balance requirement is only $1 in five of the seven states. Regardless of where you live, it's worth shopping local banks to see if they offer a lifeline account or something similar.

Those Frightening Fees

According to a study of big banks by the Federal Reserve, the banks' internal cost of maintaining a checking account fell from $7.38 a month in 1992 to $6.82 a month in 1993. By earning money on your money through lending, they reduce their cost to only $4 a month. Your costs, meanwhile, have been steadily inching up to where some of your one-time fees can range as high as $30. In other words, you're riding a down escalator while the bank's is going up—which is why you need a defensive plan to keep more of your cash.

REALLY?

Some interesting bank fee facts:

➤ Banks owe a big chunk of their good fortune to higher fee income, according to *USA Today.*

➤ Fees accounted for 25 percent of banks' gross operating income in 1993, up from 14 percent in 1989, says the Federal Deposit Insurance Corporation, the regulatory agency that monitors the banks.

➤ Banks have been raising fees at a much faster rate than inflation. For example, the typical monthly maintenance fee has jumped by 15 percent in the past two years, while inflation has averaged 2.7 percent a year.

➤ In 1993, says the newsletter *Fee Income Report*, banks charged 225 fees of all types, up from 95 in 1989.

On the fee-disclosure documents that banks hand out to new customers, we've seen one that listed 64 separate fees of all types! That's enough to throw an accounting major for a loop, much less the average Joe or Jane from Dubuque. To help you focus on fees, here's a list of the most common services that banks charge you for:

Monthly maintenance

Per-check fee

Exceeding number of monthly transactions

Dropping below the minimum balance

Using your bank's ATM

Using another bank's ATM

Higher fees if account pays interest

Bouncing a check

Depositing someone else's bad check

Stopping payment on a check

Copies of stored checks

Certified check

Cashier's check

Money order

Overdraft protection

Wire transfer

Traveler's checks

Another factor in the amount of fees you get charged is the amount of money you usually keep in your account. Banks that charge on the basis of balance don't necessarily have account tiers; often they will waive fees on the basis of higher balance thresholds or other account relationships. They will also waive fees if they're moving into a new area and looking to grow business. When most banks look at your checking account, however, they classify you as to whether you are a "low-balance," "medium-balance," or "high-balance" customer, and their fees favor—you guessed it—the high-balance crowd. For example:

➤ Mrs. Gottrocks is high-balance. Because she keeps $5,000 or $10,000 in her account she's given a better break, such as having many of her fees waived, including her monthly balance charge.

➤ Susie Smith, with $1,000, is considered a medium-balance customer. She doesn't go below her required balance during the month, so she's charged normal fees, such as monthly maintenance.

➤ Joe Doaks, with a $400 balance, is a low-balance guy, so the bank discourages him from making too many transactions that cost the bank money. They hit him with charges on a slew of services. For example? A monthly maintenance charge that may be $2 higher than what Susie Smith pays.

It doesn't seem fair, the rich getting richer and the poor getting poorer, but that's the way banks play the game. Your job is to win by making decisions that will tilt things your way.

The Clearing Game

Just because you deposited the $100 check from Uncle Louie in your bank one hour ago doesn't mean you can draw on any of the funds today. The process can take up to five days until the check clears through the national banking system. The reason it takes so long is that Uncle Louie's bank needs time to get the check back and reduce his account balance by the amount of the check. Same thing with the $500 check from Aunt Nellie. But many banks let you draw against the first $100 on the next business day, and hold the other $400 until the check clears her bank. (Regulations may *require* local checks to clear in one day. That depends on location.)

REALLY? If you deposit a $1,000 check in your account, typically the following is how much money you can withdraw against the check—depending upon what kind of check it is:

One day later, you can usually withdraw all $1,000 if it's a federal, state, or local government check; a bank check, certified check, or traveler's check; a check written on your bank by someone else; or an electronic funds transfer.

If the check was written on a local bank, you should be able to withdraw $100 of the $1,000 one day later, $400 on the second day, and the remaining $500 on the third day.

On an out-of-town check, you can withdraw $100 one day later and the other $900 five days later.

If you write checks on somebody else's check you deposited, that person's check may not clear in time for your check to be honored. If that happens, it may overdraw your account; you'll wind up paying a bounced-check charge.

There are exceptions. If you keep beaucoups bucks in your accounts and know the branch manager by name, the bank may stroke you by letting you draw immediately on any type of check you deposit.

Balancing Act

Finding out how banks calculate your balance sounds like an exercise for Einstein, but it's not. You simply need to know which method a bank uses because it will tell you when a fee will kick in on your account. The method the institution uses typically is based upon one of the following:

➤ Your *low-minimum balance*, which activates a fee if the balance falls below a certain level at any time during the month.

➤ Your *average-daily balance*, where the fee kicks in if the monthly average of each day's balance drops below a certain amount.

The average-daily balance method is better because it protects you if your balance takes a sudden, temporary dive during the month. By contrast, if you choose an account using the low-minimum method, and your balance sinks to $10 one day but is $1,000 on all the other days of the month, you will still get hit with a penalty. The dollar difference between the two kinds of accounts can be substantial, as shown in the following example.

Mary and Thelma, who have checking accounts at two different banks, normally keep about $600 each in their accounts, give or take a few hundred dollars either way. Mary's bank uses the low-minimum balance method, and charges her a $10 fee if her balance falls below $300 any day of the the month. Mary deposited her paycheck the first week of the month and her account balance went up to $950. Ten days later, after she paid her rent and other bills, Mary's balance sank to $285 for one day. But the next day she deposited another paycheck that pushed the balance up to $700. Mary's average balance for the whole month was $600, but the bank still whacked her with the $10 charge because it uses the low-minimum-balance method. Multiply that situation times 12 months a year, and you'll begin to understand why it pays to shop banks and ask the right questions.

Let's pretend Thelma's numbers were the same as Mary's—same pay, same rent, same bills, same everything. Thelma's balance dropped to $285 for just one day, just like Mary's. Even her average monthly balance was the same, $600. But she wasn't charged any fee because her bank uses the average-daily balance method. The $600 figure was all that mattered.

What Kind of Checking Creature Are You?

No one wants to go through the nuisance of analyzing their personal behavior, especially on something as small and common as a checking account. When people need to write a check they write one, period, and once a month they balance their statement and pray they have enough in the account to get through next week.

REALLY?

Eighty-three percent of consumers believe checking is the most convenient way to pay bills, according to the Gallup organization. Cash comes in second at eight percent, followed by electronic banking at four percent. On average, people use checks to pay for their retail purchases almost half the time. One in 10 uses checks 100 percent of the time. Women (53 percent) use checks more often than men (42 percent).

When you dashed over to the ATM last Sunday to get some emergency cash, you may not have thought about how many similar trips you made in the past month. Or about whose automatic teller you were using—your bank's, or a different outfit's machine across the street. But those individual actions form a pattern of your personal checking behavior. The account that's just right for you probably won't be the one that's right for your child in college or for your neighbor. They're going to need one that fits their financial lifestyles.

Take stock of how you do things. Ask yourself:

➤ How do you usually buy merchandise and pay your bills? By check, credit card, or debit card, or a combination of all three?

➤ What's the average amount of money you keep in checking every month?

➤ How likely are you to let your balance slip below that level?

➤ How many checks a month do you write?

➤ Which bank's ATM do you use? Your own bank's? Another bank's machine in the same town? An out-of-town ATM?

➤ Where do you buy your check reorders?

➤ Do you bounce checks or issue stop-payment orders?

➤ Do you ever ask the bank for back copies of your statement or copies of old checks?

> **REALLY?** The percent of U.S. families using checks rose from 85.1 percent in 1989 to 87.5 percent in 1992, the last year for which figures are available, reports the Federal Reserve. in 1992, 12 percent of those who didn't use checks said service charges were too high, up from 7.4 percent in 1989.

Next, haul out your last three or four monthly checking statements and add up all the various fees, including ATM deposits and withdrawals, check reorders—the works. Then estimate what your checking is costing you per month and per year, because those are the bottom-line costs you want to cut to ribbons. Tape that information on your refrigerator door (or put it on your desk)—and get ready to play hardball with the banks. Believe it or not, you're on your way to putting extra money in your pocketbook.

Finally, don't make the same mistake that many other consumers make and foolishly trap yourself into a high-fee account because you don't want the headache of closing out an account or haven't bothered to balance your checkbook. Get ready to switch banks by keeping a record of how many checks are outstanding and how much money you'll need to cover them. Then you won't sweat the transition.

If you don't prepare, you can wind up costing yourself some money. For example, a fellow we know wrote his ex-wife a check which she didn't cash for two months. After he closed out his account—forgetting about the check—the ex deposited the check and it came back marked NSF (non-sufficient funds), whereupon she nailed him for issuing a bounced check.

You'd Better Shop Around

Outside of mortgages, a checking account—yes, little old checking—is one of the trickiest accounts to shop. "How can that be?" you ask. "What else is there besides a few fees, and maybe an interest rate?"

Plenty. Instead of just "a few" fees, you're going to come across dozens and dozens of different ones. Rarely will you see even two banks whose fees are exactly alike, or whose account requirements are absolutely identical. The trick is to ignore all the gimmicks and focus on these two key points:

1. The account you're looking for is the one whose low-cost features tally with your personal checking behavior. (Remember?) Nothing else.

2. Pretend you're shopping for a computer or a television set, not a checking account. You wouldn't buy a TV if it cost you a buck every time you turned it on, would you? Use the same demanding buying principles when you open a checking account.

You'll never be a checking idiot if you follow these two simple rules.

Basic Shopping Tips

When you shop, don't try to compare every single, cotton-picking fee charged by every institution. Otherwise you'll go berserk and wind up in a straitjacket. There are simply too many different fees to cope with. So what do you do? You limit your comparisons to only the most common fees and charges that are apt to affect you, such as monthly maintenance, and so on.

Instead of scribbling notes on the backs of fee schedules the banks give you, organize the information on a piece of paper with headings for each fee type, bank by bank. Jot down each outfit's information under the appropriate heading, but remember to base each fee on the average monthly balance you carry in your account.

Match the fees on your shopping chart with your checking behavior that you determined earlier. Based on what you usually do with your account, what would Bank "A" cost you per month? What about Banks "B," "C," and the others? Also, ask yourself: Will your financial condition likely change in any way that would affect your decision on where to take your business? Can you change any of your old checking habits—such as reducing the number of ATM transactions or checks you write—to cut costs even further?

The more banks you shop, the better your chances of cutting your checking costs. Keep your pencil sharp and keep your eye on the bottom line. One of those outfits is going to wind up being the cheapest place to do your checking.

Before You Sign on the Dotted Line

Banks have been adding so many new fees—and increasing their old ones—that almost everything you do with checks today is going to cost you. It's critical to ask the right questions up front before you sign on the dotted line. These are the most important ones.

➤ What is the minimum deposit to open the account?

➤ Does the account pay interest? If not, what are the differences in fees between this account and an account that does pay interest?

➤ Is the account tiered? If so, what interest rate does each tier pay?

➤ What minimum balance must I maintain to avoid paying a fee?

➤ Under what conditions would you waive my fee?

➤ What is the cost per check?

➤ How much do check reorders cost?

➤ What are the ATM costs if I use this bank's machine or another bank's machine?

➤ How much is the bounced-check fee?

➤ Do you return my cancelled checks with each monthly statement? If not, how much extra would it cost?

There's No Such Thing as a Free Checking Account: Avoiding Traps

In a bid to get your business, many institutions offer "free" checking with "package accounts" that combine several of your accounts—such as savings and CDs—on one monthly statement (see Chapter 9).

Even though the free checking part of the package many seem to be a good deal, the rest of the package may not be. For example, you might be able to earn higher rates on the other accounts at different banks. You may be better off splitting up your business.

An Incentive That's Not Worth It

Often banks coax customers into opening package accounts that combine CDs, IRAs, MMAs, and so on, by offering "free" checking accounts as the lure. Those packages can be tricky to shop; you might do better by splitting your money among different institutions. This section will give you three examples.

Free Checking, My Foot!

You say you just saw a bank ad for "free checking?" Better read the fine print. Even though a Truth in Savings law (which was supposed to reduce the number of tricks that banks can pull when they advertise the word "free") went into effect in 1993, it's still fairly easy for banks to mislead you. For one thing, although they can't say an account is free if they sock you with a fee for allowing your account balance to fall below a certain minimum (or if they require you to open another account to get free checking), they can peddle the account as being "free" if there are ATM or debit card charges associated with checking.

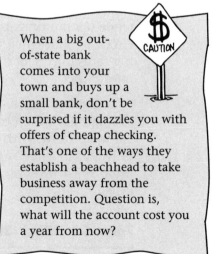

When a big out-of-state bank comes into your town and buys up a small bank, don't be surprised if it dazzles you with offers of cheap checking. That's one of the ways they establish a beachhead to take business away from the competition. Question is, what will the account cost you a year from now?

Here are some examples of when a free checking account isn't so free:

➤ You get an ATM card with your checking, but when you signed up, the small print in the agreement said you'd pay a fee for using another bank's automatic teller. If your balance slides below the minimum, you'll also pay a fee when you use your bank's machine.

➤ The bank promotes free checking even though you pay an annual fee on a debit card (which electronically uses funds from your checking when you buy something).

➤ If you do your banking electronically from your computer and are charged a fee for the service, the bank can still claim the checking account is free.

How come banks can circumvent the rules? Because the Truth in Savings law says that if the transaction is electronic, it's not really part of the checking account. Rather crafty, don't you think?

Getting the Best Interest Rate

Once upon a time, banks paid yields as high as six percent on interest checking. But when all interest rates plunged in the early 1990s, checking rates hit the basement and never came back up, even though CD rates did.

Instead, checking rates bottomed out at a disgusting 1.5 percent average, according to *Bank Rate Monitor*, and stayed there for months. So on accounts with balances of $1,000, the average customer earned only $15 in interest in a year. Monthly checking fees erased the annual interest earnings mighty fast, so customers wound up losing money! (See Table 6.1.)

Table 6.1 What Checking Interest Pays (Average Yield)

City	Percent
New York	1.49
Los Angeles	1.03

City	Percent
Chicago	1.78
San Francisco	1.02
Philadelphia	1.23
Detroit	1.74
Boston	1.42
Houston	1.61
Dallas	1.58
Washington D.C.	1.51

Source: *Bank Rate Monitor*, January 1995 Survey

Although almost all interest-paying checking accounts pay feeble rates, there are some things you can do to improve the interest rate you get on your checking:

➤ Instead of keeping all your money in a checking account that earns only 1.5 percent interest, put most of your funds in a higher-paying Money Market Account. Some out-of-state MMAs pay 5.5 percent or more. With an MMA, you're permitted to write up to three checks a month to parties other than yourself. Once a month, move enough money from your MMA to your local checking account to pay bills. You won't pay a penalty to transfer the funds, but be sure to allow at least five days for your check to clear.

➤ Get your checking account through a credit union (CU) instead of at a bank or thrift. In late 1994, CUs offered an average of 2.28 percent, while banks and thrifts paid an average of 1.50

The different institutions:

A **bank** is a depository institution that makes commercial, consumer, and residential loans and also accepts savings deposits.

A **thrift** is a depository institution that primarily makes loans for residential mortgages, but that also accepts savings deposits.

A **credit union** is a nonprofit institution formed by a common group of people, such as company employees or persons living in the same geographic area or belonging to the same organization.

percent. But at CUs they don't call them "checks," they call them *share drafts*—which operate just like checks. Note: Credit unions also pay higher rates on CDs, as you'll discover by reading Chapter 9.

Using Your Checking Account Wisely

If you find a bank that offers a higher-than-usual interest rate on checking, be suspicious—it could be just an introductory come-on rate. You could earn the rate for only a few months, then watch it plummet to the same low level as what other banks offer. Read the footnotes in bank ads to learn the gimmicks.

The biggest mistake consumers make over and over again is that they don't understand there's a cost almost every time they engage in checking activity. For example, Joe Doaks thinks he's exercising discipline by taking out only $10 whenever he withdraws checking funds from an ATM. Say he takes out 10 bucks a day for five days in a row. He forgets that each time he does this, the bank is charging him $1. That's five bucks in fees based on a $1 charge per transaction, or a total of $5. Had he withdrawn the $50 all at once, he would have been nicked only $1. This section tells you how to avoid such costly mistakes and provides some additional money-saving tips.

REALLY?

Here's why having your checks—especially your Social Security checks and payroll checks—directly deposited into your bank accounts is important. In August 1992, when Hurricane Andrew hit Homestead, Florida, although everything was being destroyed by the storm, receipt of direct-deposit payments was not interrupted. The National Automated Clearing House Association reports that 48 percent of household payroll and more than half of Social Security beneficiaries are paid through direct deposit.

Using ATMs

A machine's a machine, but whose ATM you use will make a difference in the fees you're charged. Here's the lingo banks use in their literature:

➤ Proprietary ATM: It means your bank owns the machine. A few banks still charge no fee per transaction, but most will charge between 40 cents and $1.25. The average is about 75 cents.

➤ Non-Proprietary ATM: The machine belongs to another outfit. Expect to pay $1 to $1.25 per transaction.

➤ National ATM: The bank's machine is hooked up to a national or regional network such as Cirrus, Plus, or Mastercard. You'll see their emblems on the machine. When you make an out-of-town transaction on these ATMs, the fee rises to $1.50 or $2.

➤ "Foreign" ATMs: Another way of saying "non-proprietary."

As if rising ATM transaction fees aren't enough, some banks have begun to slap a "surcharge" at ATM machines on top of all their other charges. For example, Bank One Texas has a *surcharge* (an extra charge) of 50 cents at its terminals, in addition to its regular ATM transaction fee. And this is on top of the fee your *own* bank may charge for foreign transactions. Greenpoint Savings, New York, puts a $500 temporary hold on accounts linked to an ATM card. Reason? To limit the amount a customer may withdraw until his or her check clears.

REALLY? When ATMs first appeared nearly 20 years ago, banks enticed consumers to try the newfangled machines by offering free hamburger coupons, cotton candy, and balloons for the kids. It was sort of a try-it-you'll-like-it campaign to get us addicted—and all the ATM transactions were free.

You can reduce your ATM charges if you:

➤ Keep your checking account at a bank that doesn't charge you for using its machines.

➤ Don't use an ATM belonging to an institution where you don't bank.

➤ Withdraw all the cash you'll need for the next few weeks instead of making several small transactions that run up your total ATM fees.

One final thing to keep in mind: using ATMs can be dangerous, as well as expensive, to use. To stay safe, Great Western Bank advises you to follow these rules:

➤ Memorize your Personal Identification Number (PIN) and keep it to yourself. Don't keep it in your wallet.

➤ Keep your ATM card in a safe place. It's as valuable to you as your credit card. If the ATM card is lost or stolen, report it to your bank immediately.

➤ Keep extra deposit envelopes in your car, so you can fill them out before approaching the ATM.

➤ Have your paperwork and your ATM card ready when you reach the ATM so you won't have to reach into your purse or wallet.

➤ Stand between the ATM and people waiting in line so no one can see your PIN number or your transaction.

➤ Don't accept help from strangers while you're using the ATM. If you have a problem, contact the bank.

➤ Take your ATM receipt. Put away your cash, ATM card, and receipt *before* you leave the ATM.

➤ Report all crimes to the ATM owner and local law enforcement officers immediately.

Cost-Cutting Tips

As big as the check fee world is getting, there are still a few ways to get around those little buggers. Especially now, as banks try to romance you to do business at their place instead of someone else's.

For example, many banks will waive certain checking fees if you:

➤ Keep a big balance in your account.

➤ Agree to forego getting your cancelled checks back with your monthly statement.

➤ Are older than 50 or 55 years, depending on the bank's senior checking requirements.

➤ Open a package account that combines several of your accounts, such as CDs and passbooks, under one statement.

➤ Limit the number of checks you write per month to the maximum allowed without a fee.

➤ Don't exceed a certain number of ATM transactions per month.

One of the best ways to save money on your check orders is to order your checks from an outside distributor. Checks-In-The-Mail (800/733-4443) and Current, Inc. (800/533-3973) offer a low price of $4.95 for the first 200 checks.

The Ugliest Fee of Them All

The one fee you should absolutely try to avoid is the bounced-check charge—the banks call these checks "NSFs" (non-suffcient funds). Though industry studies show it costs a bank less than $2 to handle a bounced check, the average NSF today costs a customer $19.92, according to *Bank Rate Monitor*. That's up from $15 in 1987. The NSF fee runs as high as $30 in Philadelphia and as low as $11.85 in San Francisco. (See Table 6.2).

Table 6.2   The Average Cost of Bouncing a Check

City	Bounced-Check Fee
New York	$15.90
Los Angeles	$12.60
Chicago	$19.80
San Francisco	$11.85
Philadelphia	$29.10

continues

Table 6.2 Continued

City	Bounced-Check Fee
Detroit	$18.70
Boston	$19.00
Houston	$20.25
Dallas	$20.00
Washington, D.C.	$24.50
Atlanta	$21.60
Miami	$25.70

Source: *Bank Rate Monitor*, October, 1994 Survey

If a bank decides to honor the check instead of letting it bounce, it will cost you an average of $20.33 in addition to the amount of the check. If it pays the check against your funds that haven't yet cleared, the charge is $13.05.

An outrage? You ain't heard nothin' yet. More outfits have begun to hit consumers with an NSF charge if they deposit someone else's rubber check to their account, regardless of their own balance. That cost averages $5.24. One outfit in Chicago slaps customers with a $20 fee if you deposit someone else's rubber check into your account!

Remember that if you don't have enough funds in your account, every check you write beyond your balance will bounce. If, say, your balance is $15 and you write three checks for $25 each, the bank will charge you a fee for each one. The fee will be between $10 and $30, so you could wind up with the bad checks costing a total of as much as $90!

Bounced-check charges are so out of control that it's possible for this to happen: A person writes a bad check for $10. The check is presented to his or her bank not once, but twice, and the customer gets nicked $20 each time. Plus, the person whose name is on the check gets charged five bucks. The fees add up to 45 bucks in all—just for a $10 check. Consider yourself warned!

Stop-Payments

You just issued a check to Big Bubba's garage for a new transmission in old Betsy. On your way home the transmission sounds likes a blender full of rocks, and you don't want Bubba to pocket the money until he makes good on the deal. What do you do? Immediately inform the bank to stop payment on the check. Tell them your account number, the check number, the exact amount (in dollars and cents), date of the check, and the name of the person or company you wrote it to.

The problem with stop-payments is that they don't come cheap. They'll cost you $20 or thereabouts, and fees have been going up. You will have to decide whether the action is worth it—by considering who you're doing business with on the other end, and how important it is that the other party not cash the check.

A Savings Tip That Might Not Save You Anything

Earlier we told you that you could reduce your account fees by not getting your cancelled checks back every month. The banks call this "truncation" or "check storage." It works like this: You receive only your statement, and they keep your checks in their warehouse. That will shave a few bucks off your checking fees, but if you suddenly need a copy of one of the checks—zing!—you may be charged about $3 to $5 per copy. And the process will take a few days.

Then there's something called *check imaging*: you get back miniature photos of the fronts of the checks you issued last month, printed out on a large sheet. The banks still keep the real checks.

Before you grab the bank's bait, ask yourself: Wouldn't the cancelled checks come in handy when you prepare your taxes, or if you ever get entangled in a lawsuit?

REALLY?

The first step toward preventing check forgery is to keep your checks in a locked drawer or in a safe deposit box. The institution should try to protect you by comparing the signature on the checks it receives with the signature card you filled out when you opened your account. You should have a copy of that card. It's also your proof of your legal signature.

Once a forgery is committed and it gets by the institution, there's no automatic protection. Almost all states have adopted a uniform code on forgeries, but the interpretation and execution varies by state.

As soon as possible, notify the bank if a check is forged. You'll likely discover it when reviewing your statement. Your obligation to notify the institution may be spelled out on the back of the statement. In some states, it's as short as 14 days. You can call the outfit, but your rights are protected only if you put the claim in writing.

The institution may investigate, or it may not respond. If it doesn't respond, make follow-up phone calls and write more letters. The bank may claim that you failed to notify it on time, or that you were negligent and you let other people use your checkbook.

In that case, you may be forced to sue the bank. That will be a headache if a small sum is involved. You may be able to raise enough ruckus with your letters to get some action.

The Least You Need to Know

➤ Most checking accounts are characterized by high fees and little or no interest.

➤ Knowing your personal checking habits will help you figure out what bank and which kind of checking account will cost you the least amount of money.

➤ When shopping for a checking account, limit your comparisons to only the most common fees and charges that are apt to affect you. Also, remember to read all the small type before you sign on the dotted line.

➤ Be wary of offers of super-high interest rates and free checking. The offer may be only temporary, or there might be extra fees involved that aren't immediately obvious. Again, read the small type.

➤ Getting your checking account through a credit union or putting some of your money in a Money Market Account can boost your interest rate.

➤ Remember that there's a cost almost every time you engage in checking activity. To avoid unnecessary fees, get a copy of the bank's fee-disclosure schedule, know your bank's rules regarding ATM usage, and avoid bouncing checks and issuing unnecessary stop-payment orders.

Chapter 7

How to Beat Those Low-Paying Savings Accounts

In This Chapter

➤ Recognizing the three basic savings accounts

➤ How to avoid getting tricked by promotional "bells and whistles" and other gimmicks

➤ Key steps in opening a high-paying, out-of-state account

➤ Deciding when to put your money in a CD instead

You developed a great savings habit as a kid, plopping your nickels and dimes into an old-fashioned passbook account. It was a great idea for years and years. But then came banking deregulation; banks promoted hundreds of different accounts that pay more than passbooks.

As CD rates go up, the banks keep holding passbook and Money Market Account rates down. The real reason is because people aren't complaining. They're still hooked on their old basic savings habits, to the tune of pumping $1.3 trillion into low-paying accounts. Are banks taking advantage of this situation? You bet they are. This chapter shows you how to turn those piddling-interest instruments into cash cows by doing business with safe, top-paying banks. Plus, this chapter gives you key questions to ask before you give any bank your money.

Savings Account Basics

The major advantage of savings accounts is that they're *liquid*, which means you can add to your savings or withdraw funds at any time—without getting socked with a penalty (unlike CDs). Savings accounts also can provide you with a temporary "garage" where you can park your funds while you're scouting around for a high-paying CD or other investment.

Savings accounts come in three flavors:

WHAT?

A **liquid account** lets you withdraw any of your money at any time without paying a penalty or going through any other hassle.

Passbooks   The same old account that Ma and Pa lectured about when you were a youngster. You deposit your money, and the bank gives you a little book to record your transactions. The accounts paid a regulated five percent interest until 1986, but rates have been sinking ever since—to a low of two percent or thereabouts.

Statement savings   Walks, talks and quacks exactly like a passbook, except there's no little book involved. Instead, the bank sends you a monthly statement that shows all your transactions. This, of course, reduces the time you spend bothering a teller, which is precisely what the bank wants.

Money Market Accounts (MMA)   The big new kid on the block, created in 1982. MMAs pay only a tad more interest than the other two accounts, and you're permitted to write a maximum of three checks a month (to parties other than yourself) on the account. These will come in handy to beat the miserably low interest banks pay you on checking accounts, all discussed in Chapter 6.

Fees

Nothing in life is free, especially not savings accounts. All three kinds hit you with tariffs. The following types of fees are common:

➤ A monthly or quarterly "maintenance fee," just for keeping your money in the bank. It will probably be about $3 to $12.

➤ A special fee if your account balance falls below a certain minimum in the month. Figure about $10.

➤ An ATM fee every time you use an automatic teller (see Chapter 6).

➤ On an MMA, you'll probably get a $10 to $15 charge if you write more than three checks a month. Plus, some banks will charge a $10 to $25 penalty if you close your MMA account within, say, six months after opening it.

A Word About Interest Rates

Chapters 11 and 12 focus on interest rates, but for now you need to be aware that over time, all rates are heading either up or down. That goes for passbooks and MMAs. Banks generally change their savings rates once a week, mostly on Tuesdays or Wednesdays. You'll earn the rate you're quoted today until the new numbers show up next week. (A word to the wise: Don't lose too much sleep over rates on these accounts—they're so low they look more like a dustbin than a high-powered investment vehicle.)

 Many banks will pay you higher interest if you maintain a larger balance, such as one-quarter percent more on $5,000, a half-percent more if you keep $10,000, and so on. This kind of setup is called a *tiered* account.

  When Congress authorized banks to start offering deregulated rates on Money Market Accounts in 1982, institutions paid an average of 10.35 percent. For a couple of weeks, Atlanta banks offered as much as 25 percent! That became known as "The Atlanta Sting" because shortly afterward, the banks dropped their rates down to what other banks were paying.

Over the next decade, MMA rates went up and down like a yo-yo, paying as high as 9.8 in 1984. The rates began scraping the bottom of the barrel in 1993 and 1994, dipping to an average of only 2.32 percent during that period.

Shopping for Savings Accounts

The biggest reason banks covet your basic savings and checking business? Those are their bread-and-butter "core" accounts. Once you become a customer, you're also a prospect for buying CDs, mutual funds, personal loans, and mortgages. On which, of course, you'll earn a higher rate than what the bank is paying you on savings.

The fact that interest rates on basic savings accounts are so doggone low means you shouldn't bite at the first bank offer that comes along. It may look like a rate you can live with at a "comfortable and convenient" institution. But that's not your goal: You want the highest interest rate you can find at an outfit that won't slap you silly with ridiculous fees and charges. What are the odds you can discover such an account?

➤ Ten to one that you can beat any deal at another institution in the same city. Rarely are all bank rates and fees the same, although some outfits imitate each other in their rate-setting.

➤ A thousand to one that you can come out even farther ahead—maybe even double your interest earnings—by opening a higher-yielding account at an out-of-state bank (a how-to is coming up). Some people are antsy about the whole idea of doing business with a faraway institution. But that's nonsense, for reasons we'll get to in a moment. Also, some banks have more than one savings or MMA account. With a larger balance, you might earn more, if you ask.

The sections that follow will help you steer safely through the process of shopping for a savings account.

Key Questions to Ask

Banks like to play around with names like "Master Passbook Account" and "Money Market Passbook," which do nothing except create mass confusion. You need a roadmap to figure which account is which, but you can cut through the jungle by asking the following key questions:

➤ What are the rate (before compounding) and yield (after compounding)? Compounding is explained in Chapter 11.

➤ Is the account tiered? That is, does it pay higher yields on larger balances?

➤ What is the monthly maintenance fee?

➤ Is there an additional fee if I don't keep a certain minimum balance?

➤ Is there a fee if I close my account early?

➤ Is there a per-check fee on my MMA (three third-party checks are permitted per month)? Is there an additional charge if I *exceed* three checks a month?

➤ Is there more than one version of this account?

➤ Is the account federally insured?

More Shopping Secrets

Before you sign on the dotted line, check out the following tips:

➤ The time for you to wheel and deal is *before* you sign. Since banks are paying zip in interest, basic savings accounts come cheaply to them. So, they dangle carrots like a $10 or $20 "cash bonus" and free checks to get you to agree to switch your business from another institution. Stealing the other guy's customer is the name of the game.

➤ Get a copy of the bank's "fee disclosure" document. Ask the savings representative to explain when all the bank's ugly, costly fees kick in on the account, and what you can do to avoid them. Make sure you match the fees against your normal banking behavior. Then, before you leave, courteously ask the rep one more time: "Are you sure you've told me about all ways I can earn more interest, save on my loans, and avoid fees?" You're not being a pest; it's simply good business. The squeaking wheel always gets the grease.

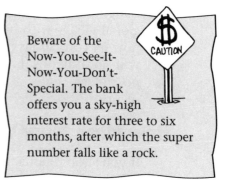

Beware of the Now-You-See-It-Now-You-Don't-Special. The bank offers you a sky-high interest rate for three to six months, after which the super number falls like a rock.

➤ Read your contract *before* you sign anything to open the account. Ditto the flyspeck footnotes at the very bottom of bank ads. It's not the time to be bashful when your hard-earned coin is on the line.

Earning More Out-of-State

To start putting higher savings yields in your pocket immediately, you're going to have to get rid of another habit: thinking there's something wrong with a bank that's 1,000 or so miles away. Nothing could be further from the truth.

In the past couple of years, the top-paying institutions nationwide have become as strong as the proverbial ox. Not only are they federally insured, most also boast three-star safety ratings by Veribanc, Inc., an independent research firm in Wakefield, Massachusetts. Veribanc uses FDIC data to diagnose each bank's financial health. No one has ever lost a dime in a federally insured bank, up to the $100,000 FDIC limit.

Of course, the whole idea of going out of state to make more money will go over like a lead balloon with your local banker. He'll tell you it's not patriotic to pull money out of your community and hand it to some faraway outfit. But gee whiz, gang, aren't big banks gobbling up little banks in other states right and left? What's good for the goose ought to be okay for the gander, too, right? And don't giant outfits like Citibank, First Interstate, First Union, NationsBank and others peddle credit cards across state lines?

So there's nothing wrong with going out of state to earn more dough on your precious savings. You're already living in a shrinking global village with new trade treaties such as NAFTA and GATT, which now let companies on the other side of the earth sell their wares in your local hardware store. Banking between New York and California is no big deal, especially when you use the information in the following sections.

How Much More Can You Earn?

If you shop financial institutions in your town, you're apt to see banks offering only two percent to three percent on MMAs. Let's even say you could top that by another half-percent by racing to maintain a large balance in the four or five figures. That's still not good enough.

In some robust U.S. markets where banks are aggressively pursuing deposits (because there's a bigger demand for loans) chances are you'll find five or ten institutions that pay between 4.5 percent and 6 percent. On a $10,000 investment, the amount of extra interest you'll pocket in a year would be $150 to $400.

All the highest-paying MMAs are ranked each week in the newsletter *Bank Rate Monitor* ($48 for 8 trial issues; $124 for 52 issues; P.O. Box 088888, North Palm Beach, Florida 33408; 1-800-327-7717). The publication lists only institutions that accept out-of-state deposits, and whose accounts are protected for up to the $100,000 FDIC limit. The list includes:

➤ The bank's name, address and toll-free phone number.

➤ Minimum deposit (anywhere from $100 to $25,000, with the average being $2,500).

➤ Basic interest rate before compounding (see Chapter 11).

➤ The compound method, usually daily or monthly.

➤ Annual percentage yield (the interest you earn per year after the compounding is figured in).

The high yields aren't confined to only Money Market Accounts. You can also get higher interest on your CD investments of six months to five years. (You can also find out about out-of-state rates from a publication called *100 Highest Yields*. Some libraries have it.)

According to *Bank Rate Monitor*, in February 1995, the *highest* nationwide yield on a Money Market Account was 5.95 percent at Lincoln National Bank, Chicago (312/868-3434). By contrast, the average MMA yield nationwide in the same month was 2.82 percent.

Here's How You Do It

These are the basic steps for investing in a high-yielding, federally insured savings account out of state:

1. Contact the institution by mail or by phone, to the attention of the person in charge of consumer deposit accounts. Some banks have a "national money desk," which handles inquiries from individuals outside the institution's local area.

2. Explain how much you want to invest and for how long.

3. Ask for the latest rate and yield on the account you are interested in. Banks are apt to change their rates on a weekly basis or more frequently. Many change their rates on Wednesdays.

4. Ask when interest earning will begin, and how many days after opening an MMA account you can withdraw funds.

5. Ask for an account-opening form and a pre-assigned account number.

6. Get the correct mailing address of the bank branch you are dealing with. A bank may have several locations.

7. If you open the account by mail, make your check payable to the institution, not to an individual. Write "For deposit only" on the back of the check.

8. If the institution doesn't provide a deposit form, attach a letter specifying how much you are depositing, the type of account, the pre-assigned account number, the check number, and the amount. Include your name, address, phone number, and Social Security number. Keep a copy of the letter.

9. Mail your letter and check to the correct bank branch.

Consider an Alternative: The CD

If you continually carry a substantial balance in your savings account, you could be costing yourself some serious cash. Confused? Let me make it clear: Even if your bank offers as much as five percent on a Money Market Account, you can earn two to three percent more with a CD. (More about these *Certificates of Deposit* in Chapter 8.)

Not convinced? Consider that while banks have been moving their CD rates up and down by as much as *eight percentage points* in recent years, passbook account earnings have been stuck in low gear. In fact, passbook rates fell so low in 1993 and 1994 that the average customer earned only 2.25 percent—less than what they earned in 1935 when Franklin Delano Roosevelt was President! More agony: When CD interest rates rebounded by by 2.5 percentage points in '94, passbooks hardly budged. They inched up by less than one-half percent. Take a look at the following table:

Table 7.1   The Gap Gets Bigger... MMA Versus CD Yields

Month in 1994	Average MMA Yield	Average One-Year CD Yield
January	2.35 percent	3.08 percent
February	2.32	3.10
March	2.32	3.17
April	2.33	3.31
May	2.35	3.60
June	2.40	3.85
July	2.42	4.06
August	2.44	4.22
September	2.49	4.42
October	2.55	4.68
November	2.62	5.05
December	2.72	5.51

Source: *Bank Rate Monitor*

Here's the reason you're getting rooked: Bank customers aren't complaining. They're behaving like a giant herd of elephants—investors who are creatures of The Great Low-Rate Savings Habit, racing to open accounts that pay next to nothing. "Heck," the banks are figuring to themselves. "Why should we pay customers a cent more? We're getting a ton of money in over the transom without lifting a finger." And the transom is getting wider. Whenever the stock market and bond market get a little shaky, more of the herd flees Wall Street and hauls even more of their cash to federally-insured banks. Result: Today there's 50 percent more money in the three basic types of savings—passbooks, statement savings, and Money Market Accounts—than in CDs.

At the end of 1989, consumers put 56 cents of every savings dollar into small-denomination CDs and 44 cents into basic savings accounts such as MMAs and passbook accounts. Five years later, 58 cents of that dollar went to savings accounts and 42 cents to CDs. Table 7.2 spotlights this trend.

Table 7.2 Where the Money Is—Annual Figures

Date	Billions of Dollars
Money Market Accounts, Passbooks, and Statement Savings Accounts	
December 1989	891.0
December 1990	920.4
December 1991	1041.1
December 1992	1183.6
December 1993	1215.5
December 1994	1145.5
Small Denomination CDs	
December 1989	1153.7
December 1990	1174.5
December 1991	1067.4
December 1992	870.5
December 1993	785.7
December 1994	818.1

Source: *Federal Reserve*

How much are American savers losing by keeping so much money in low-paying savings accounts? Plenty. Suppose that 1,000 people each keep $1,000 in a Money Market Account paying two percent interest. That comes to a grand total of $200,000 in interest per year. Now let's assume those same 1,000 customers move their MMA accounts to other banks that offer five percent—something they could easily do. The interest increases to $500,000. If the customers decide instead to put their money into CD accounts paying seven percent, the interest jumps to $700,000.

As you can see, CDs are definitely worth looking into. However, keeping a lot of money in a savings account might be the better strategy if any of the following apply:

➤ You think you might have to access the money suddenly for some reason, such as putting a new roof on the house or getting Junior a set of braces. There's no penalty for withdrawing funds from an MMA, as there is with a CD.

➤ The high-tier rate on an MMA is paying more than CDs are paying. If it is, there's something screwy going on. One-year CDs (or longer) usually pay higher interest than even big MMA balances.

➤ The bank will waive its fees in exchange for a higher balance. But the bank's deal may not be as good as the one at another outfit. Be sure to shop around.

Chapter 8 describes CDs in detail. Reading it will help you decide what your best option is.

The Least You Need to Know

➤ The three basic types of savings accounts are passbooks, statement savings, and Money Market Accounts.

➤ Basic savings accounts almost *always* pay less than CDs.

➤ Comparison shopping for the best savings account deal can really pay off. Banks vary widely in their fees and interest rates.

➤ In early 1995, you could have earned as much as six per-cent interest on your savings account if you had gone to an out-of-state bank. The newsletter *Bank Rate Monitor* is a great resource to use when shopping for the best rates nationwide.

➤ Remember, even if your bank offers as much as five percent on a Money Market Account, you can can earn two to three percent more with a CD. Read Chapter 8 to find out all the CD facts.

Secrets of CD Shopping

Ever been befuddled by which type of bank CD you should buy? Which accounts to stay away from? Or which banks are offering the highest rates? The CD world may look like a jungle, but you can tame it. The secrets are in knowing the kinds of CDs that are out there, how banks set their rates behind the scenes, and the critical questions to ask before you open an account.

Timing is the key to CD buying: Knowing when to go long-term or short-term can dramatically affect your pocketbook. But banks will try to outfox you by dangling higher rates on five-year accounts when you really should be investing the other way. They'll also offer gimmick accounts that seem to pay better rates, but don't. There are quick, easy ways to debunk what the banks are telling you and learn whether their CD deal is fantastic or a bummer. This chapter takes the mystery out of CD buying.

What Is a CD?

A *CD*, which stands for *Certificate of Deposit*, is a time deposit. With a CD you agree to deposit your money for a specific number of days, months, or years. The financial institution agrees to pay you a predetermined interest rate and yield for the period of time it keeps your money. The rate is usually fixed, but some CDs may offer a variable rate, which is often tied to an index such as the bank's prime rate.

CDs usually pay more than savings accounts, even high-earning ones such as Money Market Accounts. According to the industry newsletter *Bank Rate Monitor*, CD yields beat MMA yields by 2 to 4 percent in 1994. Here's the comparison between a one-year CD and the money market:

The most popular CDs are six-month, one-year, two-year, three-year, four-year, or five-year accounts. Though the customary time increment is six months, some CDs are for only three months—and there has been a trend toward more banks offering odd-term CDs such as five months, 11 months, and 15 months. Usually, a longer term means a higher interest rate.

You can direct the bank to deposit your money into an *Individual Retirement Account* (*IRA*). These accounts pay about the same interest rate as regular CDs, but for your benefit have separate federal insurance of up to $100,000 per person at the same institution. Unlike a regular CD, when an IRA CD matures, you must roll the money into another IRA account within 60 days to avoid paying a federal tax on your interest earnings. You can't use the money during those 60 days; the funds must remain at a bank. IRA interest continues to be tax-free until you reach age 59 1/2, or until you retire after that (see Chapter 27).

WHAT?

A **rate** is what a financial institution pays on savings accounts before interest is added.

A **yield** is what it pays after interest is added. The amount of interest is determined by how the interest is compounded (see Chapter 11).

Compounding is simply interest added to interest (see Chapter 11).

An **index** is a well-known interest rate (such as the bank's prime rate) that an institution may use to set a savings or loan rate. It adds or subtracts so many percentage points to or from the index rate to determine the rate you earn on a CD, or what you pay to borrow.

Withdrawing Your Money Early Will Cost You

When you open a CD account, you promise the bank to keep a certain amount of money (the *principal*) in the account for a certain amount of time (the *term*), in exchange for a certain amount of interest (the *rate*). If you break your promise and withdraw money from the CD account before the time is up (before the account *matures*), you pay a penalty.

How stiff are these penalties? It varies. Many institutions sock you with six months' worth of interest if you yank out any money on a CD with a term of more than one year. For CDs of less than one year, often the charge is three months' worth of interest. On a *floating* (variable) *rate* CD, an institution may calculate the penalty by using the average rate they paid every day up to the day you withdraw. If you read your CD contract carefully, you'll see that often the bank even has the right to take away part of your principal (the amount you deposited) if not enough interest has built up to cover the early withdrawal penalty!

Pretend you open a $10,000, 2 1/2-year CD paying a yield of 6 percent, but one month later you have a personal financial emergency and need cash. The bank's penalty for early withdrawal is six months' interest on CDs of more than one year. You wind up with less money than you started with.

You deposited $10,000

Penalty (6 months' interest) $300

Balance. $9,700

Some banks, however, may not tap into your principal.

Some Penalties Aren't as Stiff

There are a few "no-penalty" CDs kicking around. For example, a bank may skip the penalty if it limits the CD term to six months or a year, or waive the penalty any time after the first seven days. It may also require a minimum deposit of $2,500 and partial withdrawals of no more than $1,000. Any amount above that may involve a penalty. Some outfits may eliminate the no-penalty feature when you renew your CD.

Many institutions promote accounts with "no penalties," but they're really Money Market Accounts, not CDs (see Chapter 7). CDs by law must charge a penalty within the first seven days, even if they're hyped as "no-penalty." Otherwise it's not really a CD, but an MMA, which has no early withdrawal penalty.

> **REALLY?**
>
> As of December 1994, according to the Federal Reserve, there were $818.1 billion in small-denomination CDs. These are CDs with low minimums such as $1,000 to $25,000, as opposed to high-minimum accounts ($100,000 and up) called "jumbo CDs." In comparison, the amount of money consumers keep in ordinary savings accounts—such as Money Market Accounts, passbooks, and statement savings accounts—is even greater (about $1.145 trillion).

How Banks Brew Up Their Rates

Ever wonder how banks set their interest rates? Something must be going on in the back room, right? Else why do the rates keep changing all the time? Let's take a look-see into the bank's kitchen and see how they make their soup.

The first thing you should know is that banks typically change CD rates every week, generally on Tuesday or Wednesday. Say it's Thursday, and you just waltzed into the lobby of Megabuck Bank. You notice that the white plastic interest-rate numbers on the black felt sign in the lobby are higher than they were last week. The one-year CD that paid 5 percent last week has edged up to 5.50 percent. How come? Nobody in the bank is going to tell you. Chances are the bank didn't even explain why to its employees.

What banks pay on CDs generally depends on the health of the U.S. economy. When the economy is getting stronger, interest rates tend to rise; when it's getting weaker, rates usually fall. But it also can depend on other factors. For example, say that when Megabuck's rate-setting committee met on Tuesday they noticed that a whole bunch of things occurred since last week:

➤ Treasury rates moved up at the federal government's auction the day before.

➤ Many of the country's biggest banks also raised rates.

➤ Just before the Tuesday meeting, a Megabuck secretary made cold calls to eight or nine other local banks and found their rates, too, had climbed.

➤ The morning paper says consumer prices and housing starts were higher last month than the month before—signals that the economy is getting stronger.

➤ Megabuck's loan officer reports more of the bank's consumer and business customers have been borrowing, which means the bank has to pull in some new money to replace what it has loaned out.

Not only did Megabuck learn that interest rates were heading up across the country and in its home town, but Megabuck also had to guess where rates would be a year or two down the road. Banks don't just set rates based on what happens today, but on what they expect to happen tomorrow. That's why you saw the one-year CD rate on the lobby sign increase to 5.5 percent. Had Megabuck gotten different information—if, for example, consumer prices and housing were down instead of up, and if other banks were dropping their rates—Megabuck might have lowered its rates.

The direction banks believe interest rates are headed is based on what they pay on long-term CD rates, such as 2 1/2-year and five-year accounts. If banks think rates will continue to go up for a long time, odds are they'll raise rates on those CDs faster than rates on six-month or one-year accounts. By contrast, when long-term CD rates come down faster than short-term rates, banks foresee a rate decline. You don't have to be a wizard to plot the trend. Simply pick out five big banks in your hometown, and then track their short-term and long-term rates for five or six weeks in a row. This will tell you which way the wind is blowing.

There's a Higher Rate in Your Hometown

On any given day in most cities in the U.S., and on the very same kinds of CD accounts, you'll find rate differences bank by bank. It could be anywhere from one-quarter of a percent to a full percent between the lowest- and the highest-paying institutions. That's not exactly chicken feed. Why the different rates? Because some banks are more aggressive than others; they've figured out that even by hawking a rate higher than the other guy's, they can still lend out your money (or invest it) at a profit.

For example, our old friends at Megabuck Bank may be peddling five-year auto loans like crazy at a rate of 9 percent. By hiking its five-year CD rate a half-percent above what the competition pays, say to 6.5 percent, Megabuck can pull in more deposits. For five years it will make a profit on what you earn on savings and what it charges you to finance a car.

It pays to shop! Table 8.1 shows what different banks and thrifts offered on CD investments on the same day in Detroit in February 1995. The yields varied by as much as 2.5 percentage points. On a $10,000 CD, that amounted to a difference of $250 in earnings in one year.

Table 8.1 Banks Pay Different Yields

Institution	6-month CD	1-year CD	5-year CD
Comerica	3.50%	4.25%	5.50%
First of America Bank	4.55	5.00	6.00
Huntington Banks	4.85	5.61	7.45
Michigan National Bank	5.60	6.25	7.01
NBD Bank	4.40	5.00	5.75
First Federal Michigan	4.00	5.20	6.15
First Nationwide Bank	4.70	5.55	6.35
Great Lakes Bancorp	6.00	5.50	6.39
Standard Federal Bank	4.30	5.50	6.39
TCF Bank Michigan	4.10	5.25	7.00

Source: *Bank Rate Monitor*

Where You Live Makes a Difference

Where you live influences what the CD rate is. The average rate that banks pay on accounts is different in every city. On the same day, the range could be from 5 percent in one market to 6 percent in another town. How come? Three reasons:

➤ The higher-paying cities have stronger economies. Businesses and consumers are borrowing more, so institutions are chasing deposits more feverishly. According to a recent survey by *Bank Rate Monitor,* Chicago outfits were paying an average yield of 5.44 percent on six-month CDs, while Philadelphia bank customers had to settle for only 4.3 percent. That's a difference of 1.1 percentage points—or an extra $110 per year for Windy City savers who deposited $10,000!

➤ Banks in the same town tend to "shadow" each other when they set rates. We've heard lots of bankers proclaim, "We set our rates based on local market conditions." Well, that's partly true, but it's also part baloney. There's a lot of monkey-see-monkey-do going on. When Megabuck Bank monitors the latest CD rates of the competitor across the street, and then chimes in with similar rates to stay in the ball game, how scientific do you think that is?

➤ Banks pay what *you* will accept. If you're willing to accept three percent on your money, there's no reason for a bank to shell out five percent. It's money that cuts into their profits. If you carry nothing else away from this book, remember that although we would be lost without our banks, they essentially pay and charge what they can get away with—period.

CD investors in certain U.S. metro areas earn more on their savings than people living somewhere else. Table 8.2 shows the average CD yields in each of the top 10 cities as of February 1995, according to *Bank Rate Monitor.*

Table 8.2 Some Cities Pay More

City	6-month CD	1-year CD	5-year CD
New York	5.37%	6.04%	7.07%
Los Angeles	4.49	5.82	6.59
Chicago	5.44	5.21	7.15
San Francisco	4.29	5.74	6.53
Philadelphia	4.30	5.24	6.64
Detroit	4.60	5.31	6.35
Boston	4.86	6.07	6.87
Houston	4.91	5.72	7.06
Dallas	4.78	5.81	7.07
Washington	4.82	5.78	6.82

What the Rates Mean to You

Should you have jumped at Megabuck's 5.50 percent offer? No way. Here's why:

A half-percent increase in a CD rate is pretty hefty. A more typical gain—when rates are rising—is more like two-, three-, or four-hundredths of a percent. The half percent tells you something is up. Either all rates are rising in a strong up-cycle, Megabuck is bringing its one-year CD more in line with what competition is paying, or it is getting a greater demand for loans.

Assuming it's an up-cycle that's causing the rise, it means interest rates probably will also go up next week, too. That's what you call momentum. It's like a Fourth of July rocket taking off. It can't stop in its tracks. Interest rates behave the same way. Any idiot knows the rocket will keep going in the same direction until it runs out of steam.

When you see the rocket (rates) start to slow down and not rise as high—or even start coming down—that's the time to buy your CD. And the longer the term the better. That's the biggest secret of all—

knowing when to time your buys. Chapter 12 explains exactly how you can figure out where interest rates are going.

Had you grabbed Megabuck's new 5.50 percent rate on a one year CD, the bank would win and you would lose. Here's why: All Megabuck would have to pay you for 12 months is the 5.5 percent, instead of a higher rate if you had waited. Example: If you open a $10,000 one-year account now at that rate, you'll earn $550 in interest. But if the rate goes to, say, 6 percent within a month, you'll earn $600, or $50 more. That's provided you don't withdraw any of the funds. Had you bought a longer-term CD—say, five years—you would have made an even bigger mistake. Reason: You'd be horsecollaring yourself with the same rate for five years while rates are rising.

How badly can you get stung by not paying attention to which direction rates are going? Ask the folks who got hoodwinked by banks in 1994. Early that year, CD rates began rising after a long, ugly downfall that had lasted almost five years. (Rates had plunged so low, in fact, that the average one-year CD paid only 3 percent, according to the newsletter *Bank Rate Monitor*.)

So when the rates turned upward, what CDs did the banks begin pushing like mad? Why, five-year CDs, of course. They were paying only 4.65 percent at the time. That kind of number looked good to savers and investors who were sick and tired of the low rates they had been getting. What did a lot of them do? They grabbed the bait.

The banks were no idiots. By locking people in at 4.65 percent until 1999, they attracted billions of dollars in deposits that cost them beans. By the end of the year, the average five-year CD was earning 6.67 percent nationwide. The customer who bought his or her $10,000 CD too early lost a total of $1,010 in interest over the five years. They would have lost less, of course, if they had bought the highest five-year rate they could find. Moral to the story: Timing is everything in the CD game. And you need to be careful. Even economists with the most sophisticated computers make mistakes.

When you try to figure how much you're really earning on a CD, you've got to figure the current rate of inflation—how fast the price of goods and services is rising or falling. For example, if your CD earns 7 percent interest over the next year and the inflation rate is 2.5 percent, you're 4.5 percent ahead (7 percent less 2.5 percent), not the 7 percent quoted for the CD. In other words, inflation chews into your real earnings. What you want is the biggest cushion you can get.

Inflation is measured by the Consumer Price Index (CPI), which is reported in your newspaper's business news section and in financial magazines. By tracking the CPI you'll learn whether the cost of goods and services is going up or down. Your goal: Buy CDs that pay a rate that is as high as possible over the rate of inflation. This takes a little luck, but if inflation is low (for example, 3 percent), that's the time to lock into a CD of 7 percent or higher.

Shopping Strategies

Before venturing into the CD jungle, ask yourself a couple of key questions:

1. How much can you afford to invest? For how long *won't* you need the money?

2. How nervous are you about risk? If you're the skittish type, federally insured bank CDs are probably for you. No matter what gossip you've heard, no one has ever lost a dime in an FDIC-insured CD, up to the $100,000 maximum protection.

Once you know what you're looking for, use the tips in the following sections to get the best deal.

Key Questions to Ask Before You Buy

Never open a CD account until you ask the bank some questions. Here's our top ten list:

1. What are the rate and the yield, and how is the interest on the account compounded (the more frequently, the better—such as daily compounding)?

2. Is the rate fixed or variable? If variable, what index is the rate tied to, and how often does the index change?

3. For how long is the rate effective?

4. What is the minimum deposit to open the account?

5. Can you add to the account later on? If so, at what rate? Do any added funds mature at the *same time* as your original deposit?

6. How much will you receive in interest—in dollars and cents, not percent—when the account matures. Note: If the bank can't answer this question, say goodbye and take your business elsewhere.

7. What is the penalty if you withdraw any of your funds before the account matures?

8. How and when must you notify the bank if you decide to withdraw all of your money when the CD matures, to avoid rolling the CD over at the new rate that will be in existence?

9. What other benefits do you receive as a CD customer, such as the bank waiving fees and charges on checking, savings, ATM transactions, or annual fees on credit cards?

10. If you're over 50, are there any special benefits for senior citizens?

When you shop rates around town, instead of just reading newspaper adsor calling one of those telephone "Rate Lines," talk to a live bank officer—not an account representative. You'd be amazed at how many lower-echelon bank personnel don't know what their institutions are paying on a certain day!

Some banks may allow you to add to your CD account at the rate in effect on that day, instead of the rate you earned when you opened the account.

When you do sign on with the bank, remember to keep copies of all your account-opening documents in a safe-deposit box or another secure location.

Monthly Check Deals Pay Less

If you elect to take your CD interest through monthly checks mailed to you by the bank or directly deposited into your account, remember these pointers:

➤ Odds are that your CD interest will be less—say, by one-quarter percent—than what customers who don't receive monthly checks earn.

➤ If an outfit offers extra-high interest on a CD, it may not allow you to exercise a monthly check option or withdraw any money at all. You might have to leave all your funds in the account until it matures—that could take years.

Thrifts Pay More Than Banks

As a rule, savings and loan associations (sometimes called "thrifts") offer higher CD rates than commercial banks. The gap runs about one-quarter of a percent on all CD terms. You may need a roadmap to tell banks and thrifts apart; after the S&L bailout mess in the late 1980s frightened a lot of people, a whole slew of thrifts dropped the words "savings and loan" from their names and substituted the word "bank."

You'll Earn Even More at a Credit Union

Have you thought about joining a credit union? They are nonprofit institutions that carry the same $100,000 federal insurance protection on your savings, but on average pay up to a half-percent more on CDs than a bank or thrift. Table 8.3 puts it in black and white.

Table 8.3 You're Better Off at a Credit Union

Institution	MMA	6-month CD	1-year CD	5-year CD
Banks	2.71%	4.54%	5.61%	6.68%
Thrifts	2.83	4.69	5.83	6.78
Credit unions	3.82	5.42	6.17	7.04

How are credit unions able to do this? Because they are nonprofit and have lower overheads. CUs exist primarily to help their members—who are members for life once they join. CUs have membership requirements, such as working within a particular industry or company, but if your Aunt Mabel or cousin George belongs to one, you may also be eligible. Credit unions are definitely worth checking out. Look them up in the Yellow Pages.

There's an Even HIGHER Rate in Another State

You may find a bank 2,000 miles away that not only pays you 2 percent more on your hard-earned cash, but may also be stronger than your present outfit. By going out-of-state, the only difference is that you'll be doing business by phone and by mail. You already do this with your credit cards, don't you? Most of the banks have toll-free 800 numbers so you can check them out on their nickel. For low-minimum CDs, you'll need between $100 and $25,000 to open an out-of-town CD, but it's more likely that the minimum will be between $500 to $2,500.

Here's how to deposit money out of state. Besides asking the same basic account-opening questions covered earlier in this chapter, you'll need to know how to transmit your funds. If you follow these steps, the transmitting of your money will be as safe as if you had done business with a local bank.

If you open an account by mail:

1. Make your check payable to the institution, not to an individual, endorsed "for deposit only."

2. If the institution doesn't give you a deposit form, attach a letter that states how much you are depositing, the type of account, the account number, the rate and yield, the check number, and the amount.

3. Include your name, address, phone number, and Social Security number.

If you open an account by wire:

1. Have your local bank or thrift wire the funds. Wired funds usually arrive the same day and begin earning interest that day or the next.

By law, banks are required to include complicated language in their CD ads. It usually winds up as flyspeck-size footnotes. But banks also use that tiny gobbledygook to hide little facts about how an account really works. When you read a bank CD ad, examine the tiny-type footnote at the bottom of the ad first, and the offer in big type and pictures in the top of the ad last. For example, a bank offers 15 percent on a two-year CD. But the footnote, which you need a magnifying glass to read, says: "The 15% rate is an introductory rate only. After 30 days the rate is reduced to 6 percent for the remainder of the 24-month term." Translation: you've been had. The 15 percent is a low-ball rate for a short time only. And other banks in the area were probably paying more than 6 percent on the same 24-month account.

2. Ask your local institution how much it will charge you to wire the funds. If your deposit is less than $5,000, the wiring cost may be higher than the extra interest earned by using wire rather than mail.

3. Include all key information in your wire. Ideally, you would send the wire directly to the branch with which you're doing business, routing it with the bank's *ABA number* (that's a number to identify the bank within the U.S. banking system). The wire should go to the attention of the person who is helping you open your account.

4. Be sure to include the correct name and location of the institution. Don't forget to include your name, address, phone number, and Social Security number.

5. Make arrangements for the institution to call you, or for you to call it, to confirm that the wire has arrived. You should normally allow about four hours for the wire to arrive, but it could take longer.

Use a "Ladder" to Hedge Your Buy

If you're in a situation where you're not sure whether interest rates are going up or down and you want to cover yourself just in case, one strategy is to "ladder" your CD buys by dividing up your money and opening several accounts with different terms.

Here's an example: You've tracked the banks' rates in your home-town for several weeks. It appears they're going up, but you're not sure. They could just as easily go down. Solution: You split your investment of, say, $10,000 into four different CDs of $2,500 each, with terms of three months, six months, and two years.

Why? If rates continue to rise for a few more months, you can renew the three-month CD in three months at a higher rate. Or you could switch to a CD with a longer maturity (such as six months or a year), which probably will pay an even higher rate. If rates start to go down, you could lock in your maturing CDs for a longer term (such as two or five years) to protect you from the falling rates. If rates took a big dive a few months down the road, your one-year and two-year CDs in the "ladder" would be fixed for that long.

A typical $10,000 laddered buy might look like Table 8.4, assuming rates continued to climb by *a half-percent a year*. Just for the sake of showing how your money would grow, we've stretched the ladder over five years, with the further assumption that you kept rolling over each CD for the same period of time. The three-month CD would be renewed for three months, the six-month CD for six months, and so on. Remember, you don't *have* to do that. You're *flexible*. You can move your money to any different CD term upon maturity. Generally, the longer the term, the higher the rate.

Table 8.4 A Laddered CD Buy

	3-month	6-month	1-year	2-year	TOTAL
$$$ invested:	$2,500	$2,500	$2,500	$2,500	$10,000
1st year rate:	4.05%	4.90%	5.80%	6.40%	
Grows to:	$2,525	$2,531	$2,539	$2,540	$10,133
2nd year rate:	4.55%	5.40%	6.30%	6.40%	
Grows to:	$2,554	$2,565	$2,576	$2,581	$10,287
3rd year rate:	5.10%	5.90%	6.90%	7.40%	
Grows to:	$2,587	$2,601	$2,621	$2,629	$10,438
4th year rate:	5.60%	6.30%	7.40%	7.90%	
Grows to:	$2,623	$2,642	$2,669	$2,678	$10,612
5th year rate:	6.00%	6.80%	7.90%	8.40%	
Grows to:	$2,662	$2,607	$2,722	$2,734	$10,806

Watch Those Gimmick CDs!

"Gadzooks!" you exclaim. "Look at the big CD rate Calamity National is offering!" Hold your horses before you buzz on down to the bank. Banks keep inventing tricky CDs to lure you in the door. You've got play Mr. or Ms. Skeptic—always looking under the rug, always reading the fine print—to learn how these CD critters really work.

Some CDs may fit your financial goals to a T; others could cut into your wallet, or worse still, explode in your face. You'll see gimmick CDs promoted with far-out names as if they were invented on Mars. The most popular types, and their pluses and minuses, are listed in the following sections.

Rising-Rate or Step-Up CDs

The bank offers, say, a 30-month CD whose rate starts out low, then rises by one-half percentage point every six months to a higher rate—sort of like climbing up five stairs from the ground floor.

The Plus: By the time you get to the last six-month period, the rate has gone from a beginning number of, say, 4 percent in the first period to 6.5 percent in the final period. Naturally, the bank will pump up that "6.5" real big in the ad to dazzle your eyeballs.

The Minus: Suppose you leave all your money in the account for the entire 30 months. You don't earn 6.5 percent on the CD. What you earn is an *average* of what the bank pays during each six-month period—5.25 percent. You could have found something better at another outfit.

Bump-Up CDs

The bank allows you to increase the rate one time during the life of the CD, at whatever rate then happens to be in effect.

The Plus: You enjoy a hedge against rising rates. Instead of being locked in at the opening rate, your CD moves up to a higher rate.

The Minus: There are several downsides to bump-ups. There is no guarantee that rates will continue to rise. Often you can find a higher opening rate elsewhere; also, many banks raise the rate when they extend the term. If rates are in a long upward cycle, you would be better off buying a short-term, high-rate CD (for example, a three-month), and keep renewing it at a higher and higher rate.

Odd-Term CDs

Instead of advertising CDs with six-month increments, such as one year, two years, or three years, the bank offers weird terms like seven months, 11 months, or 15 months.

Why? Because the longer the term, usually the higher the rate. A seven-month CD at 4.5 percent looks like a better deal than a 4.25-percent six-month CD. Another reason: Banks like to "balance" their money by matching their deposit terms with some of their loan terms. They just might "need" extra funds for the next seven months instead of six.

The Plus: Banks often are so hungry in their balancing act—or anxious to outsell their competition—they may jack up an odd-term CD rate way above average. We've even seen seven-month CDs outpay one-year CDs at the same institution.

The Minus: None, if the rate is super compared with other banks, and the CD term matches your personal financial game plan. However, don't be fooled by a seven-month CD that "seems" to pay more than a six-month term. It simply follows the standard practice of banks that pay a higher yield on a longer term. Often the odd term is purposely timed to renew automatically at a time when there is little competition for deposits (a low-rollover period). Thus the institution can pay you less upon renewal. Also it's harder to compare rates for odd terms, so institutions can get away with lower rates.

Remember that the yields on all CDs are expressed as "annual percentage yield" (APY) regardless of the term. APY is what a CD earns in a year, not six or seven months. For example, if you invest $1,000 in a six-month CD with an APY of 4.25 percent, you won't earn the full 4.25 percent on your money. You'll only earn *half* of the 4.25 percent because the money was on deposit for only half a year. The same applies to a $1,000 seven-month CD with an APY of 4.5 percent. It would earn $45 in a year, but over seven months it only earns $26.25.

115

Stock-Indexed CDs

Like to gamble? Your CD earnings will be tied to how well the stock market performs. If stocks go up, your CD interest goes higher. But if stocks take a bath, you lose the interest. Though there have been only a little more than two dozen of these gizmos launched around the country—still relatively few—they've received way too much publicity.

The Plus: If the stock market makes a big gain during the life of your CD, you earn healthy interest. But that's a big if.

The Minus: If the stock market goes nowhere fast—or dips as it did in 1994—you earn zip. In fact, under the complicated formulas bank promoters use for these CDs, you could wind up with less money in your pocket than what you started with. So far, most customers who got burned by stock-indexed CDs would have earned higher interest by buying a plain-vanilla CD without the bells and whistles—without suffering palpitations because of the ups and downs of Wall Street. But many offers had not yet matured as of this writing.

Brokered CDs

The new kids on the block are brokerage houses who peddle bank CDs that offer the same federal insurance as other standard CDs. The brokers team with banks to sell their accounts for them, and some of the country's biggest brokers (such as Merrill Lynch and Dean Witter) have gotten into the act in a big way. It's a faster way for banks to raise cash—having an army of broker salespeople—than attracting funds through other means.

There is a secondary market on brokered CDs; you might be able to trade a brokered CD and avoid paying a withdrawal penalty. On the other hand, depending on the environment, you may or may not be able to sell it for what you invested.

Are brokered CDs your cup of tea? Yes and no. Yes, because they usually earn more than what the average CD pays at banks. No, because if you personally do business directly with the highest-paying bank, you'll probably earn about one quarter of a percent more than you can get from a broker. Reason: Nothing is for nothing in the financial world. The broker has to get his cut somewhere.

The Least You Need to Know

➤ When you open a CD account, you promise the bank to keep a certain amount of money (the principal) in the account for a certain amount of time (the term) in exchange for a certain amount of interest (the rate). If you withdraw money from the CD account before the time is up (before the account matures), you pay a penalty.

➤ What banks pay on CDs generally depends on the health of the U.S. economy. When the economy is getting stronger, interest rates tend to rise; when it's getting weaker, rates usually fall.

➤ When rates are on the upswing, banks try to peddle you long-term CDs such as for five years. During a down-cycle, they try to get you to buy a three-month CD. In both situations, you should take the opposite strategy.

➤ To get the best rates, buy a CD from a credit union or a strong out-of-state bank.

➤ Be wary of "gimmick" CDs such as rising-rate CDs and bump-up CDs. Be sure you weigh their advantages and disadvantages against your financial goals.

➤ Banks sometimes base their CD rates on their loan business. If there is a big demand for loans, banks need to attract more deposits to replace the money they lend out. That tends to boost CD rates. When loan demand is weak, banks may be apt to raise their CD rates more slowly. They tend to book a loan for a specific period that matches the CD terms they offer.

Chapter 9

Relationship Packages— Good or Bad Deals?

In This Chapter

➤ How package accounts work

➤ Key questions to ask before you fall for a line

➤ Special package accounts for seniors

For years, banks have been selling you separate savings accounts, CDs, checking accounts, and personal loans. Well, now they've figured out how to bundle some of those accounts together in what they call *relationship packages*. It's their shrewd way of trying to get *all* your business instead of just part of it.

To get you to combine your accounts at their institution, banks dangle bait such as free checking accounts and discounts on loans. They also waive a slew of different fees that you ordinarily pay if you open separate accounts. Packages look great—on the surface. But are they your best deal? This chapter takes the whole package notion apart—and explains why it may not be the most sensible route to go.

How Package Accounts Work

First off, you may not even see a bank call a "package account" by that name. It might use the term "relationship package" because the different accounts in the package are tied to each other. More than likely, the bank will give the package a confusing, meaningless name like "MoneyMaster Deluxe," "Premier Super-Duper Savings," or something even crazier.

Whatever they're called, all package accounts work on similar principles. First, there's typically more than one account in the package, such as a Money Market Account, CD, checking, and maybe a credit card. Each bank creates its own mix of accounts. Frequently you get a combined statement showing how those accounts are doing.

The package may require a minimum amount of money to qualify or avoid fees. The funds can all be in one CD account or a combination of CDs and other savings accounts—including Individual Retirement Accounts and checking. Some outfits let you also include the amount of your loans at the bank. How much do you have to deposit? Probably $5,000 to $10,000, but the range can be as low as $2,000 and as high as $25,000 or even $50,000. Sometimes, the higher your combined balance in a package account, the more freebies the bank will give you.

Even so, don't fall for a package account unless you first determine the *real value* of what's being offered. Just because the bank tosses in things like a free safe deposit box and free traveler's checks doesn't necessarily make the account a good deal. You should be more concerned with the interest rates on your savings accounts, the rates you pay on loans, and the cost of all the fees!

How does a typical package account work? Corestates Bank in Philadelphia offers several packages, including Core-Flex1, which gives customers these benefits:

➤ Free check-writing

➤ Free ATM transactions

➤ Free first order of checks

➤ No-annual-fee credit card

➤ No "low-balance" fees on certain savings accounts

➤ Combined monthly statement

➤ No annual fees on lines of credit

➤ Overdraft protection (in case you bounce a check)

➤ Credit toward mortgage closing costs

How does the customer get all that? One of two ways. By having a checking account that *doesn't* pay interest and keeping $2,000 in combined accounts. Or by getting a checking account that does pay interest and keeping $4,000 in the accounts. The downside is if your combined balance falls short any one month, there's a $12.50 fee.

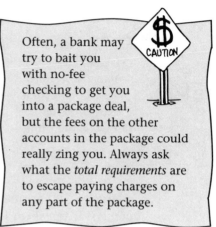

Often, a bank may try to bait you with no-fee checking to get you into a package deal, but the fees on the other accounts in the package could really zing you. Always ask what the *total requirements* are to escape paying charges on any part of the package.

Sounds great and looks convenient, right? You get something for nothing. You don't have to scramble all over town to conduct transactions at different banks. And balancing your accounts is so much simpler every month. Not only do you feel more *efficient*, you believe it's about time your bank rewards you for all the business you've been giving them. But hold on. That's just the first half of the story. You need to look these gift horses in the mouth, as you should any type of bank account.

What's the Bottom-Line Value?

Deciding whether a package account is right for you is not easy because no two accounts are the same. Each individual bank hitches a bunch of different features to its own particular package, and that can boggle your mind. If you try to shop three different outfits, it's like trying to compare an apple and a pear with a banana. What you're looking for— bottom line—is the *real value* of a package deal versus what you could get elsewhere. That means investigating other banks, or skipping packages altogether and opening separate accounts at more than one institution.

For example, say you keep $3,000 in a two percent Money Market Account and $2,000 in a six percent CD at one bank, *and* $1,000 in non-interest-bearing checking at a third outfit. That's $6,000 altogether. Checks cost you 25 cents apiece, and you write 20 a month. You use an ATM maybe three times a month, at an average cost of $1 per transaction. Your credit card at one of the banks has no annual fee, and the interest rate is meaningless because you pay off your balance every month. You have no IRA accounts.

Make sure you comparison-shop when looking for a "free" checking account and/or a relationship package.

When you add everything up, you're earning a total of $180 a year on your savings and shelling out $60 for checks and $26 for ATMs. Now do the math: $180 minus $26 means you're coming out with $154 to the good every year.

Another bank offers this deal: a $5,000-minimum package that pays five percent on the same CD and three percent on MMAs. It waives all per-check charges and ATM fees, but charges a $40 annual fee on credit cards. It also pays an extra one-half percent interest on IRAs. Is it for you?

You could switch your $5,000 in CD and MMA money to qualify for the package, and earn $190 instead of $180 on these investments. But after deducting the $40 credit card fee, you'd have $30 less than where you bank now. Plus, the extra IRA interest isn't going to help because you don't have an IRA.

Shopping packages can get complicated when you run into more exotic accounts with loads of bells and whistles. How can you put a yardstick against each one to be sure which is best? You can't. You have to come up with a foolproof set of questions that will tell you the roses from the weeds.

Ask the Right Questions Before You Leap

Don't let the complicated packages fool you. There's a way for you to cut through the clutter and get to the real pluses and minuses of each account. For openers, get answers to these questions before you buy:

1. What is the combined minimum amount to qualify?

2. How much money must you invest, and for how long?

3. What is the minimum balance to avoid fees?

4. What are the interest rates on other accounts in the package (such as credit cards)?

5. What's the charge if you somehow slip below the combined minimum amount you must keep on deposit?

6. What fees and charges will the bank waive? How many of the bells, whistles, and freebies will you need?

7. Are there any extra incentives—such as reducing the rates on your loans by one-half percent if your monthly payments are automatically deducted from your checking account?

8. Compared with your *current banking behavior*, how much more will you probably earn—or lose—if you bundle all your business into one package account?

By splitting your savings accounts at different institutions that pay higher rates, you can earn more on your money than you can by lumping it into one package at the same outfit.

Remember: It's not the glitz and glamour of the package that counts. It's the bottom line.

Romancing the Mature Market

Seniors are attractive customers for the financial industry; they are thought of as being affluent and debt-free. In fact, a Gallup poll for *Bank Advertising News* reports that folks 55 years and older are significantly less likely than younger folks to own a debit card (12 percent total). The over-55 crowd (41 percent) is among those least likely to own an ATM card. Many of these people are concerned about their money because they lived through one of the roughest financial eras in history: The Great Depression. Banks, thrifts, and special *money-management centers* (bill-payment centers that will help pay bills for seniors—it's like having a secretary to handle personal bills... for a fee) are vying to capture this growing sector of the population. They are increasing the number of banking services aimed at the seniors market, as the following examples demonstrate:

There's a trend toward banks requiring only one account (such as $100-minimum checking) to lure you closer to a package—especially if you're a senior citizen. Their goal is to sell you other accounts by offering a high rate on a CD, for example, or a low-rate credit card. Remember: Their goal is to lock up as much of your business as they can.

➤ Since 1987, First Chicago has been offering its "Renaissance Checking" accounts to consumers 55 and older.

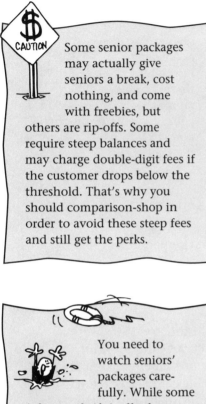

Some senior packages may actually give seniors a break, cost nothing, and come with freebies, but others are rip-offs. Some require steep balances and may charge double-digit fees if the customer drops below the threshold. That's why you should comparison-shop in order to avoid these steep fees and still get the perks.

You need to watch seniors' packages carefully. While some (often at thrifts) offer free checking with no strings attached, others (though they may have numerous perks) charge steep fees—or drop your membership—if balance requirements are not met. Sometimes they include items that seniors are not likely to use, such as credit cards and debit cards.

The bells and whistles include unlimited checking, no minimum balance requirement, no service charges on ATMs (unless it's a Cirrus machine—then there's a $1 charge), and no monthly service fees. It's a checking account that pays interest from the first dollar that's deposited. And for a $3.50 monthly fee, seniors get discounts on travel programs, $100,000 accidental death coverage, and an extended warranty on items purchased by check. Plus, there's no requirement for direct deposit of Social Security checks.

➤ Cole Taylor Bank touts its "New Horizons" program for consumers 50 years and older. Clients must meet a total minimum balance requirement of $15,000—which could be in the form of several accounts, such as CDs, savings, and NOW accounts. Seniors receive a free safe deposit box, free check ing, money orders and cashier's checks, and discounts on group travel programs. If your balance drops below $15,000, Cole Taylor Bank will drop your membership (although they tell us that your $14,999.99 balance will be taken into consideration)

➤ PNC in Pittsburgh offers a "Priority 50-plus" checking account. For $4 a month, seniors get 15 additional benefits, which include (but are not limited to) a quarter-percentage-point bonus rate on CDs and identical discounts on loans. Other perks? No-fee traveler's and cashier's checks and $100,000 accidental death travel insurance.

So are they worth it? As long as you meet the minimum balance requirements and shop around for competitive pricing, a seniors' package may be advantageous in the long run because of the money you save on trips, travel programs, and discounts on loans. Make sure you find out *exactly* what fees are involved in each program before you sign up for that three-day cruise to Pago Pago.

The Least You Need to Know

➤ A package account involves opening two or more accounts at the same bank—checking, savings, and CDs, for example. Customarily, you must either keep a certain amount of money in combined deposits (and/or loans) at the bank in order to avoid fees, or you have to open one account to get another one "free."

➤ Some incentives that banks offer to convince you to open package accounts include free check-writing, no ATM fees, and no annual fee for credit cards.

➤ Some banks may waive checking fees with direct deposit of Social Security checks.

➤ To see whether a package account is for you, compare its interest rates and fees to the interest and fees involved in your current banking setup.

➤ In order to attract the lucrative senior market, banks have created special package accounts that involve incentives such as travel discounts, free accidental death insurance, and free safe deposit boxes.

➤ Always examine the *real value* of the freebies that come with a package account. How much are you really saving?

Chapter 10

NO. JUST GO.

When It's Time to Kiss Your Banker Goodbye

In This Chapter

➤ The big tip-offs on when to make the move

➤ Why you shouldn't feel embarrassed or guilty

➤ Critical steps to cover yourself during the change

Parting is such sweet sorrow—but not when you're being ripped off by a bank's lopsided savings and loan rates, or when you need the special pampering you're not getting. Most people dread the inconvenience of switching banks, even though it takes very little time and energy. The result is worth it, because it's your money that's on the line—not how close the institution is to your home or office.

This chapter examines the important issue of whether you should change banks or stay with your current bank. If you do move, this chapter tells you the step-by-step procedures you should follow to avoid fees or a bad credit record that will haunt you forever.

Should You Switch?

You're hopping mad. You're almost at the boiling point because your bank just screwed up on one of your accounts. Is it time to kiss those guys goodbye? It is if you keep you keep running into these problems:

➤ **Other banks pay more than your bank on savings and checking accounts.** If you haven't checked your bank's rates lately, do it. Rates have been flipping and flopping all over the place in the past year. Just because your outfit offered the highest rates in town a few months ago doesn't mean that's the case today. Compare all their rates, not just a few of them.

➤ **The bank's loan rates are moving much higher than its savings rates.** Do you know what that means? The bank is fattening its profits at your expense. Before you yank your accounts, try negotiating by asking the bank to lower your loan rates. If they say no, you have another reason to switch.

➤ **The bank's fees have increased.** Study the fine print in your monthly statement. Compare your latest statement with one from a year ago. Notice any difference in those nickel-and-dime fees? We thought so.

➤ **They don't bend over backwards for you.** Does the bank ever bend over backward when you need a special favor or make an innocent mistake? You may not know it, but some customers may get sweeter treatment than you get. Here's an example: If you don't have the funds in your account to cover a check that comes through, will the bank courteously phone you first thing that morning and let you race over to cover the check before it bounces?

➤ **The old personal service is missing.** Banks are like any personal service business. You're happy when they are pleasant and courteous, cater to you when you need it, and go that extra mile when you have a special problem. But we all know that as banks have expanded by buying up smaller community institutions, their turnover in personnel has been humongous. Plus, they've shifted to ATMs and electronic banking; as a result, a lot of the old "personal touch" has disappeared. At big outfits in particular, you're more a number than you are a name. If any of these things bother you, you're a prime candidate for finding a new home for your money.

Today's banking industry is very competitive. Even if you're fairly happy with your current bank, it may be worth it to switch for the special deals offered to new customers elsewhere.

➤ **The teller lines always go around the block.** Sure, automatic tellers have cut your banking time down considerably, and many institutions have extended their weekday hours and are open on Saturday mornings. But suppose you've got a question, and the only time you can make it into the bank is late Friday afternoon—when everybody and his brother, sister, and cousin is depositing a paycheck, and they're all ahead of you? Time is money; you shouldn't spend it cooling your heels in a line.

➤ **They just closed the branch in your neighborhood.** It's happening more and more. Megabuck Bank buys up little old Friendly Federal, whose name disappears along with the Friendly branch where you've been doing business for years. To keep your business at a Megabuck branch that's farther from your home (and where nobody knows you), you'll probably have to spend more on gas than you'll earn on your meager savings account. It's definitely another reason to split.

➤ **They still apply the old, tough credit standards.** After applying very strict criteria to those who qualified—or didn't qualify—for loans in the early 1990s, most banks today have relaxed their lending rules. They are making personal and mortgage loans—and issuing credit cards—to folks who couldn't get to first base before. If your outfit hasn't yet hopped on the easier-credit bandwagon, this alone is a big reason to change banks pronto!

➤ **The bank doesn't offer any special rate breaks.** Do you get special rate breaks if you maintain a big balance? Many outfits will pay higher interest on CDs or knock a half-percent off your loan rate if you keep beaucoups of bucks on deposit, such as in a relationship account (see Chapter 9) or have your monthly payments automatically deducted from your checking or savings.

➤ **The bank doesn't offer good information.** What are the brochures in the lobby like? Are they superb dollars-and-cents information that you can use to

An excellent way for you to check out the financial soundness of any bank is to phone Veribanc, Inc. in Wakefield, Massachusetts, at (800) 837-4226. For a very small fee, this independent and respected research company will provide you with a report of the institution, including its safety rating.

make your money grow? Do they address your toughest financial problems? Or is the literature blue-sky propaganda that only hustles your business? When was the last time your bank explained how interest rates behave, what credit cards really cost, or the total cost of a fixed-rate versus adjustable-rate mortgage? Not recently? We thought so.

➤ **Your bank hasn't been making a profit recently.** Your bank's probably more financially sound than you think, but there's no harm in checking. The average person would need a Ph.D. in math to understand all the numerical gobbledygook that banks put into their annual and quarterly financial reports. You want to know how safe the institution is—in plain English. Stick with a bank that has made a profit at least five quarters in a row. If it hasn't, simply say, "See ya!"

Dealing with the Guilt

You've looked at the facts and decided that this relationship is no longer working for you. Don't worry about how your old bank will view your decision. There's nothing awkward or embarrassing about changing banks, nothing whatsoever. After all, the bank employees may be awfully nice people, but the bank has been making money on you all along. It's your hard-earned cash that you care about. Anyway, the day you leave, they'll pick up other new customers and probably won't miss your business one iota.

Okay, You've Decided to Switch. Now What?

Take a tip from how the apes and monkeys swing through the trees in a jungle. They never let go of one branch until they have a hold on another one. The same goes for changing banks. Don't let go of the last one till you've shopped and found a better one. (For more secrets of bank shopping, see Chapters 6 through 9.)

Once you've found your new bank, some basic housekeeping chores are necessary to protect you and your money:

➤ Make certain all your checks have cleared your checking account, otherwise you could wind up liable for high bounced-check charges.

➤ Write the bank a dated letter—be sure to keep a copy—informing them that you are closing out your account(s). List each account number and the name(s) on the account(s). Otherwise, you could run into a problem. For example, if you have a checking account and haven't formally closed it, you could get zapped with an "inactivity" or "dormant" fee after as little as six months. That could run as much as $5 to $10 a month. Watch it!

➤ You have to be careful if you have a relationship package account (see chapter 9). Close out all your accounts at once or you risk getting hit with fees on the remaining ones.

➤ Review your old bank's account-closing fees. Increasingly, outfits will slap you with a $10 to $25 charge if you close out an account within 90 days to six months after opening it. That's particularly common in tourist areas. You might want to wait until that period expires before you act.

➤ Hold onto your old checks when you leave. If you open a new account, many institutions, hungry for new checking business, will offer to pay you a few bucks for your old checks.

➤ If you don't turn in your unused checks at your old bank, be sure to destroy them, along with any unused deposit slips *and* any credit cards from your old bank. This will prevent them from possibly falling into the hands of someone who could abuse your accounts.

➤ Don't forget to turn in your old safe deposit key! Most folks don't remember this. Otherwise, you could pay a fee.

➤ If you're leaving the area, don't forget to leave a forwarding address for your loans. Just because you move doesn't mean your outstanding balances won't follow you on your credit record. Plus, if you miss a bill, it doesn't mean the interest will stop piling up.

➤ Don't burn your bridges behind you. You never know when you might need those guys again!

Once you've made the switch, don't forget to change your records at other places where you do business, such as supermarkets and drug stores. It's something many consumers forget to do when they switch banks. The reason for doing this is that one day, for some reason, the store may try to contact your bank to verify that you have an account there. (Yes, it's a big hassle to have to go through this, but the inconvenience later could be even worse.) *Tell the store your new account number in person—never over a cordless phone.* As paranoid as it may sound, your conversation on that type of phone can be picked up by other people. Where your money is concerned, better safe than sorry!

The Least You Need to Know

➤ Stay informed about what your bank is doing. Have they been raising fees? Raising loan rates? Not earning a profit? If so, it's probably time to find another bank.

➤ Compare what other banks are paying and charging. Do they offer higher interest on savings? Lower loan rates? Better customer service? If so, it may be worth switching.

➤ Lack of personal attention and an unwillingness to be flexible when you have a personal financial problem are good reasons to switch banks.

➤ Have a heart-to-heart chat with the branch manager before you close your accounts. Is the bank willing to negotiate any of your interest rates or fees before you bid them adieu?

➤ Make sure all your checks have cleared, and then close your accounts in writing to avoid any misunderstandings later on.

➤ Avoid fees related to closing accounts by making sure your checks have cleared before you close an account, leaving a forwarding address for your loan bills, and turning in your safe deposit key.

➤ Don't feel any guilt or embarrassment when you change banks. Your old bank won't, and some poor sap will come along and take your place.

Part 3
Interest Rates: How to Ride the Roller Coaster

And what a roller coaster it is! Millions of Americans can testify that the ups and downs in interest rates makes them feel woozy… and unsure of their investment decisions. We saw proof in 1994 when short-term interest rates were raised six times in just one year. Just what the heck is going on? And what can you do to time your investment and buying decisions when there's a flip-flop interest rate market?

Plenty! This section will expose the simple secrets behind those confusing numbers and help you learn how to track the latest rate trend the easy way. Really! Hang on, as you discover one of the most important lessons that will affect all your financial planning decisions. Are you ready?

Chapter 11

Easy Crash Course in Interest Rate Math

In This Chapter

➤ How banks calculate the interest on your money

➤ How to think in "dollars and cents," not "percent"

➤ The key difference between rate and yield

➤ Which compounding methods work harder for you

The average bank customer is bewildered by the confusing array of mathematical methods that banks use to figure the interest on consumer accounts. They see "rates," "annual percentage yields," and "compounding" mentioned in newspaper ads and bank brochures. The jargon can be alarming to anyone who is not a skilled accountant.

As a result, millions of people invest their money without ever knowing how and why some yields are higher than others—even when everything else about the accounts may look the same. Yet, every dollar they deposit in a bank is affected by the specific math formula the bank uses to manipulate the saver's hard-earned cash. Math is the least-understood part of banking, but you can handle it—and make more money—by learning the ABCs outlined in this chapter.

Knowing a Few Math Basics Can Go a Long Way

Don't worry. This isn't about calculators and slide rules. It's simply a down-to-earth explanation of the most popular mathematical games that banks play to compute the earnings on your savings investments.

If you know their formulas, you can decide which type of interest will put more money in your pocket. You won't be confused by "rate versus yield," or the information on compounding that they hide way down at the bottom of their ads.

It doesn't take a whiz to understand the most basic tricks. Just a smidgen of the right knowledge can make a difference of several hundred dollars on your savings in CD, Money Market, and checking accounts. Some other math gimmicks on all types of accounts are covered in chapters 6, 7, 8, 13, 16, and 18. But on all forms of savings, these are the important ones to remember.

Time Is Money—More or Less

On a savings account, the longer you agree to lock up your money, the higher the interest rate. Reason: It's an enticement to keep your cash in the bank's vault for a longer period. The bank can count on the money staying there, instead of having to chase after new money day after day. Other factors, of course, also come into play—such as where the banks think interest rates might be months or years from now (see Chapter 12). They try to balance their savings-account maturities against their loan maturities.

Regardless of the CD term, learn the formula that determines the yield the bank offers you.

Rate Versus Yield: Knowing the Difference

All savings offers are quoted with an *interest rate* and an *annual percentage yield*. The rate is the base number that the bank uses to make the rate grow to a higher number called the *annual percentage yield (APY)*. The formula can be one of several different compounding methods that produces the final APY.

An APY is what your money earns on an annual basis, regardless of the CD term—less than one year or more than one year. This figure enables you to compare apples with apples on whatever CD term you are shopping. If you didn't have APYs to work with, you'd have to cope with a zillion different numbers and never know which account would pay you the most interest.

REALLY? Which would you rather have? An outright gift of $1 million, or a penny in a savings account that doubles every day for 30 days? Better think this one through before you answer. At the end of the 30 days, the $1 million will still be worth one million bucks. But the penny will have grown to an astounding $5.37 million! That's not a misprint; get out your calculator and check it for yourself.

Compounding: Interest on Top of Interest

Compounding is simply interest added to interest. The more frequently the bank compounds your money, the more interest you earn. If the compounding is done daily, that's one of the two best methods of all. Compounding is like depositing $1 the first day, and having the bank add interest of one cent on the second day to increase the balance to $1.01. Then on the third day, the bank adds more interest on top of the $1.01 to build the account to $1.02, and on the fourth day it piles even more interest on the $1.02 to build the balance to $1.03.

For example, if you deposit $1,000 earning 5 percent interest compounded monthly, your account grows to $1,051 at the end of a year. But if the compounding is less frequent (say, on only a quarterly basis), your balance grows to just $1,016. Look for frequent compounding when you shop. Banks generally use one or more of seven different compounding types when they compute interest on savings accounts: continuous, daily, weekly, monthly, quarterly, annual, and simple interest.

Say you have $1,000 to invest. Megabuck Bank and its competitor Friendly Federal both offer one-year CDs with an "interest rate" (the base rate you start with) of six percent. Megabuck compounds your money daily. Friendly Federal compounds its CD annually. Because it compounds more frequently, Megabuck's APY comes to 6.18 percent and your $1,000 grows to $1,062. By contrast, your balance at Friendly Federal would rise to only $1,060—despite the fact that both institutions started with the same stated rate.

Here's an example of how the different compounding methods can affect what you earn, based on a $10,000 investment yielding six percent. Pretend you are investing $10,000 in a savings account for one year, but don't know which of seven basic types of compounding will grow your money fastest. The following table shows how much will be in the account at the end of each quarter over the next year.

Note that at the end of the year there is no difference in the amounts for "simple interest" and "annual compounding," both of which pay interest at the end of the year. There *would* be a difference if you left the money in the account for a second year. With annual compounding, the interest in the second year would be added onto the interest in the first year. But with the simple interest method, the interest you'd earn in the second year would only be on your original $10,000 investment.

Compound Method	First Quarter	Second Quarter	Third Quarter	Fourth Quarter
Continuous	$10,152	$10,305	$10,460	$10,618
Daily	10,151	10,305	10,460	10,618
Weekly	10,151	10,304	10,460	10,618
Monthly	10,151	10,304	10,459	10,617
Quarterly	10,150	10,302	10,457	10,614
Annual	10,000	10,000	10,000	10,600
Simple interest	10,000	10,000	10,000	10,600

Banks Are Cashing In on Your Ignorance

How many people do you know who can walk into a bank, discuss opening a new savings account, and figure exactly how their interest

138

rate will be computed? Not many. Banks have been around for hundreds of years, and along the way they've designed a slew of different formulas for every kind of account they offer.

Few customers ever ask how the numbers work. That gives banks a big advantage. They can sell you an account based on a complicated mathematical computation that earns you less money than you can earn somewhere else. You may never realize you've been had. As one bank customer complained, "I'm getting smoked by all those numbers."

To help consumers, the federal government today requires banks to provide disclosure documents that explain how they arrive at their rate computations. They also must print disclosures in their advertising.

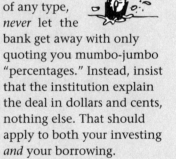

Before you sign up for a bank account of any type, *never* let the bank get away with only quoting you mumbo-jumbo "percentages." Instead, insist that the institution explain the deal in dollars and cents, nothing else. That should apply to both your investing *and* your borrowing.

The Chiseling Gets Down to Pennies

Wait'll you hear this one. We all know there are 365 days in a year. Well, not all banks use that many days when they compute your interest. Some work with a 360-day year. That shaves your earnings by only pennies—but it saves the banks millions of dollars a year.

Say you deposit $10,000 in an account that pays seven percent interest. If the bank uses a 365-day calculation method, you earn $709.72 in interest; with a 360-day method, the interest comes to $700 on the same account.

"Indexed" Accounts Protect the Bank More Than You

Indexed accounts have become the rage in the past decade because they allow the bank to set the rates they pay you on savings or charge you on loans, based on a known benchmark. It can be the bank's prime rate, a U.S. Treasury bill, or some other known index that moves up or down with the economy.

An index gives the banks a predictable, controlled device that protects the bank from swings in interest rates. If their costs rise (such as having to pay you higher interest on CDs when the economy gets stronger), their indexes on rates for credit cards, home equity credit lines, mortgages and other loans will also rise. If banks didn't protect themselves that way, it would cut into their profits.

Key Math Questions You Should Ask

➤ What are the interest rate and the annual percentage yield?

➤ Is the interest rate tied to an index? If so, how often can the index change?

➤ How often is the account compounded?

➤ Based on the compounding method, how much money will I have in the account in dollars and cents at the end of the first year, or when my CD matures if the account is less than one year?

The Least You Need to Know

➤ Use the Annual Percentage Yield to compare CDs of different terms and figure out which really offers you the best deal.

➤ The more frequently the bank compounds your money, the more interest you earn. Accounts that compound daily are best.

➤ Get the bank to explain the deal to you in dollars and cents instead of percentages.

Chapter 12

Reading the Interest Rate Cycles

Don't get turned off by the mumbo-jumbo words "interest rate cycles." Believe it or not, they're not just for egghead economists and professors who wear horn-rims and tweed jackets. Any idiot can learn how the cycles work in just a few minutes—and turn that new knowledge into smart investment moves that earn a lot more money.

The trick? Simply knowing that cycles always go up and down like a roller coaster. You can accurately call the shot on when—and when not—to buy a short-term or long-term CD, or when to purchase a new home or finance a new car. This chapter breaks down rate-cycle gobbledygook into simple language that anyone with a tenth-grade education can understand.

The Great Rate Roller Coaster

You're usually vaguely aware of when rates are getting higher or lower, aren't you? You don't have to be a brain surgeon to detect that, when you're in a bank or talking to a mortgage lender, the numbers keep changing. The rates they quote you today aren't the same rates as last week.

What you probably don't realize is that if you kept track of interest rates for only a few weeks, you'd see the numbers form a pattern as clear as a bell. They go up and down over time, forming a picture that looks like a roller coaster. And that's exactly what rates behave like—a roller coaster. The rates go in one direction for a long time, and then they change direction and go the other way. But unlike a roller coaster, each trip lasts for a few years instead of a few hundred yards.

When the roller coaster gets to the top of a ride, or the bottom of one, it pauses for a short while and then takes off into the next part of the cycle.

➤ The pause at the top of the ride is called a "peak." That's when interest rates reach their highest point during an up-cycle.

➤ The pause at the bottom of the ride resembles a "valley." That's when interest rates hit their lowest level.

Timing is the single most important secret in investing. It's almost as simple as tying your shoes—yet even many high-level stockbrokers and financial experts we've bumped into don't understand how to take advantage of interest rate cycles. Why? Because they're so obsessed with what the market's doing that day, or will do tomorrow, they never step back 100 paces and take a *long view* of where rates have been and where they're headed. What's a long view? *Years*, not days.

If those financial wizards were paying attention, they'd make themselves rich instead of constantly asking us, "Where do you think rates are going?" We hear that question every day. Well, let's take the whole "economic cycle" rigmarole and break it down into plain English. In fact, let's not use the whole economy at all—let's just look at the impact rate cycles can have on *what you earn on your savings and other investments*.

Enjoying the Ride

Okay, let's pretend you're on the rate roller coaster (you're already on one, whether you realize it or not). To give your investments the biggest money-making ride of all, remember this secret:

> **Pick the right time to save when rates are high, and the best time to borrow when loan rates are low.**

By doing that, you can earn hundreds or thousands of dollars more, and cut costs by just as much when you buy a new home or finance a new set of wheels. But how can you tell whether rates are at a peak or in a valley? Good question. This section tells you the secrets to reading the rate cycle.

By using the same cycle-tracking methods described in this section, in early 1994 we were able to predict that a new rate up-cycle had indeed begun. We accurately forecast that:

➤ Rising rates were no fluke.

➤ The Federal Reserve and banks would keep raising rates throughout '94 and into '95.

➤ Consumer savings and loan rates would rise by about two percentage points during '94.

Ten months later, in November 1994, the respected weekly financial newspaper *Barron's* published an article quoting a major prediction by Columbia University's center for International Business Cycle Research. The Institute, no idiots they, forecast that the up-cycle would carry into mid-1996 or early '97, after which the country would slide into another recession.

Which Direction Is the Roller Coaster Going—Up or Down?

There are a couple of ways to figure which way rates are going. The simplest is to check your newspaper's bank rate tables week by week and keep track of the average rates banks pay on deposits and charge on loans. A more reliable way is to follow the average national rates published in the newsletter *Bank Rate Monitor*. Do either of those things for six to eight weeks, and you'll learn where rates will probably be tomorrow.

How Long Has the Roller Coaster Been Going in That Direction?

Roller coaster rate-rides usually last for a couple of years. More precisely, the average ride, up or down, lasts an average of one-and-a-half to three years. To figure out where rates are headed in the future, you need to calculate for about how long the coaster has been on its current ride. The easiest way is to visit your library, or cozy up to your bank and ask them to do a little research for you. Find out what rate the bank paid on one-year CDs last month, six months ago, one year ago, and two years ago.

Aha! Now the roller coaster picture is taking shape! With a little imagination, you'll be able to figure when the current ride began. Match this against the fact that cycles usually last one-and-a-half to three years, and you'll be able to estimate how much farther the roller coaster has to go.

How Long Can the Ride Last?

If the roller coaster is only a few months into the ride—up or down—odds are it has more than a year or two to go. If it's up, your savings rates and loan rates are bound to go higher before they start going lower. A one-year CD paying six percent likely will go to seven percent (or even eight percent) before the up ride is over. Ditto borrowing costs—they're going to climb, too.

If the ride has been two years or longer, chances are the roller coaster may be getting near the end of its trip. So hang on for a downward ride soon. That seven percent CD eventually will fall back to six percent and even lower, but the good news is that auto loan and mortgage rates also are going to drop.

How Fast Is the Roller Coaster Going?

Economic wizards love to point out that interest rates don't go up and down in a vacuum. Rather, rates are influenced by economic growth that expands or contracts like a rubber band. When the country is in a recession, rates are low, as they were in the early 1990s. When the economy picks up steam and there's fear of inflation, the Federal Reserve steps in and raises rates to slow the economy. If the Fed tightens up too drastically, the slowdown could push the country back into a recession.

144

You need to know this because it will help you figure out, during an up-cycle, how much your CD rates might rise over the next few weeks. If rates are going up by only two-hundredths of a percent a week (say, from 7.00 percent to 7.02 percent) that's a slow ride. Rates could continue to move up slowly, or even pause in their tracks. If they're rising faster—say from 7.00 percent to 7.10 percent—it means a longer upward ride.

Suppose you watched two roller coasters, one with a 10-horsepower motor and the other with a 100-horsepower motor. If you pointed them both on an upward track, which one would generate the faster speed? Right, the 100-horsepower job. Which roller coaster would go farther up the track? Or down the track, if rates were dropping? Again, the 100-horsepower coaster.

It's the same with interest rate cycles. Just think of how much the banks are increasing or decreasing their rates each week and you'll know the strength of the latest cycle. The higher the horsepower, the longer rates will continue in that direction. Even a lot of "experts" haven't learned that, as the following examples demonstrate.

Not long ago, when banks were boosting their CD rates by nearly a tenth of a percent a week, a famous economist said on television, "No one knows for sure where interest rates will be tomorrow afternoon." Horsefeathers. Did he really think the 100-horsepower roller coaster was suddenly going to stop cold on the track and not climb any farther? The only way his comment would have made sense was if bank rates had been standing still, or barely inching up or down for several weeks.

In late 1994, Orange County, California went bankrupt because it invested its money in the belief that interest rates were going lower. Anyone tracking rate cycles knew that a new up-cycle had started in February of that year.

How Many Banks Are on the Roller Coaster?

An important factor in figuring out the horsepower of the rate roller coaster is knowing how many banks are pushing the coaster up or down at the same time. Pretend there are 10 bankers in town. Only two jump on the roller coaster, and each raises savings rates by only one-hundredth of a percent this week. That's not many horses, is it?

But if all 10 bankers climb aboard and hike rates by 10-or 15-hundredths of a percent, that's more like a 200-horsepower effort. You can bet your bottom dollar the coaster is going up again next week, because of how many banks were pushing rates upward. To measure this horsepower, count how many banks in your area are changing rates each week, and by how much, and track it for several weeks.

Know What Else Drives the Engine

Sure, it's tough for the average Joe or Jane to sift and sort through all the headlines about the economy. One day some pundit says things are getting better; the next day another wag swears they're getting worse. That shows you how confused those guys really are.

What you should watch:

The Federal Reserve (the Fed)   It lowers its key rates depending on whether it thinks the economy is weak and needs rate cuts to stimulate business activity. If it believes there's an inflation threat ahead, it raises rates to cool down the economy to prevent rates from going out of sight. It's a tricky job—keeping the economy growing without stalling the motor.

The highest-yielding banks in the country jump out of the pack first, and raise rates even faster than your average hometown bank, because these institutions are more aggressive and want to beat other banks to the draw. Remember: It pays to look beyond your own backyard when dealing with banks.

Economic data   As tons of data pour out of Washington, the Fed and the economists—and the banks—study every piece of information they can get their hands on. Employment reports, producer prices, consumer prices, new plant equipment, housing starts, you name it. Even the federal deficit and the soundness of the dollar have an influence on the Fed's decisions. When the data show very strong gains, the economy may be tilting toward inflation. Data suggesting a weaker economy, such as higher unemployment and lower housing starts, suggest the opposite.

The prime rate   Typically, as the Fed moves, so go the banks. They immediately increase or decrease their *prime rate* (supposedly what they charge their most creditworthy business customers to borrow money) by the same amount as the Fed's move. And when the prime rate changes, so do your savings and loan rates.

But note that savings rates go up more slowly than the prime rate, and that lag gives banks an edge. Their loan rates increase by more than the increase in savings numbers. When rates start to fall, that's another story. Typically your savings rates will come down first, followed by loans. Again, score one for the banks. A good guideline to remember is that every time banks boost their prime rate by one-half percent, average CD rates rise by about one-third to four-tenths of a percent over the next eight weeks.

REALLY?

An exception to this rate-lag rule occurred in early 1994, when an up-cycle caused savings rates to take off faster than loan rates. The reason behind this was that banks were so stuffed with cash to lend out that they had to hold loan rates down, for fear they'd lose business to the competiion. Within a few months, loan rates finallly began to catch up.

What Happens in Tokyo Affects the Interest You Earn in Peoria

You know how you keep hearing that we live in a global village? It's true. Events overseas (such as foreign government money policies, the price of oil and other natural resources, saber-rattling by a kooky foreign military leader, and acts of nature) have a direct impact on the savings yields, investment decisions, and monthly mortgage payments in this country.

For example, higher oil prices in the Middle East affect the price you pay at the pump. When prices rise, that's inflationary. Bond yields go up, which ultimately affects your decision of what bond maturities you should buy. And when those things go up, they take mortgage rates with them. Then the Federal Reserve steps in and raises its key rates, such as the federal funds rate, and that boosts your short-term savings yields as well as the cost of your auto loans, home equity

The best sources for tracking changes in the economy are the business pages of your local newspaper, or national newspapers such as *USA Today*, *The Wall Street Journal*, and *The New York Times*.

loans, and seven out of ten credit cards.

The strength of the U.S. economy affects your rates *exactly* the same way. Follow the latest data on housing, unemployment, and prices. The greater the possibility that inflation is in the wind, the higher your interest rates will be, and vice versa.

Heady's Five Critical Laws of Timing

Okay, you've done your roller coaster homework. You know how the cycles go up, down, then back up again. Now you're ready to put your new knowledge to work. You're going to invest based on where the roller coaster is on the track. By following these laws religiously, you should be able to add a substantial amount of coin to your personal treasury.

➤ **Law 1: Go short when rates are rising.** If rates just started to take off, say, up by a quarter-percent within a few weeks after the up-cycle started, don't touch a 2 1/2- or five-year CD with a ten-foot pole. Why? You'll be trapped into a low rate for a long time. Instead, open a three-month CD—no longer—and plan to renew the account when it matures, perhaps at a different bank if it's paying more then.

Make sure you ask the bank how they will notify you before your CD matures. Whatever you do, don't let the CD "automatically" roll over at the same institution, because its new rate may be too low compared with what other banks are offering. You may elect to switch your account pronto.

An optional plan is to park your funds temporarily in a high-paying, out-of-state, federally insured money market account (MMA). It'll probably pay more than two percent above the average MMA. That way you can continue to shop as the up-cycle gathers steam. If you find a red-hot three-month rate, you can withdraw your MMA funds with no penalty. See Chapter 8 for more information.

➤ **Law 2: Go long when rates peak.** When rates peak, it's a sign that rates could start falling in a new down-cycle. Grab a three-to-five-year CD for all it's worth. You'll keep earning that same high rate while all other rates are falling.

REALLY? In 1984, when CD rates hit their highest peak ever, smart cycle-followers locked in five-year CDs at an average rate of 12.5 percent. That's what they pocketed through 1989! Similarly, during the 1989 peak, five-year accounts topped out at 9.2 percent. Customers who bought then enjoyed that yield through mid-1994. And the really smart five-year investor who jumped from peak to peak in '84 and '89 earned a total return of $17,647 on his $10,000 investment over 10 years!

➤ **Law 3: Watch the indicators, especially the Federal Reserve, economic data reports, and the banks' prime rate.** These are the three main indicators discussed earlier in the chapter, and they're the ones to keep your eye on. At a bare minimum, at least follow your daily news headlines to detect whether the economy is getting stronger or weaker.

➤ **Law 4: When the Federal Reserve changes rates, move quickly behind it.** As an investor, your key is the Fed's discount rate, the rate the Fed charges banks for loans. Once the Fed moves, the banks follow suit. For example, in 1994 the Fed raised rates several times—and almost every time the Fed boosted its rates, the banks increased their prime rate by the same amount *within 24 hours*.

CD rates instantly began following, and rose by as much as a half-percent within four to eight weeks. In other words, the banks don't hang around and wait. They march in step with the Fed like tin soldiers—but your rates bring up the rear.

➤ **Law 5: The longer interest rates have been falling, the shorter the CD term you should select.** Let's say the numbers have been dropping steadily for two years. Odds are the down-cycle is going to end soon, so you want a CD that will carry you past the bottom—or valley—of the down-cycle and into the next upward cycle. This would not—repeat, NOT—be the time to buy a two- or five-year CD, because you'll miss out when rates start rising again.

By obeying the laws of timing, you'll maximize your earnings—while the rest of the crowd gets white knuckles from riding the roller coaster the wrong way.

The Least You Need to Know

➤ Interest rates are like a roller coaster—they have peaks and valleys, and are in constant motion.

➤ To make the interest rate work for you, you must pick the right time to save when rates are high, and the best time to borrow when loan rates are low.

➤ Most up-cycles or down-cycles last an average of 1 1/2 to three years. If you know how long the interest rate has been in its current cycle, you can predict where it's heading in the future.

➤ Watch economic indicators such as the Federal Reserve, economic data reports, and the bank's prime rate to figure out where rates are going.

➤ Buy short-term CDs when the interest rate is rising, and buy long-term CDs when the rate has reached its peak.

Part 4
Credit and Loans—
Getting Money When
You Need It

Oooh… a credit card. The plastic that makes you feel fantastic. They are seductive, aren't they, with their instant-millionaire credit lines? Unfortunately, credit cards and loans are necessary in the world of financial planning. If you want to buy a house or car—or if you need to take out a loan—you need credit. In order to get credit, *however, you* need *credit, right? Makes the quizzical chicken-and-egg scenario seem easy to answer.*

Getting money when you need it for major purchases doesn't have to be difficult. Once you learn how those credit-rating agencies score your credit application, it'll be a snap. But the credit world doesn't stop there. You will find out how to beat those 18-percent rip-off rates that credit cards offer and save yourself some dough. Plus, you'll discover how to finance a car—without being taken for a ride—and how to shop the real bottom-line costs when you're looking for a mortgage.

Chapter 13

How to Cut Your Credit Card Costs in Half

In This Chapter

➤ A quick crash course on the credit card jungle

➤ How—and where—to get a card that will cost you NOTHING

➤ How to avoid the credit card debt trap

➤ Which fees and charges will hurt you most

➤ Where to get a card even if you have bad credit

There's no bigger rip-off than credit cards. Banks are getting away with murder—charging you 18 percent or more because you've become addicted to the convenience of plastic.

The plastic picture is also getting more confusing. More banks and more companies have jumped into the credit card business because it's one gigantic gold mine. But the credit card pie is just so big; that's why card issuers are dangling low-rate offers, freebies, and rebates to grab your account away.

You need to see through these offers and cut a cheaper deal, including switching your cards to low-rate, no-fee institutions. More importantly, you should learn how to avoid falling into the card debt trap and hurting your credit record. This chapter explains how credit cards work, who offers the best rates, and how to trim your costs to the bone.

Can't Live With 'Em, Can't Live Without 'Em

Notice how more credit card offers have been bombarding your mailbox lately? Card companies sent out more than one billion offers to consumers in 1994 alone. Why? Two reasons:

➤ Credit cards represent enormous profits for banks and other card issuers. They sock cardholders with rates of 18 percent or more while they pay puny interest on savings.

➤ More card outfits are competing for your business, so they're tempting you with lower rates and rebate deals.

Americans are hooked on plastic, plain and simple. Convenient? You bet. We simply whip out our cards; no money leaves our wallets. That's a good feeling—temporarily. Only… later, when the monthly bill comes in with all your charges plus interest, it's pay-up time. Sure, the bank will let you get away with a teensy minimum payment. But that practice could keep you in debt forever. And if you fall behind in your monthly payments, you'll wind up with an ugly blemish on your credit record that will haunt you for years.

How Credit Cards Can Cost You

You can make purchases with your credit card up to a certain dollar limit decided by the card issuer. As you use the card, you're constantly borrowing against your limit and repaying the money. Say your credit limit is $1,000 and you buy a garment for $100, or take a $100 cash advance against the card. You have $900 left. When you repay the $100 (plus the interest charges), you again have $1,000 in available credit.

If you're like the average American, you're what the credit card companies call a "revolver"—a person who doesn't pay off his monthly balance, but instead "rolls" part of the bill over to the next month. Nearly seven out of 10 cardholders do this, and the average amount they roll over every month is $1,700.

Let's set it straight: Banks and other credit card outfits *want* you to do this. They make their profits by making it easy for you to finance your balance. If you paid off your bill every month, they wouldn't make a dime.

How expensive can credit cards be? Take the case of a cardholder with a balance of $2,500 who pays 18.5 percent interest. If he or she made only a minimum monthly payment of two percent of the unpaid balance—which many card issuers permit—it would take more than 30 years to pay the card off. Even worse, the total interest would come to $6,500. All for a $2,500 loan!

Using Credit Cards Wisely

Skip credit cards entirely? Just try it. In today's society, a credit card is almost as important as a birth certificate. You need plastic to rent a car, buy an airline ticket, reserve a hotel room, order from a mail-order catalog or TV shopping network, or rent movies. A woman we know moved into a new town and tried to deposit $20,000 in a bank. She had her driver's license and voter's registration card, but the bank insisted on seeing a credit card before they'd accept her as a new customer. She didn't have one, so they declined her business!

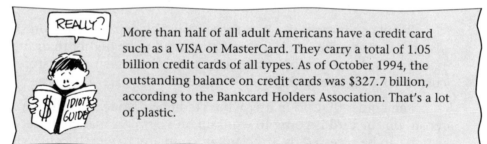

REALLY? More than half of all adult Americans have a credit card such as a VISA or MasterCard. They carry a total of 1.05 billion credit cards of all types. As of October 1994, the outstanding balance on credit cards was $327.7 billion, according to the Bankcard Holders Association. That's a lot of plastic.

Credit cards are definitely useful. The key to avoiding credit card trouble is to be smart about how you use credit. For example, did you know that

➤ You can get a free card if you pay off your balance each month?

➤ You can cut your card costs nearly in half if you have good credit?

➤ You can even get a card if you've had credit problems or haven't had a chance to build up a credit record of your own?

The following sections will help you become a smart credit card user.

Kinds of Credit Cards

The main types of credit cards are

➤ Fixed-rate cards.

➤ Variable-rate cards.

➤ Gold cards.

➤ Secured cards.

➤ Credit cards with gimmicks such as rebates.

The sections that follow explain each of these types in more detail. Besides those standard cards issued by banks, thrifts, and credit unions, consumers may qualify for an American Express card—provided their financial condition is eligible for a minimum credit line of $5,000. You pay no interest rate with an AmEx card, but the annual fee is $75. AmEx makes its money from these fees, and from merchants and other businesses that will accept the cards. The merchants pay AmEx a small percentage of any amount charged on the card.

Retail credit cards (such as those issued by department stores) are also big business, but their interest rates tend to be higher than the rates banks charge on their standard cards. We've seen many stores slap customers with rates as high as 21 percent.

Remember that no matter what credit card you use, your payment record on the card is going to wind up on your personal credit report— which can be accessed by any bank or company to which you apply for credit.

Fixed-Rate Cards

This is your ordinary, everyday, plain card. The interest rate is *fixed* at a certain percentage. Whatever you buy, that's the percent interest you pay. This type of credit card has become an ugly duckling because the average rate is about 17.5 percent, according to the newsletter *Bank Rate Monitor*. In cities such as San Francisco, the rate is even higher— an astronomical 19.5 percent!

To avoid paying these high fixed rates, shop the best card deals nationwide. You'll find rates as low as nine percent. It's a perfectly safe and smart thing to do; after all, most big card-issuers are national anyway. The only catch is that the lower the card rate, the more difficult it will be for you to get your credit approved. Tougher standards may apply. But if your credit is good, give it a shot!

Table 13.1 shows the best fixed-rate credit card deals in the U.S., according to the newsletter *Bank Rate Monitor*.

If you're carrying one of these high-rate plastic monsters, complain to an officer of your bank. Nowadays, because of stiff card competition, there's an excellent chance the bank will give you a lower rate such as 14 or 15 percent.

Table 13.1 Best Deals for Persons Who Carry Balances

Institution Location Phone Number	Interest Rate	Annual Fee	Interest-Free Days/From
Pulaski Bank & Trust Little Rock, Arkansas (800) 980-2265	8.75%	$35	25/billing
Wachovia Bank New Castle, Delaware (800) 842-3262	9.00%	$88	25/billing
Metropolitan National Bank Little Rock, Arkansas (800) 883-2511	9.24%	$25	25/transaction
Federal Savings Bank Rogers, Arkansas (800) 374-5600	10.20%	$33	25/billing
Arkansas Federal Little Rock, Arkansas (800) 224-7283 (Arkansas) (800) 477-3348	10.25%	$35	25/billing

continues

Table 13.1 Continues

Institution Location Phone Number	Interest Rate	Annual Fee	Interest-Free Days/From
Simmons First Nat'l Bank Pine Bluff, Arkansas (800) 636-5151	10.25%	$35	25/billing
AFBA Industrial Bank Colorado Springs, Colorado (800) 776-2265	11.00%	$35	25/billing

Source: *Bank Rate Monitor.*

You can also switch banks to get a better deal on your credit card. The new bank may give you a special "account-closing" check to pay off your balance at the old bank. The balance then will show up on your new card account at the outfit to which you switched your business—or you simply pay off your old balance and open a new account at another bank. Either way, cut your credit card in half, and enclose it with your check and a letter to the old bank. Advise them you are closing your account (give the number) and keep a copy of the letter.

Variable-Rate Cards

To get customers in the door, banks may offer a very low introductory variable rate such as 4.9 percent. After six months or a year, the rate jumps to a much higher figure. These introductory rate deals are okay if they're good for at least a year. You can switch from your old high-rate card to the new bank, then switch to another low-rate card when the year is up.

Choosing a *variable-rate* credit card will cost you less in the long run. With this type of credit card, your interest rate changes according to an index used by the bank. Often, the rate is tied to the bank's prime rate plus six percentage points. For example, if the prime is at 8.5 percent (which it was at the end of 1994), the variable rate on your credit card would be 14.5 to 15.5 percent. Because variable rates have been less than fixed rates in recent years, more than 70 percent of all credit cards now are variable-rate.

Variable-rate cards are great when the prime rate is low, as it was in the early 1990s when the prime stood at only six percent. Then, the average variable rate was only 12 percent. But when rates start rising, as they did in 1994, variable-rate plastic becomes less and less attractive. The average today is about 15 percent.

Table 13.2 shows the best variable-rate credit card deals in the U.S. as of February 1995, according to the newsletter *100 Highest Yields*.

Table 13.2   Best Deals for Persons Who Pay Off the Entire Balance Monthly

Institution Location Phone Number	Interest Rate	Annual Fee	Interest-Free Days/From
USAA Federal Savings Bank San Antonio, Texas (800) 922-9092	12.78% V	$0	25/billing
AFBA Industrial Bank Colorado Springs, Colorado (800) 776-2265	14.50% V	$0	25/billing
Amalgamated Bank Chicago, Illinois (312) 822-3130 (Illinois) (800) 723-0303	14.50% V	$0	25/billing
First Western Bank New Castle, Pennsylvania (800) 837-6669	15.40% V	$0	25/billing
Transflorida Bank Boca Raton, Florida (407) 347-0007	15.40% V	$35	25/billing
Bank One Lafayette Lafayette, Indiana (800) 395-2255	16.40% V	$0	25/billing

Source: *Bank Rate Monitor.* V = variable rate

Gold Cards

The secret to shopping for gold cards lies in their perks: emergency roadside service, buyer protection plans, cash back if you spend thousands of dollars. All too often, though, cardholders choose gold cards as a "status" symbol. The only thing a gold card *can* promise you is a higher credit limit—and sometimes expensive annual fees. Gold card applicants require a stronger credit record; the cards come with mandatory benefits such as $150,000 travel-accident insurance.

Secured Cards for Those with Bad (or No) Credit

There are more than 400 issuers of *secured* credit cards for folks with a poor credit history or no history at all. Anyone who's been hanging his head because he lost his card during bad financial times now has new hope.

A secured card works like this: You keep $200 to $500 on deposit with the bank. It issues you a card with which you can make purchases for up to your deposit amount. More and more institutions also pay you a small amount of interest on your deposit, such as two to four percent.

Don't jump at the first secured card offer that comes along, no matter how plastic-hungry you are. With so many banks beating the bushes for business, you should shop these cards as you would anything else.

The interest rate you pay on a secured card is a little stiff, anywhere from 17 to 21 percent, but it's temporarily worth it for you to start rebuilding your credit. Banks used to charge an application fee of $20 to $40 on secured cards, but that's fading as competition heats up.

Why the boom in secured cards? Because banks have discovered a huge, new market of people with damaged credit, young people applying for a card for the first time, divorced people who don't have their own personal credit records, and new workers, including immigrants.

Who can get a secured card? Almost everybody, with a few exceptions. Requirements vary. Many card issuers will accept those with bad payment records; a few will even take customers with bankruptcies that are at least six to 12 months old. Others insist you be employed for one year or have no excessive credit card debt or federal tax liens. Income requirements range from $165 a week at Key Federal Savings Bank, Havre de Grace, Maryland (800/228-2230), to $15,000 a year at Surety Bank, Hurst, Texas (800/624-8472). First Consumers National Bank, Beaverton, Oregon, requires an opening deposit of $150, and lets cardholders charge up to 150 percent of whatever they deposit, to a maximum of $2,500.

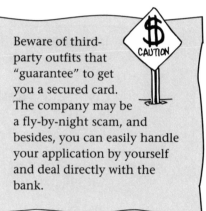

Beware of third-party outfits that "guarantee" to get you a secured card. The company may be a fly-by-night scam, and besides, you can easily handle your application by yourself and deal directly with the bank.

Is a secured card for you? Yes, if your credit needs repair and you don't mind paying the high interest. If you mind your manners and make your monthly payments on time, that will be a plus on your credit record. Six to 12 months later, you might be able to ask the bank to increase your credit limit, or apply for a standard card. For example, Key Federal Savings Bank allows you to apply for their unsecured credit card if you have maintained a good track record on your secured card for 24 months.

Table 13.3 is a rundown of the different outfits that offer secured cards, based on a *Bank Rate Monitor* survey. Note: Citizenship, age, employment, credit record, region, residency, income, account minimum/maximum, and other restrictions may apply.

Table 13.3 Who Offers Secured Credit Cards

Institution	Location	Phone Number
American Pacific Bank	Portland, Oregon	(800) 879-8745
Bank of Hoven	Hoven, South Dakota	(800) 777-7735
Bank One	Lafayette, Indiana	(800) 395-2555
Bank One	Phoenix, Arizona	(800) 544-4110
Chase Manhattan Bank USA	Wilmington, Delaware	(800) 482-4273

continues

Table 13.3 Continued

Institution	Location	Phone Number
Citibank	Sioux Falls, South Dakota	(800) 743-1332
Community Bank of Parker	Parker, Colorado	(800) 779-8472
Federal Savings Bank	Rogers, Arkansas	(800) 290-9060
First Consumers Nat'l Bank	Beaverton, Oregon	(800) 876-3262
First Nat'l Bank Brookings	Brookings, South Dakota	(800) 658-3660
First Nat'l Bank of Marin	San Rafael, California	(800) 588-5170
First Premier Bank	Sioux Falls, South Dakota	(800) 584-7097
Household Bank	Salinas, California	(800) 395-6080
Key Federal Savings Bank	Havre de Grace, Maryland	(800) 228-2230

Source: *Bank Rate Monitor.*

Gimmick Credit Cards

Credit cards with bells and whistles are popping up all over, as every card outfit and its brother tries to get a piece of the credit card pie. The main gimmicks are discounts on merchandise and services, and promises of cash rebates. The more you use a particular card, the more rebates and freebies you get. These can range from discounts on new cars to free air travel and cut-rate hotel rooms. Sounds groovy, but the questions you must ask yourself are:

➤ Could I get a better deal with another card that offers a lower interest rate and lower fees?

➤ Do I really need the "free" merchandise, discounts and whatever? If the card gives me points toward buying a Chevrolet sedan, but I'm in the market for a Ford pickup, it doesn't make much sense.

The offers have lots of different twists—you're going to see more of them this year—the most popular being money-back gimmicks that rebate a percentage of your purchases. For example, Chase Manhattan in Delaware (800/282-4273) rebates one percent of monthly purchases, as does Fidelity Trust Co., Salt Lake City, Utah (800/323-5353). Colonial Bank USA in Delaware credits one point for every $1 charged, toward U.S. Savings Bonds. If, say, you carry a balance of $1,000, you'd rack up 3,000 points—enough for a $50 bond. If customers pay off their $1,000 balance in full, Chase and Fidelity forks out $30 in cash.

As with any credit card, it's not the gifts and pizazz that count, it's what you wind up with in your pocket. Compare the bottom-line costs—after the rebates.

Key Fee Factors

Okay, you've got the types of cards down pat. Now you need to know the *key cost factors* you could be hit with. The three main ones are interest rate, annual fee, and grace period. The kind of card you want depends on the way you pay off your credit card bills. If you're a "revolver," that is, if you finance your balance every month, you want a credit card with a very low interest rate. If you pay your balance off in full every month, you want a card with no annual fee. This card will cost you nothing.

The *interest rate* is what you're charged to borrow the bank's money to finance what you purchased with the card. If you're in the habit of not paying off your monthly balance, you want the cheapest, rock-bottom interest rate you can find. If you don't pay off the full balance, interest keeps accumulating on the unpaid amount. The meter begins ticking the moment you buy something with the card, or more likely the day the card issuer bills you for what you owe.

The interest could keep you in bondage forever if you don't use your noodle. For instance, says Bankcard Holders of America, it would take eight years and eight months to pay off a $1,000 balance at 16.5 percent of you only paid the minimum payment. The minimum is normally 2.5 percent of the amount owed. You'd wind up paying $766 interest on your $1,000 loan. But you could pay off the debt in three years and pay $500 less in interest just by adding an extra $10 a month to your payment.

163

You pay the *annual fee* just to have the right to have the card for one year. The fee is usually $20 to $50, but many banks charge no fee at all. If you're the meticulous type and always pay your monthly card balance in full, you should carry a no-annual-fee card and nothing else. The card will cost you nothing. It will be like having a free card.

Double-check the rates and fees you're now paying on your cards. The rate may have gone up over the past year if you're carrying a variable-rate card that is tied to some index. If your rate today is 16 to 19 percent, you're being taken to the cleaners. You might have missed the fine print on a bank notice, stating that the card's annual fee has been raised. The most you should pay is $50.

The *grace period* is the number of days you have to pay off all new purchases without being hit by a finance charge. The usual grace period is 25 days. Typically, if you don't pay off your entire bill, all new purchases get clobbered by finance charges immediately.

For example, two brothers, Eenie and Meenie, both carry credit cards with an 18 percent rate. Each has a $1,000 balance on his card, on which there's no annual fee. Eenie pays off the entire $1,000 before the 25-day grace period is up. The card costs him zero. But Meenie only makes a minimum payment, $20, and gets charged 18 percent interest per year on the remaining $980. If you can't pay off your credit card entirely, always be sure to pay at least the minimum payment on your card before the grace period expires. Late payments will go over like a lead balloon at the next place you apply for credit. You'll probably get rejected.

Other niggling card costs:

➤ **Late fees:** You'll usually be nicked with a flat $15 charge, or two percent of your outstanding balance, if you don't make at least a minimum payment by the due date shown on the bill.

➤ **Cash advances:** You can borrow money against the card, but the interest rate you pay for this type of transaction is apt to be higher. Plus, there's usually no grace period and you may also pay a small fee.

The Biggest Secret of All—Watch Your Habits!

Americans are up to their ears in debt, and the credit card got them there. Bad card habits have caused divorces, bankruptcies, lost dreams, and emotional wreckage. You can avoid the credit trap by following these simple rules:

➤ Know your credit limit based on your income, amount of current debt, and credit history. A rule of thumb is that your total monthly debt should not exceed 38 percent of your monthly income; for a review on managing your debt, check out Chapter 3.

➤ Carry only the number of cards you need, even though you haven't used up your credit line. Creditors look at how much you're able to go into debt when they review your record.

➤ Don't apply for more than one card at a time. Some creditor may think you're going to charge like mad and take off for Brazil.

➤ Consider joining a credit union to take advantage of their lower interest rates. In 1994, for example, the average credit union offered a fixed-rate credit card at 12.98 percent, versus the national average of 17.95 percent, according to *Bank Rate Monitor*.

➤ Remember that a bad credit record will dog you for years. Nothing can screw up your life faster than going overboard with credit cards. Your card payment record will shadow you in everything you do, including buying a home (or renting), getting a job, and opening a checking account.

➤ Pay against your balance ASAP. Don't let bills hang around. Every day you wait is going to cost you more in interest.

➤ If you can't make your payments on time, or if you want to dispute a charge, contact your card issuer immediately—and put everything in writing.

➤ Don't get fooled when card issuers lower your minimum payments. It only makes it easier for you to stay in debt, and increases the total interest you'll pay. This is a tar pit if ever there was one.

➤ If you run into severe financial problems, contact one of the personal-credit counseling organizations listed in Chapter 17. They've helped millions of people, and can probably help you at no charge, or for a small fee.

The Least You Need to Know

➤ Credit cards are so profitable that competition for your credit card business has increased dramatically in recent years. You can use this to your advantage by shopping for a card that best meets your needs, such as a low interest rate, no annual fee, or rebates that could save you money.

➤ The basic types of credit cards are fixed-rate cards, variable-rate cards, gold cards, secured cards, and credit cards with gimmicks such as rebates.

➤ To figure out how much a credit card is costing you, you need to be aware of the interest rate, annual fee, and grace period. Extra fees are also involved when you get cash advances, or are late with a payment.

➤ Don't carry more cards than you need, and always pay more than the minimum monthly payment to avoid drowning in credit card debt.

Chapter 14

Financing a Car—Without Being Taken for a Ride

In This Chapter

➤ How to avoid the biggest rip-offs of all

➤ How to find the cheapest financing

➤ Buying versus leasing

You'll buy many cars in your lifetime, but how much are you really paying? If you're like most consumers, you'll never learn the nervy, shocking back-room tactics used by car dealers to drive up the cost of your car. Their rip-off tricks run into the hundreds, beginning the moment you walk into the showroom. A dealer can trap you with overcharges on things you don't need, from "undercoating" to "credit life insurance"—and inflate your financing costs without you ever knowing it. Result: You can be scammed into paying thousands of extra dollars on that shiny new set of wheels.

The same goes for leasing a new auto instead of buying it. Although leasing today may appear to be the cheapest way to get behind the wheel, leasing is loaded with mathematical schemes the average person doesn't understand. This chapter strips away the mystery of buying a car versus leasing one, explains the key steps of shrewd buying, and points out how *not* to be taken for an expensive ride!

Knowing the Biggest Rip-Offs

When you go into a store to buy a television set or washing machine, they tell you the price and maybe the cost of an optional service contract. And that's about it, right? Not so with a new car. Auto dealers are the gimmick-and-add-on champions of all time. Besides the financing rip-offs, which we'll discuss a little later, the list includes:

➤ Invoices and stickers that could have been created by somebody in the back room, not the manufacturer.

➤ An outrageous delivery charge. Shouldn't the cost of hauling the car from Detroit be included in your price?

➤ The dealer's "setup and preparation" charge. What did they do besides a wash and vacuum? After all, the car didn't arrive in bits and pieces from the manufacturer, did it?

➤ A whole bunch of options—a power sun roof, for example, or power seats—all priced sky-high.

➤ Dealer maintenance which you can buy more cheaply somewhere else.

➤ Extended warranty plans that they scare you into buying because Nick, the mechanic, does work at "$70 an hour."

➤ Dealer interest rates that have been booted up higher than what you could get from a bank.

➤ Vehicle undercoating. Forget it. You don't need to spend the extra couple hundred bucks. Do you think manufacturers are stupid enough to build new cars that rust out overnight?

➤ Credit life insurance. You're not required to buy it, and you shouldn't. Insurance experts have pointed out that of every $1 people spend on this scam, only 40 cents

You probably can't do much to avoid setup-and-prep charges, but this chapter does discuss other ways you can foil a dealer's adding to the price. For one thing, the window sticker on most new cars shows an "MSRP" price (Manufacturer's Statement of Retail Price) at the bottom. That's what the car maker has determined to be the optimum retail price for the options shown on the sticker. You won't be able to escape the delivery (freight) charge on the MSRP, but the dealer's charge for setup-and-prep is a tip that the dealer has that much room within which to discount the selling price. (You can always shop another dealer's window stickers for comparison.)

is paid out in the form of claims. Most people are already covered by life insurance policies or other assets if the borrower dies.

➤ Trade-ins. The dealer promises to lower your monthly payment if you trade in Old Betsy. But he's already figured how much it will cost him to spruce up the car and how much he can sell it for at auction. He knows exactly how much money he has to play with to get your business. He'll take his cost of that old clunker out of your hide one way or another.

You don't need any rip-off extras the salesperson will try to load on you. They only increase the debt you'll have to finance, and boost the salesperson's commission. Even so, consider options carefully, and make your own decisions. You may wish to include certain attractive options you plan to sell the car a few years later. Reason: Today many options—for example, power windows, cruise control, and a cassette player—have become almost-standard equipment that your future buyer will expect when he or she buys the car from you.

Used Cars: Buying Right and Selling Right

A new car depreciates the moment it is driven off the dealer's lot. The amount of depreciation can vary, but we've heard of as much as 20 to 30 percent in the first year.

When you finance a used car, expect to pay an interest rate of two to three percentage points above the rate you pay on a new car. If a new car costs 9.5 percent to finance, chances are a used car will cost 11.5 to 12.5 percent in the same town. (If your credit is bad, prepare to get hit with a rate that may be 18 percent or higher.)

The best source of information on what a used car is worth is the National Automobile Dealers Association's *Official Used Car Guide*. It covers domestic and imported cars and small trucks. On the pages of the guide you'll find three columns of numbers for each auto make and model:

➤ **Trade-In Value** shows what the car is worth in trade at the dealer—*if* the vehicle is in tip-top condition in both appearance and mechanics.

➤ **Loan Value** normally determines how much a bank will lend you to finance the car.

➤ **Retail Value** tells you what price the car will fetch in the marketplace, whether you sell it to someone or buy it from the dealer. The value assumes the car is in great shape. If it isn't, the value will be less.

How to Get Top Price When You Trade In or Sell a Used Car

Look at the vehicle you're trying to trade or sell. Ask yourself, "Would I buy this car if someone offered it to me?" If not, invest a few bucks at an auto detail shop, a complete car wash (including wax), and a mechanic if necessary. On many used autos, this couple-hundred dollars of investment could bring an extra $500 to $1,000 in the selling price or trade-in value.

On a trade, the new car dealer is saying to himself, "Let's see, if I accept this clunker against the price I'm going to try to get from this customer on a new car, there's some fixin' I'm gonna have to do. Like new carpets, a couple of tires, wash and wax, maybe an engine tune-up and other stuff." The dealer figures he'll sell your slightly-renovated car for, say, $5,000 at an automobile auction; he offers you $4,000 for Old Betsy. He spends $300 to get it in shape, and pockets the $700 difference.

Now you know rule number one when you trade your car in on a new one: *Do some preliminary shopping around* before *you let a dealer know that you have a used car to trade.* First try to negotiate a new-car price at a discount off the dealer's sticker price. Dealers tell us that this discounted price may be between $1,000 and $1,500 less than what the sticker price (MSRP) shows. (Don't expect a big discount if there is an industry shortage of a particular model. In that case, the discount will be less.)

The dealer may try to low-ball you by saying it will cost him much more to get your car into "ready-to-go" condition. Don't believe it.

170

Then, using the discounted price, ask the dealer how much he'll pay you for the car you'll trade in. This strategy will go over like a lead balloon with the dealer, but at least he'll know you're no idiot.

Stifle Those Emotions When You Go to Buy!

Follow these rules whenever you are buying a new or used vehicle:

➤ Don't get excited about the vehicle. The salesperson can read you like a book. If he or she senses you're falling in love with that little two-seater with the stick shift and double carburetor, it's going to cost you.

➤ Don't be anxious to close the deal on the same day.

➤ Shop at least one other dealer who offers the same car. Dealers know from experience you're going to do this, and that's what will give you clout in negotiating the cheapest price.

➤ As mentioned before, start negotiating a discount off the sticker price right off the bat—before you reveal that you have a car to trade.

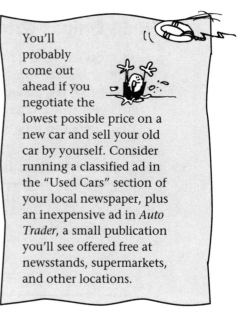

You'll probably come out ahead if you negotiate the lowest possible price on a new car and sell your old car by yourself. Consider running a classified ad in the "Used Cars" section of your local newspaper, plus an inexpensive ad in *Auto Trader*, a small publication you'll see offered free at newsstands, supermarkets, and other locations.

Getting the Best Financing

Competition in the new car market is so ferocious that many dealers earn more of their living from the finance charges than from the profit they make off their autos. This section explains how you can avoid the pitfalls and walk out with the best deal.

Avoid Dealer Financing

Want to save one to two percent on your loan right off the bat? Avoid dealer financing altogether. And don't even think about going to an independent finance company where the rates are even higher—unless, of course, your credit is so shot that there's no other way out.

Go to a bank or thrift institution and obtain a preapproved loan for the amount you plan to finance. Better yet, join a credit union if you're not already a member. CUs are big in car loans, and their interest rates always beat what banks charge, as you'll see in Table 14.1, which shows what the average credit union charges for a new car loan versus what you'd pay at a bank or thrift institution, according to the industry newsletter *Bank Rate Monitor*.

Credit Unions Offer the Cheapest Rates

It's less expensive to finance a new car through a credit union than through a bank or thrift. Besides offering cheaper rates, a credit union will provide you with information on the dealer's *real* cost of the car. A CU will also arrange special sales with local dealers who guarantee CU members special low rates.

Table 14.1 Auto Loan Interest Rates

Type of Institution	Interest Rate
Credit union	8.21%
Bank	9.85
Thrift	9.76

When you walk into the dealer's showroom armed with a preapproved loan, you'll have enormous clout for two reasons. First, the dealer knows you're a red-hot, live prospect—and he won't let you out the door until he gives you his best deal. Second, he won't try to flim-flam you with his own financing (which is more costly), because you already have the cheapest one in your pocket. A nice position to be in.

Get a Simple Interest Loan

With a simple interest loan, you'll be paying interest only on the remaining amount of the loan. How come? As you make your payments month after month, you'll be steadily paring down what you still owe on that original $15,000. Say you make 10 monthly payments of $373. At nine percent interest, your first payment of $373 is on the whole $15,000. Of the $373, $112 is interest and the other $261 reduces the principal you still owe to $14,739.

After the tenth payment you will have whittled the principal down to $12,302. But your monthly payment will stay the same. Here's why: When the bank sets up your simple interest loan, it figures a flat amount of how much total interest you'll pay on the (say) $15,000 you're borrowing. You can arrange your payments so that they'll still be $373 every month. That's easier for you, because you wouldn't want to start out with a gigantic payment and have it get smaller every month. You might not be able to afford the payment in the early months.

Simple interest loans are commonly offered by banks, whereas many finance companies will charge higher interest through front-end loans. If a finance company does offer a simple interest loan, it will probably be at higher interest rates than what you'd pay at a bank. If the applicant has a poor credit history, the rate could shoot up even higher.

Example: On a four-year (48-month) loan, the total interest comes to $2,917. Divide 48 payments into $2,917 and you get a monthly interest payment of $61. The bank gets its $15,000 back, plus the $2,917 interest. You can budget for a steady monthly payment figure.

What you should avoid is a "front-end installment loan." Unlike the simple interest example you just read, with the installment loan *you pay interest every month on the original $15,000 you borrowed*. In this case, your total interest cost would work out to $5,400, or $2,483 more than with the simple interest loan. Your monthly payment would be $425 instead of $373. Better that money goes into *your* pocket instead of the dealer's (or the bank's).

Other Financing Secrets

The following tips will help you stay focused on the bottom line of buying a car:

➤ **Don't slide into the low payment mentality.** This is where many folks never learn. Car dealers are no idiots. They know the average person is more concerned about being able to afford their monthly payments than they are about the total cost of the loan.

So what do dealers—and banks—often do? Suggest you stretch the loan term to five years instead of three. They say it will "make it easier on you." Humbug. All lower monthly payments do is jack up your financing cost.

Here's an example. A $15,000 loan financed through a bank at nine percent for three years comes to $477 a month, with a total cost of $2,172. But over five years, though the monthly payment drops to $311, your loan cost jumps to $3,683. Not much of a deal, huh?

➤ **Make as big a down payment as you can.** Generally, you'll be required to make a down payment of 10 to 20 percent when you buy a new car, although we've seen credit unions finance 100 percent of the price. Some banks will do that, too, but only on luxury models. Why a bigger down payment? Because the more you put down, the lower your interest rate is apt to be.

➤ **Be wary of manufacturer financing.** Boy, are they enticing— those car dealer ads with low-ball financing and the promise that you can drive the car home by five o'clock! Car manufacturers have captive finance companies to help their dealers wheel and deal. They desperately want your business, and they'll turn cartwheels to get it—including a super-low interest rate and same-day credit approval, even on Sundays.

However, this type of financing has several downsides. First, the low-ball rate may only apply to certain models, like that little convertible over there with the purple stripes and no trim. Other regular models may cost more to finance. Second, if you do get the dealer's low manufacturer rate, the dealer may take it out of your hide by charging you more for the car. Third, manufacturer financing is less apt to give you a simple interest loan.

➤ **Stay away from variable-rate loans.** Most car loan rates are *fixed*—that is, you're charged the same interest during the entire loan term. Some car financing rates are *variable*—meaning the rate can go up or down, depending on which direction all bank rates are going. If rates rise, as they did in 1994, your car loan rate could go up by as much as two to three percentage points in a year.

If that happens, the bank may make it "easier" for you by keeping your monthly payment the same—but stretching the term of your loan. Result: Your 48-month loan could turn into a 50-month loan. You wind up paying a bigger finance cost.

➤ **Take advantage of car rebates.** If Bubba's Auto Showroom says the manufacturer has a special $1,000 "rebate" offer, you may want to grab it—that is, *if* the rebate applies to the exact auto you want. Here's why:

Say you're working with that same $15,000 example at nine percent bank interest for four years. The loan payment is $373 per month. The total cost of the car is $17,917. On the other hand, if you take the $1,000 rebate and apply it to your down payment, you'll reduced your monthly payment to $348. The total cost of the loan will be cut to $16,723.

➤ **Check whether you can pay off your loan early.** Some lenders will let you do it, others won't. So before you sign for a loan, ask if you can pre-pay the loan without a penalty. Are there any extra fees or charges? If a pre-pay is okay, be sure to note on your payment checks how much is going toward reducing the principal and how much is going toward the interest. This way you'll have proof if you're ever challenged by the dealer or the bank.

REALLY?

Some lenders have a complicated little gizmo built into the way they calculate your payments. It's called the "Rule of 78s." It's complicated as heck—and depends on state law—but it simply means that most of your early payments are going toward the interest, not the principal. In that case, you won't save very much by paying off the loan in advance.

➤ **Get a tax deduction on the car by hocking your house.** It's a little bit risky, but lots of people do it. You can no longer get a tax deduction on a straight car loan—the IRS did away with that in 1990—but you can get one by borrowing against your home. How? By opening a home equity line of credit. First, you figure how much of your home you own—what the house is worth, minus what you owe on your mortgage. Banks, thrifts, and credit unions will usually lend you up to 75 or 80 percent of that amount (see Chapter 18).

Example: If your home's appraised value is $100,000 and you owe $40,000 on the mortgage, your equity in the house is $60,000. If the bank lends you 80 percent of that $60,000, the amount of the principal is $48,000.

If the interest rate on the home equity loan is less than the rate on a car loan, you'll save on your financing costs. Plus, if you're in, say, the 28 percent tax bracket, you'll save money compared with the taxes you'd pay on a straight auto loan. Reason: The IRS allows you to deduct the interest expense.

Buy or Lease?

How popular has leasing gotten? Today, 27 of every 100 new car deals is a lease, up from three out of 100 a decade ago. And leasing will get bigger: Last year leases expired on 2.5 million U.S. vehicles. Why the big growth?

There are several reasons. Auto prices have been going up: The average car cost $18,200 last year, versus $10,725 10 years ago. It's now cheaper for you to get into a leased vehicle. Plus there's no more tax write-off on the interest you pay to finance a car. Consumers also have less disposable income to play around with, and there's more competition for the dollars they have. And the idea of "turning in your car to get a new one every two or three years" has caught on in a big way.

Knowing that, dealers have learned how to gouge people with complicated lease agreements that only an accountant can understand.

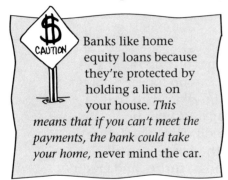

Banks like home equity loans because they're protected by holding a lien on your house. *This means that if you can't meet the payments, the bank could take your home,* never mind the car.

Dealers have been pulling so many shenanigans on customers that consumer advocate Ralph Nader and the attorneys general of 22 states have demanded that leasing laws be overhauled to protect the average Joe. Leasing was no problem when big corporations did most of the leasing, but now Joe is the key customer—and he knows zip about the subject. This section will help you figure out whether leasing is for you—and how to get the best deal on a lease.

How a Lease Works

In a nutshell, leasing is just like buying a car except that you pay only a portion of the principal with your monthly payments. When the lease expires you can do one of two things:

➤ Walk away from the car and owe nothing. That's called a *closed-end lease*. It's outlawed in some states, but it's the most popular type of lease nationwide.

➤ Consider buying the car. That's an *open-end lease*. Your monthly payments may be lower, but you could wind up on the short end of the stick, as you're about to find out.

At the beginning of the lease, the dealer's figured how much your car will probably be worth at the end of the lease, say, in three or four years. That's called the *residual*—what the dealer thinks the street price of the car might be at that time. When the lease is up, you can buy the car for the residual value, or *buyout price*.

Dealers may talk you into a lease by using language that sounds like you're purchasing the car instead of leasing it. For example, one Detroit auto maker instructs its dealer sales staff to never use words like *lease, interest rate*, and *residual* when they chat with you in a showroom. Instead, they're instructed to use words such as *buying, equity*, and *guaranteed future value*. And you have the option to *trade or sell* after a couple of years.

REALLY?

Some dealers figure the residual value in two or three years instead of four or five. That tips the scales in his favor. Why? Because a car can depreciate by 10 percent the moment you drive it home, and maybe by another 20 percent two or three years later. The younger the car, the higher the residual value. If you get a three-year lease and the dealer has figured the value after two years, you'll have to spend more than you should to buy the car when the lease expires.

Look at the Bottom Line

Let's say you're deciding between leasing or financing a $15,000 vehicle, but don't have the $3,000 down payment (20 percent) to go the financing route. Under a lease, the dealer will typically want—up front—the first month's payment of, say, $250 plus $15 in taxes—and another $250 as a refundable security deposit. That makes a total cash deposit of $515. Assume the lease is for four years, and the residual value is $8,000.

If you finance the car, you'll be borrowing $12,000 for four years after making your $3,000 down payment. Assume you pay six percent in taxes up front, and that your interest rate is 10 percent. Your monthly payment will be $350. So far, the lease gets the nod. But how will your wallet really make out in the long run?

With the straight loan deal, in four years you'll own the car outright after paying a total of $4,800 in interest, $373 in taxes and $12,000 on the principal. Had you leased, you'd probably make a $240-per-month payment and could simply turn the car in after four years and say good-bye. You wouldn't own a dime's worth of the vehicle and would still need new wheels. To buy the leased car, you would have to pay the dealer the $8,000 residual value.

But suppose the street value of the car has declined to only $6,500? You'd be out the $1,500 difference, because you could probably buy a similar car for $6,500. It would only be a good deal *if* the residual value was *less* than the street price. In that case, you'd be foolish not to pay the residual value and keep the car. You could sell it at a profit and use the money as a down payment on another set of wheels.

The key to getting the best deal on a lease is to do your homework. Check out these sources before and after you lease:

➤ You can get an excellent checklist and brochure on auto-leasing tips by sending a check or money order for $1 to Consumer Task Force for Automotive Issues, Reality Checklist, P.O Box 7648, Atlanta, GA 30357-0648.

➤ What's your leased car worth now? Call *Automotive Lease Guide*, a bimonthly publication, at (813) 536-8093. For $12.50 you can learn the residual value of any used car or other model.

➤ Go to the library and look up the market value of your car in the *National Automobile Dealers Association Used Car Guide*.

➤ Check the classified ads in your local paper to determine your car's value.

178

Don't Touch That Pen Until You Read This

Before you sign any lease, go over these points as though your life depended on them:

➤ Lease for no more than three years. That's the most you want to get stuck with if something unforeseen happens.

➤ Dealers are pushing shorter and shorter leases, such as two years. One reason: Their warranties from manufacturers to cover any possible problems with cars may only be for that long.

➤ If you turn the car in before the lease expires, the dealer will sock you with an early termination charge of $250 to $500. Insist that the charge be calculated by the *level yield method*, which means the dealer only recovers his charges for services and depreciation—no more.

Say you lose your job and can no longer make the payments. When you turn the car in, that's called *voluntary early termination*. You'll still be responsible for all remaining monthly payments, plus the pre-set residual value. In that case, the total due could be twice the value of the car!

➤ How many miles a year do you drive? If you've exceeded that estimated mileage when the lease ends, the dealer will hit you with an extra-cents-per-mile charge. Be honest up front. If they tack on a higher mileage cost at the beginning, it will probably be *less* than what you would be charged when the lease is up.

➤ A lease may require higher insurance limits. Insurance is your responsibility, not the dealer's.

➤ What does the dealer mean by "normal wear and tear"? If the car is dented and dinged all over, and the seat cushions are ripped and torn, it's gonna cost you.

➤ You may have to keep documents to prove the car maintenance was done by a reputable outfit.

➤ Check all the fees and payments under the lease. According to the "Truth in Leasing Law," you have a right to see them.

➤ Negotiate. Dealers can wheel and deal on leases just as on a sale.

➤ If there's a chance you might move, check to see whether you are restricted from taking the car to another state. Some dealers are finicky about this.

The Least You Need to Know

➤ Just say no to vehicle undercoating, credit life insurance, extended warranties, and other unnecessary charges the car salesperson will probably try to talk you into.

➤ When you negotiate a low price on a new car, get the dealer's discounted price *before* you mention that you have a trade-in.

➤ Whether you're trading in your old car or selling it yourself, spend a few bucks to get the vehicle into top cosmetic and mechanical shape. You'll make more money on the deal.

➤ Don't show any emotion when you inspect a new car, and do not close the deal the same day you visit the dealer's showroom.

➤ Always shop the same vehicle at more than one dealership.

➤ Get pre-approved for a loan through a bank or credit union before going to the dealer. Not only will you save money on interest rates by not financing through the dealer, you'll have more negotiating power because you have the money in hand.

➤ Other ways to save on finance costs include getting a simple interest loan, paying a higher down payment, and taking advantage of manufacturers' rebates.

➤ Leasing a car is not as simple as your dealer may lead you to believe. To avoid being taken for a ride, make sure you're aware of all the terms of the lease and compare the lease to the cost of buying the car outright.

Chapter 15

So You Want to Buy a Home

In This Chapter

➤ Simple math to help you figure out your buying power

➤ Common mistakes and how to avoid them

➤ All about home inspections

➤ Reducing your real estate tax NOW

It's May 1st and you're writing out the check to pay your rent, *again*. Nine-hundred and fifty dollars down the tubes—no tax breaks whatsoever. You can't even wallpaper the walls, change the color of the carpeting, or hang a chandelier. You've been living like this for three years, paying rent (on time, of course) on the first of every month. Where has it gotten you? $34,200 in the hole. Of course you need a place to live, but at one point or another in your life you're going to have to make a decision: to continue to rent or to buy your first home.

It's the American dream: a place you can call your own. You can hang as many chandeliers as you want and install green carpeting if you want. After all, it's your home and your decision! When most folks look to buy a home, what they really buy is the cozy Norman Rockwell

If you want to learn more about buying a home, check out *The Complete Idiot's Guide to Buying and Selling a Home* by Shelley O'Hara. It's packed with helpful information.

idea of owning a home, which is what many real estate professionals use to hook potential homebuyers. It is a financially—and emotionally—rewarding experience.

What some of these real estate pros won't come out and tell you is all of the headaches that go along with home ownership. It's more than just a leaky faucet or a broken air-conditioner that *you* are now responsible for. This chapter helps you determine whether or not you should buy a home, how to seal the deal, and how to save a few bucks during the inspection process.

So You're Thinking of Taking the Plunge

Whether you buy or rent a home, the decision is based on more than just finances. It's also based on what your expectations are for your future lifestyle. Do you mind having to mow the grass every Saturday? Would you rather have the building engineer fix your stopped-up toilet? You are the only person who can answer those questions.

The Ups and Downs of Home Ownership

The major advantage to buying a home is the equity or ownership you build over time as you pay off your mortgage (as long as your home appreciates in value). If your home appreciates in value as a result of good maintenance and it's in a good location, congratulations. You have a chance of considerable appreciation over time.

Other advantages? Owning a home may reduce both your federal and state income tax burdens by allowing you to deduct 100 percent of your mortgage interest. Local property taxes are also deductible from your federal income tax. Plus, if you sell your home, you don't have to pay a capital gains tax on the profit as long as you invest the proceeds in another home of equal or greater value within two years.

> **REALLY?** If you are more than 55 years old and sell your home, you qualify for a great exemption! When you sell your house, you receive a one-time exemption from capital gains taxes of up to $125,000.

But there are disadvantages, too. Because a home is considered an illiquid investment, you may not be able to sell your home if the real estate market takes a turn for the worse. Homeowners who have adjustable-rate mortgages (which you'll learn about in the next chapter) risk higher mortgage payments if interest rates shoot up.

Also, some people may have difficulty affording the large chunk of money initially required to buy a home. It goes beyond the down payment; there are closing costs, mortgage application fees, and in some cases, transfer taxes you have to pay. And because people often sacrifice their entire lifestyle by sinking 40 to 50 percent of their income into home ownership costs, they tend to lead stressed lives.

When to Keep Renting

Renting does have some advantages over buying. For one, the extra money you save from not paying into home maintenance costs can be invested in stocks, bonds, and mutual funds, which often rise in value faster than home prices. Additionally, if your housing needs are constantly changing, either because of your career or family additions, renting doesn't lock you into a long-term commitment as a home can.

Of course, renting also has a downside: no ownership, for one. And all of the money you pay on monthly rent doesn't benefit your taxes in any way (unless—depending on the circumstances and IRS rules—you have a home-based business where you can write-off a portion of your rent as a business deduction).

If you decide to continue renting, keep the following points in mind when choosing a place to live:

➤ Make sure you can afford the monthly rent *and* have money left over to invest so someday you can afford to buy a home with the money you've saved.

If you decide to keep renting but someday want to own a home, consider waiting until the real estate market has bottomed out to try to get a good deal on a house.

➤ Don't rent the first home or apartment you find. Do your homework because the more time you take to do your research, the more likely it is that you'll come across a better deal.

➤ Unlike an inspection you'll get before you buy a home, you have to do your own rental inspection. Make sure you check all of the appliances from top to bottom. So what if the rental agent thinks you're goofy because you check the water pressure in the shower. *You* are the one who has to live there.

REALLY?

If you like your rental home, you can always ask your landlord whether he or she would consider a "rent with option to buy" situation. Rent-to-own agreements are gaining popularity, and the beauty of them is that you are not obligated to buy if you don't want to. If you do consider a rent-to-buy option, make the term as short as possible. If another prospective buyer comes along with ready cash, you won't be encumbered by a long-term contract.

Three Times, My Foot

People say that you typically spend about a third of your income on housing. Maybe that's true, but potential homebuyers often take that one step further and assume that they can afford a house that is three times their annual income.

Wrong! Why? You need to take into account your assessments and taxes and other outstanding liabilities you have now. For example, a lender will ask you if you own a car. "Sure," you say. "But I have five more years worth of payments on the car." The lender then says "Then you don't really own the car—the bank does."

You must consider all of your outstanding liabilities when determining how much you can afford to pay for a house. Otherwise, you'll inflate what your buying power really is!

Figuring out how much you can afford to buy shouldn't be a long, involved process. Complete the following worksheet to determine what you can manage to buy.

A. Gross Annual Income: $_____
(before taxes)

B. Gross Monthly Income: $_____
(Line A divided by 12)

C. Monthly Allowable Housing Expense and Long-Term Obligation
(Line B multiplied by .36): $_____

D. Monthly Allowable Housing Expense: $_____
(Line C minus long-term obligations *or* Line B multiplied by
.28, whichever is less)

E. Monthly Principal and Interest: $_____
(Line D multiplied by .80; estimate since taxes and insurance will
vary)

F. Estimated Mortgage Amount: $_____
(Line E divided by the appropriate factor from the interest rate
chart (see the table below) and multiplied by 1,000)

G. Estimated Affordable Price Range: $_____
(Line F divided by .80 or .90, depending on down payment)

Example interest rate factors for 15- and 30-year mortgages are
listed below:

Interest Rate	15 years	30 years
8.00%	9.56	7.34
8.25%	9.70	7.51
8.50%	9.85	7.69
8.75%	9.99	7.87
9.00%	10.14	8.05
9.25%	10.29	8.23
9.50%	10.44	8.41
9.75%	10.59	8.59

When in doubt, check these out! Here's a list of figures you need to check at your real estate closing:

➤ The broker's commission

➤ Monthly payments

➤ A charge for loan fees that have already been paid

➤ A charge for utility bills that have already been paid

➤ A professional (such as an attorney, contractor, or appraiser of the contract) who has not yet been paid

Buying Blunders to Avoid

The following are common buying blunders you should avoid:

➤ **Keeping your realtor on board even if you don't like him.** If you don't like your realtor, don't keep him or her. You're not obligated. If you're in the process of looking for a new home and your realtor just doesn't cut the mustard, make the switch. You can cancel the existing agreement with a buyer's broker.

➤ **Not getting pre-qualifed.** Forget scouting the real estate section of your newspaper to see what you want to buy. Get pre-qualified first! Talk to a lender (a bank, credit union, or mortgage broker) about all the costs involved. Although the worksheet on the previous page gives you a good start, a lender will help you determine not only what you can afford based on your income and debt obligations, but also what you can afford including taxes, condo association assessments, or private mortgage insurance—depending on what you're looking for and how much your down payment is.

➤ **Not shopping around for a lender.** Basically, you're buying money when you apply for a mortgage, right? Because you'll be giving this person the most intimate details of your financial life, you should find someone you're comfortable with and who will offer you a good deal. Just what are those good deals you should be scouting out? You'll find out in the next chapter.

➤ **Thinking that a large down payment will cancel out any previous blemishes on your credit report.** Wrong! In fact, a lender would rather choose someone with little to no money to put down and a squeaky-clean credit report than someone who has a 20 percent down payment and black marks up to his ears. In fact, the down payment for those people with credit problems may be larger; it depends on the lender. Correct any erroneous information on your credit report and give explanations for the blemishes that you can't get rid of.

➤ **Not looking at the broker's commission.** If a buyer is looking at five properties similar in price and condition, a broker may loosely "suggest" the property that he or she would generate a bigger commission from. Check what the broker's commission is on the listing sheet. If you can't find it, just ask. Why do this? The broker might push a property he has a listing agreement on. That nice real estate agent might be a direct employee of the seller.

➤ **Getting emotionally involved if you miss an opportunity.** One Chicago real-estate maven tells us that potential home buyers become so emotionally involved when they miss out on one deal that they often botch up the offer on the next home they want to buy.

➤ **Not doing your homework.** The best way to avoid this glitch is to get a printout of all similar homes in the potential area that have sold in the past six months. The house you want should be selling in the same price range. If not, maybe the homeowner upgraded too much and the price is not justified.

Inspector Clouseau, I Presume

Anyone see the movie *The Money Pit* with Tom Hanks and Shelley Long? It's a home inspector's nightmare. Detecting problems is what a home inspector does. What you, as a potential homebuyer, hope for is that there aren't too many problems.

Once you "put a contract" out on the property you want to buy, there's a seven-day inspection approval. Inspections usually cost around $300 to $400, and the buyer pays for the inspection to find out if anything is wrong. If you're feeling squeamish about taking your real estate broker's word for "this really good guy I know," you can find a professional inspector by contacting The American Society of Home Inspectors at (708) 290-1919. Keep in mind that your realtor can recommend an inspector too, or just comparison shop using the Yellow Pages. You can get out of the contract if the inspector finds things wrong with the property, such as leaking plumbing or a schlocky furnace. (Or, you could have the home owner agree to fix the problems before you buy the house.)

Challenging the Tax Collector

If homeowners could have one wish, many of them would wish they didn't have to pay real estate taxes—and with good reason. Real estate taxes can run as high as thousands of dollars for some folks if the assessed value of the house increases. But life isn't that simple: the tax man cometh, and the homeowner payeth. You can't do anything about your real estate taxes, but you do have an alternative. Challenge your assessments.

➤ **Show that the property is overvalued or that your assessment is higher than that on comparable properties in your area.** How? You can have your real estate agent pull up all the nearby listings on the Multiple Listing Service to compare properties. Or, simple compare nearby sales in the real estate section of your local newspaper. Do it before you make any necessary repairs from damage or deterioration on your property that has lowered its value.

> If you still want to buy the property, it's much better to settle for a reduced price than to take a "credit" that your broker offers. Why? Since the broker makes his or her commission based on a percentage of the sale price of the house, of course he or she will want you to take a "credit" instead of a reduction in price. Plus, if you get the price reduced, you'll have to finance a smaller amount.

➤ **Check the tax records for a description of your property and income.** Local tax records often show big boo-boos in overstating size or income.

➤ **Figure out the ratio of the assessed value to the present market value.** You may have to consult a real estate broker to help you compare this ratio with the average ratios of similar properties sold in your area recently.

The Least You Need to Know

➤ Buying a house can be a good investment and save you money on taxes. However, if you don't have a nice chunk of cash available up front and aren't willing to devote a lot of time and money to upkeep, you may want to continue renting for a while.

➤ Avoid common buying blunders by getting pre-qualified for a loan, not letting your broker boss you around, and doing your homework.

➤ Once you find a house you like, make sure you have it inspected before you commit to buying it.

➤ Don't be afraid to challenge your assessments if you feel you're being overcharged on your real-estate taxes.

Chapter 16

Which Mortgage Is Best for You?

In This Chapter

➤ Which kind of mortgage will be kinder to your pocketbook?

➤ How adjustable rates (ARMs) really work

➤ What's more important—rates or "points?"

➤ The best loans to get if you're strapped for cash

A home mortgage loan is probably the single biggest hunk of money that you'll ever have to lay out for anything. It's for the number-one asset you own—your house—and the bottom line is that it will cost hundreds of thousands of dollars.

But mortgages are trickier and more complicated than any other money transaction in your entire life. Taking out the wrong mortgage at the wrong time—or borrowing an amount that cripples your budget—can cost you dearly. You need to know when to make your move on interest rates, what type of loan to get, and the secrets of keeping hidden charges to a minimum.

You also need to learn how to strengthen your credit record so your loan application will be approved. And even if you're cash-poor, there are lenders who will accept lower down payments and ease up on credit restrictions.

This chapter helps solve the mortgage-rate guessing game, explains how to get a loan that fits your pocketbook, and teaches you how to get around the confusing mortgage math that throws most people for a loop.

Key Mortgage-ese You Should Know

Let's start with the lingo; the mortgage process is chock-full of confusing terminology. The following definitions should help clarify things a bit:

Appraisal: A professional estimate of what a house is worth, based on its style, appearance, construction quality, improvements, usefulness, and the comparable value of nearby properties.

Up-front charges: What you are charged at the beginning of the home-buying process, such as for an appraisal of the property.

Closing: The final settlement of the transfer of property. It involves the buyer's signing of the mortgage and mortgage note, and a change of title to the home.

Closing costs: Fees and other charges paid by the buyer and seller at closing.

Conventional mortgage: A mortgage *not* insured by the government (such as an FHA or VA loan).

Deed: The document that transfers the title from the seller to the buyer.

Down payment: The buyer's payment to the seller at closing. The payment is based on a percentage of the purchase price required by the buyer's mortgage loan.

Earnest money: Money paid by the buyer to the seller at the time an offer to purchase the home is presented.

First mortgage: A mortgage that is a first lien on the property pledged as a security.

Mortgagee: The lending party under the terms of the mortgage.

Mortgage note: A signed promise to repay a mortgage loan in regular, monthly payments under pre-agreed terms and conditions.

Offer to purchase: A legally-binding, written contract that declares how much a buyer will pay for property, provided certain conditions are met.

PITI: Principal, interest, taxes, and insurance—the four main parts of a monthly mortgage payment.

Points: One point equals one percent, or one one-hundredth, of the total mortgage amount.

Qualify: To meet a lender's mortgage-approval requirements.

Title: The right of ownership and possession of a property.

Title insurance: A policy that protects a buyer against errors, omissions, or defects in the title.

The ABCs of How Mortgages Work

A *mortgage* is nothing more than a loan. If you don't have the money to pay all cash for a house, a mortgage lender may loan you up to 95 percent of its appraised value. You deposit the rest up front as a down payment. The lender holds a lien on your home until you fully repay what you borrowed—meaning that if you default on your payments, the lender can take the house.

We're not talking about small change in mortgage loans, folks; we're talking in the hundreds of thousands of dollars. That's the total tab of a 30-year mortgage when you add up the amount you borrow plus the huge interest you'll pay on the loan.

You'd think that with that kind of dough involved, more people would understand what makes mortgages tick. Not so. The guys in the mortgage business have made these loans so complex that it takes a mathematical wizard to figure them out. What you need to do is dissect this monster one piece at a time.

The key to getting the right mortgage is learning which type of loan will fit your present and future budget to a T. There are two major types of "conventional loans" (as opposed to government-insured loans, also discussed in this chapter).

The two biggies are *fixed-rate* and *adjustable-rate* mortgages (ARMs). Trying to make a simple comparison between the two is enough to blow your mind, But you can do it. Just keep asking yourself this one basic question: How will each mortgage gimmick make an impact on my pocketbook? The odds are in your favor, because today mortgage lenders are knocking themselves out trying to get your business.

How to Prevent Your Payments from Bouncing Up and Down

A fixed-rate mortgage locks in your interest rate—and your monthly payments—for the entire life of the loan. Most fixed-rate loans are for 30 years or 15 years, but there's a whale of a difference in how much either one will cost you.

Suppose you borrow $100,000 at nine percent interest, which was the approximate average fixed rate at the beginning of 1995. The $100,000 is called your *principal*. With a 30-year term, your monthly payment would be $805, and your total *interest cost* over all 30 years would be $189,664. By contrast, the monthly payment on a 15-year loan would be higher—$1,014—but the total interest over 15 years would be sensationally less—$82,568. You'd save a whopping $107,096 with the 15-year loan!

A 15-year loan is a good option for middle-aged and older buyers who can afford the higher monthly payment. First, in addition to saving you interest cost, a 15-year fixed-rate is slightly cheaper than a 30-year fixed-rate. You're also building up your equity in the home a lot faster. The disadvantage is that there's less tax-deductible interest on a 15-year loan. Plus, people with low incomes probably won't qualify as borrowers because their budgets can't handle the stiffer payments.

A 30-year fixed-rate loan has its advantages, too: It's a good investment when interest rates are low. There may be considerable tax benefits, especially in the early years. Your payment stays the same even if rates rise, regardless of inflation. The one disadvantage is that your equity builds up more slowly with a 30-year loan.

ARMs: Initial Payments Are Lower, but Could Shoot Up Later

Suppose someone lends you $1 today. He charges you a dime in interest this year, but next year he starts working with a different formula that could increase your interest each year until it gets up to a maximum of a buck-and-a-half. That's sort of how adjustable-rate mortgages (ARMs) work. You start out paying cheap interest, but later the rate can zoom.

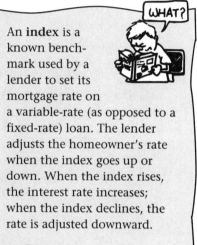

An **index** is a known benchmark used by a lender to set its mortgage rate on a variable-rate (as opposed to a fixed-rate) loan. The lender adjusts the homeowner's rate when the index goes up or down. When the index rises, the interest rate increases; when the index declines, the rate is adjusted downward.

The only thing ARM rates have in common with a fixed-rate mortgage is that they're both usually for 30 years. But unlike a fixed-rate mortgage, the ARM interest rate can adjust periodically—typically every year or six months. The adjustment is based on which index the lender ties its ARM rate to. The rate can go up or down according to the index—and so does your monthly payment. But your indexed rate may not start showing up until the second year of your loan.

Here's how it works: Lenders discount their first-year ARM rate as a ploy to get you in the door. As a result, their introductory ARM rate looks mighty good to you—it's probably two percent to three percent less than the interest on a fixed-rate. So far, so good. But beginning in the second year, the ARM rate jumps to the index rate plus a margin that the lender tacks onto the index. This produces your indexed rate. If the index continues to rise, your ARM rate keeps going up as well.

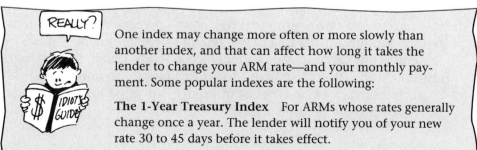

One index may change more often or more slowly than another index, and that can affect how long it takes the lender to change your ARM rate—and your monthly payment. Some popular indexes are the following:

The 1-Year Treasury Index For ARMs whose rates generally change once a year. The lender will notify you of your new rate 30 to 45 days before it takes effect.

The 11th District Cost of Funds   Used mostly for ARM rates that are adjusted monthly. The index is calculated by the Federal Home Loan Bank of San Francisco. Your new rate is usually determined by the index value 30 to 90 days before the next rate change.

LIBOR—the London InterBank Offered Rate   This is the most volatile index; it can jump up or down more frequently, with no set pattern as to how often.

Before you start wondering why anyone would get an ARM, keep in mind that a lender will usually cap any annual increase in the rate so that it will never rise by more than two percentage points above the rate you paid in the previous year. The lender also has a "life-of-loan" cap (currently around six percentage points), meaning your rate can't ever be higher than six percent above the rate you started out with in the first year of the loan. That's why many ARM formulas as expressed as "two and six" deals.

ARMs are a good strategy for younger, first-time home buyers who may be short of cash for a few years, but who believe their income will increase. ARMs are also best bets for people who plan to move within four years.

5/25s and 7/23s—Cheaper in the Early Years

Say you can only afford a low monthly payment, and don't plan to stay in the home for more than a few years. Suppose interest rates are rising, and you prefer to lock into a fixed rate instead of gambling with an ARM rate that could increase by two percentage points a year. A *5/25* or *7/23 mortgage* may be for you.

With these mortgages, you take out a 30-year mortgage for which you pay a fixed rate for the first five or seven years. At the end of either term, your rate adjusts to a new fixed rate (which may be higher) for the remaining 25 or 23 years. Lately a few lenders have been offering customers an option to convert to an ARM mortgage after five or seven years. Either way, these types of mortgages are good for first-time home buyers with more income ahead.

Another Possibility: Cheap Government Financing

Can't afford a big down payment and four-figure closing costs? There are ways to get into a new home through government programs that are ideal for new, young families and folks who don't have a lot of cash. Lenders are now pushing the programs for two reasons.

First, rising mortgage rates have dried up much of the lenders' conventional business; fewer people qualify for higher monthly payments because of higher rates. Lenders are looking elsewhere to make a buck.

The federal government is also clamping down on lenders—especially banks—if they fail to help provide affordable housing for low and middle-income families. In 1991 alone, the government set aside $3.4 billion for these efforts—and in hundreds of cities across America, local governments have come up with "free money" for down payments and closing costs. The key programs are the following:

➤ **Federal Housing Administration (FHA) Loans**   The federal government doesn't actually *lend* the money for these loans; rather, it insures or guarantees the loan for the lender under several different mortgage programs. The down payment may be only three to four percent, and the fixed rate is lower than what you'd pay for a conventional 30-year loan. The downside is that the credit limit on how much you can borrow will be lower— $151,700 in most areas. The term can be 30, 25, 20, or 15 years.

Beware of *negative amortization*! This is the ugliest of all types of mortgages, and it is usually found on adjustable-rate loans. Negative amortization is a little confusing, but basically it works like this:

Say the ARM interest rate is 9 percent, and pretend your payment is $800 per month, including principal and interest. The lender puts a "cap" on how much interest may be included in your monthly payment. If rates rise, theoretically the interest portion of your payment would also increase. But it doesn't.

Instead, because of the cap, the extra interest is added *to the balance of your loan.* Your monthly payment stays the same—but you *could* wind up having to make payments on your mortgage for more than the normal 30 years because the amount you have to pay off is greater. When that happens, some lenders will offer you an option to make extra monthly payments to reduce the larger debt, or extend the period of the loan.

➤ **Veteran's Administration (VA) loans** These loans are also federally insured or guaranteed, with no down payment and some of the same features as with an FHA loan. Borrowers must have current or previous military service. Loans may be for a 30-year or 15-year fixed-rate, or for a 30-year ARM.

➤ **Community Home Buyer's Program** This may be the cheapest deal of all. The down payment requirement is only five percent, and 2 percent of that can be a gift from family or friends. The two percent doesn't show up on your credit report, so it doesn't count as a debt you owe. Plus, you don't need cash reserves to cover two months' worth of mortgage payments (normally you need them with other low-income loans).

Comparing the Big Two: ARMs Versus Fixed-Rate

When interest rates are low, more home-buyers choose a fixed-rate because it locks in their monthly payment for 15 or 30 years. When fixed rates start approaching 10 percent, more people tend to shift to ARMs because the low introductory rates are typically two to three percentage points below a fixed-rate.

For example, when the average fixed rate was 6.8 percent nationwide in 1993, and the ARM rate was 4.01 percent, almost all home buyers chose the fixed rate. Buyers avoided ARM rates because, despite the cheap 4.01-percent financing, the rate could rise. By early 1995, however, the fixed rate had climbed to 9.1 percent and the ARM was at 6.8 percent. Then the reverse happened; most consumers began choosing ARM mortgages instead.

Table 16.1 How Rates Go Up... and Down... and Up

Mortgage Type	1989	1990	1991	1992	1993	1994	1995*
ARM		8.91%	8.17%	7.02%	5.46%	4.42%	6.18% 6.73%
30-year fixed-rate	10.26	10.01	9.09	8.27	7.18	8.99	8.95
15-year fixed-rate	10.25	9.67	8.76	7.80	6.66	8.50	8.58

* First quarter of 1995

To understand how an ARM might work, let's look at an example. In the first year, your introductory ARM rate is 6.75 percent. Your monthly payment on a $100,000 mortgage would be $649. In the second year, the lender starts to set your new rate based on the index. Say the index is 6.5 percent. The lender adds the margin, typically 2.75 percentage points. That increases your rate to 9.25 percent (6.5 plus 2.75), but because of the two percent cap, your new rate can't go any higher than 6.75 plus two, or 8.75 percent. That's the maximum rate you pay in the second year; your monthly payment increases to $784.

In year three, let's assume the index has now gone up to 8.5 percent. Add the 2.75 percent margin again, and your ARM rate becomes 11.25 percent (8.5 plus 2.75), but because of the annual cap, the most your rate can rise is by 2 percentage points above the previous year's rate of 8.75 percent. That's 10.75 (8.75 plus two). With that rate your monthly payment jumps to $926 in the third year.

Play out that same scenario through the fourth year. Your ARM rate can go up by a maximum of another two percent, to 12.75 percent (10.75 plus two), and the payment rises to $1,072. At this point, four years after you took out your ARM loan, which type of mortgage would have been the better deal—the ARM or a fixed-rate? Table 16.2 will give you an idea.

Table 16.2   ARM Costs Can Rise

	ARM	Fixed-Rate (9%)
First year	$6,717	$8,972
Second year	$8,626	$8,908
Third year	$10,523	$8,838
Fourth year	$12,407	$8,761
Total interest cost, first year	$38,273	$35,480

Of course, ARM rates can go down as well as up, depending on what happens to the index. The indexes that ARM rates are tied to will change periodically. The higher the index, the higher your ARM rate (based on a formula the lender uses). In strong economic times and during periods of inflation, the index will probably rise. During a recession, such as the one between 1990 and 1993, the index will fall. Table 16.3 illustrates by how much two popular ARM indexes changed between 1990 and 1994, and between 1994 and 1995. (Remember: An index is only a benchmark that the lender uses to figure the ARM rate you are charged.)

Table 16.3 ARM Index Changes

Adjustable Index	1990	1994	1995
1-year Treasury	8.09%	3.66%	6.88%
11th District Cost of Funds	8.48	3.88	4.59

In other words, the mortgage buyer who takes out a fixed-rate loan only pays the rate in effect at that time for 30 or 15 years. The person who gets an ARM rate instead will start out with a lower rate, but later see the rate go up or down depending on the index—which is influenced by the economy.

Worst-case scenario: If the fourth-year ARM rate in the example we gave stayed at 12.75 percent for the remaining 27 years, you'd wind up paying a murderous total of $275,491 in interest over the life of the loan—*plus* the $100,000 principal you owe. By comparison, with a 30-year fixed-rate at 9.75 percent, you'd pay a total of $209,303 in interest, in addition to the $100,000 amount borrowed.

What's It Gonna Cost Me?

You'll probably make a down payment of between five percent and 20 percent on that little house with the picket fence. You'll also have closing costs that run 4 percent to 5 percent of the amount borrowed. And you'll be forking out for not-so-incidental things such as moving, new-house fix-ups, and any outside legal fees attached to the purchase.

That's a lot of cash outflow. So it's not wise to plunk down *all* your money into a down payment. There's a better way around it. To budget for the house, you should ask yourself two questions:

How low do I want my monthly payment to be?

How long do I plan to stay in the house?

You also need to take rates, points, APR, fees, and closing costs into consideration when figuring out how much this mortgage is really going to cost you.

Which Should You Watch Most—Rates or Points?

So far we've discussed only rates. However, there's another little animal in the mortgage jungle that directly affects the cost of your loan. It's *points*. A point is nothing more than one one-hundredth of your loan amount. On a $100,000 loan, each point is $1,000. Lenders charge points to cover the costs of completing a mortgage application and to earn income. The buyer pays the points at closing, for example, when buyer and seller sit down together and close the sale. If a $100,000 mortgage comes with three points, that's $3,000.

Mortgage shoppers often ask, "Which is more important, rates or points?" It depends on your situation. The *rate* is probably key; it determines your monthly payment of principal and interest. But points can directly influence the rate you pay, even though the two are completely different things.

Points come into play when the lender determines how much of a monthly payment you can afford. Since that payment is influenced by the interest rate, one way to bring the rate (and your payment) down is to increase the number of points. Many lenders have five or more rates-and-points combinations; some may have a dozen. For example, a lender that quotes a rate of nine percent with one point might also have quotes of 8.88 percent with two points, and 8.75 percent with three points.

As you can see, rates and points move in opposite directions. The higher the rate, the lower the points, and vice versa. If you want to lower your monthly payment, you can "buy down" the rate by paying more points. The lower rate can also reduce your interest expenses. On

$100,000 borrowed at nine percent for 30 years, the monthly payment would be $805. Over the first five years of the loan, total interest would be $44,157. If you lowered the rate to 8.5 percent by paying more points, the monthly payment would drop to $769 and total interest for five years would decrease to $41,625. The lower rate would save you more than $2,500 in interest, but the benefit would apply only to the first five years.

That five-year period is important. Why? Because it takes at least that long, and more likely seven years, to recoup the cash outlay of more points with lower monthly payments. If you don't have a lot of ready cash or aren't planning to stay in the house for more than five years, taking fewer points and a higher interest rate would probably be the better strategy.

The "APR" Tells You the REAL Cost!

What's an "APR?" It stands for "Annual Percentage Rate," a complicated term that throws almost any mortgage shopper. An APR helps you compare apples with apples when you try to stack two loan offers side by side to decide which one is the better deal. The Consumer Credit Protection Act of 1968 requires that lenders disclose their APRs.

The APR may be higher than the rate, but it reflects *the real cost of your loan on a yearly basis*. Why? It also includes a bunch of other charges in addition to the rate. That creates a more level playing field for you to judge all the different mortgage deals. For one thing, the APR includes the points *and* many of the fees you're charged on your loans. Starting to get the idea?

Suppose (as in Table 16.4) that Megabuck Bank offers a 30-year fixed-rate loan at nine percent. Friendly Federal's rate is only 8.5

If you can afford a higher rate with higher monthly payments, some lenders may offer you a no-points deal.

percent. That makes Friendly's offer the better deal, right? Maybe not. You could pay five points for Friendly's loan compared with only one point at Megabuck. Plus, Friendly might have forgotten to tell you about other fees such as mortgage insurance premiums, prepaid interest, and its cost of originating the mortgage. That could total a few thousand bucks.

On the surface, it *looks* like Friendly Federal has a cheaper mortgage based on the rate alone. But when all the costs are figured into the APR, the cheaper mortgage is Megabuck's.

Table 16.4 The Lowest Rate May Not Be Your Best Deal

	Megabuck Bank	Friendly Federal
Rate	9.0%	8.5%
Interest	$8,972	$8,471
Points (based on a $100,000 30-year mortgage)	$1,000 (1 point)	$5,000 (5 points)
Closing costs	$500	$2,500
Total cost in first year of mortgage	$10,472	$15,971

Learn the Up-Front Fees and Closing Costs

Besides the cost items that go into your monthly payment, there are other costs on the front end and back end of a mortgage loan. Ideally, you want to do business with an outfit that doesn't rook you at either end. Most lenders will charge you up-front fees; others may not charge anything at all to get your business. Beware of lenders who load on extra costs like photos, document charges, notary, and so forth. These can run into hundreds of dollars.

When you shop, always ask lenders for their APRs on fixed-rate loans versus ARMs, and how these compare with other lenders' APRs in the area.

Typically you should only pay:

Up-front: Appraisal and credit report.

Closing costs: Points, recording fees, documentary stamps, mortgage insurance, document preparation, and inspection.

Remember that you must have enough cash for closing costs, which have to be paid when the final papers are signed. Most lenders will provide you with a "good faith" estimate of these costs in advance. Typically, closing costs run between two percent and six percent of the loan amount.

The Quick, Easy Way to Find the Cheapest Mortgage

Okay, so you now know all the major costs of getting a mortgage, but you're probably thinking, "How am I going to remember all this stuff? I feel like I'm drowning in an ocean of rates, points, formulas, and other mathematical gobbledygook. There's gotta be an easier way!"

There is. Try this simple solution. It works like a charm. First, pick out a half dozen or more of the lenders in your area that seem to be offering the best combination of rates and points.

Second, assume you'll be in your new house for five years—which is about the average length of time most families stay. (Five years also happens to be the magic cut-off point for deciding between a fixed-rate and an ARM, remember?)

Then ask each lender to tell you its:

➤ Total up-front fees *and* charges on the types of loans you'd consider.

➤ Total interest charges (not counting the principal) for *five years*, in actual dollars and cents, not percent.

➤ Total closing costs.

Then add up the total cost of the mortgage—those three items—for five years at each lender, and compare the various deals. Voilà! You immediately see who offers the best deal! When you shop for the lowest mortgage cost among several different lenders, add up the three main cost areas (shown in Table 16.5, the Mortgage Shopping List) for each lender, and compare.

Table 16.5 Mortgage Shopping List

	Lender A	Lender B	Lender C	Lender D
Up-front charges	$ _____	$ _____	$ _____	$ _____
Interest cost (first 5 years)	$ _____	$ _____	$ _____	$ _____
Closing costs	$ _____	$ _____	$ _____	$ _____
Total cost (first 5 years)	$ _____	$ _____	$ _____	$ _____

> REALLY?
>
> Lenders are super-hungry for business. The sharp rise in interest rates has cut their mortgage volume by as much as 40 percent in some markets over the past year. Plus, their refinancing business is shot because high rates no longer pay homeowners to trade their old mortgage for a cheaper one. As a result, many lenders are reducing their down-payment requirements, discounting their financing costs (for example, a $250 cash bonus applied to closing costs), approving higher percentages of debt for applicants, and permitting buyers to lock in their rate 30 days *before* closing instead of *at* closing.

Who Lends the Money

Lenders fall into one of three categories:

➤ **Financial Institutions, such as Banks, Thrifts, and Credit Unions**   Sometimes the institution offers the loan, sometimes it's a mortgage company owned by the institution. You can't tell the difference offhand in most cases; it's more a technicality than a real difference anyway. For example, if your bank directs you to a loan office somewhere else, you'll probably be dealing with a mortgage company owned by the bank.

➤ **Mortgage Companies**   The term may be loosely applied to an organization that specializes only in mortgages, or to a bank or thrift that has an affiliated mortgage company (hence the term "mortgage banker"). Mortgage companies can be big national outfits such as Countrywide Mortgage or Norwest, or small home-grown lenders. They make the same loans that banks make. Size isn't important, especially if you're getting a standard 30-year loan.

➤ **Mortgage Brokers**   They're like mortgage bankers (although they are not connected with financial institutions), but they can be part of a national loan company. But there's an important distinction: Brokers don't actually fund mortgage loans. Instead, they put borrowers and lenders together. They call on a number of loan sources to arrange the best possible match. They can be a great help if you've had past credit problems because they can locate lenders who will be more flexible than others.

Doing business at a bank where you have a checking account or another loan can be an advantage. Why? You may be able to apply at the same branch where people already know you. Plus, because you have the other accounts, the bank may discount your mortgage rate by (say) one-quarter of a percentage point if you agree to have your monthly payments debited automatically from checking.

A broker makes money by collecting a fee from the lender, not the borrower. Since the lender and the broker sometimes split some of the fees you're charged on a mortgage, it shouldn't cost you any more to borrow through a broker.

Should you choose one over the other? Not unless you have a special circumstance. If a bank will give you a better break because you're already a customer, that's good. If a mortgage banker will cut its rate to get your business, that's fine. And if a broker can get you a loan when others have turned you down, that's even better.

No matter who you do business with, you should always shop around for the best possible lender. When you talk to a bank or mortgage company, ask for references from other customers. In the case of mortgage brokers, talk to lenders the broker regularly uses.

How to Play the Mortgage "Lock-In" Game

Unpredictable mortgage rates can drive home buyers batty. They nervously watch rates dance up and down, week after week. But knowing exactly when to lock in their rate is like a cross between playing Blind Man's Bluff and Las Vegas craps. Even the "experts" can't tell you how high or low rates will be a week or a month from today. So what do you do if you want the best possible rate on the day you're supposed to close?

If you believe rates will drop between now and the closing date, skip, postpone, or shorten the lock-in because you might cut a better deal later. If you think rates are going up, tell the lender you want to lock in the current, lower rate for a certain number of days (such as 30, 60, or 90). But it will cost you something in return.

As part of the game, the lender may tempt you with different rates and points for different lock-in periods. For an extra half-point or so, you might be guaranteed the current rate for *X* number of days. For every $100,000 borrowed, that would cost the borrower $500. (Remember: A point is one one-hundredth of the loan amount.)

You say you'd rather gamble and save the $500? Consider what happened to a couple we know. Their builder promised them their new home would be ready in 45 days. So they skipped paying the $500 to lock in a lower rate for 60 days. Guess what. The builder didn't finish the house for 90 days. Meanwhile, mortgage rates climbed by more than a half percent. That added thousands of dollars to the couple's total mortgage cost.

When you play the lock-in game, follow these rules:

➤ When rates are rising, lock in immediately. When they're falling, stall for as long as you can.

➤ Learn the lock-in choices and how much each one costs. In general, the longer the lock-in period, the higher the points. You may discover the lender won't lock in the rate.

➤ The lock-in period should be spelled out in a document provided by the lender. You will likely be required to sign this sheet. The document should explain what will happen to your rate if the lock-in expires before you close on the house purchase.

207

What happens when the lock-in expires? Your rate should then float up or down to the current rate at closing. Sometimes, if rates have fallen, you'll pay the original rate that was in effect when you applied for your loan. If rates have risen, you'll pay the new, higher rate.

How to Speed Things Up

Beware of lenders who drag their heels in processing your loan. It could happen, especially when rates are going up, because that increases the lender's profit, and the result is that the rate jumps and you'll be forced to make higher monthly payments.

Bear down on your loan officer. You don't have to be a pest, but you should keep on top of your application. Call in regularly with questions about your loan status. Find out if the appraisal has been ordered, completed, and reviewed. Ask the loan officer if he or she needs any additional information from you.

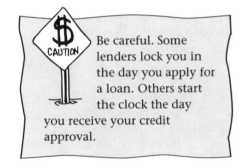

Be careful. Some lenders lock you in the day you apply for a loan. Others start the clock the day you receive your credit approval.

You may find that the appraisal has been done, but it mistakenly got routed to Joe or Sally, or it's still in that big stack on Harry's desk. A couple of phone calls can get things back on track. Each step of the way, note in writing what the lender tells you. Keep a complete record; give the loan officer a report each time you talk. That way the lender will know you're ahead of the game.

Get Your Credit Record in Shape Now!

How do lenders think home buyers make mistakes when they set out to buy a house? They'll tell you that too many consumers wait until the last minute to get their credit in order. The process, they say, should begin six months before you apply for the loan (unless, of course, you have megabucks in the bank and have a squeaky-clean credit record). Here's what to do:

➤ Get a copy of your credit report. (To learn how, see Chapter 17.)

➤ If you have four or five credit cards, trim the number down to only one.

➤ Pay off as many of your debts as possible.

➤ Don't apply for any more credit until you go for a mortgage. A bunch of new inquiries could show up on your credit report; that's a no-no in the eyes of lenders who are considering you for a mortgage loan.

➤ If Aunt Matilda promised to give you a present of $20,000 next year, ask Auntie to help by letting you have the money now, to build up your bank balance before you go for a mortgage.

You Pay Through the Nose in the Early Years

The way lenders calculate the payback on your mortgage loan, you get socked with tons of interest in the early years of the loan. Very little of your monthly payment amounts go toward your principal. It's not until the later years that your monthly payments begin to reduce the principal substantially.

Assume you borrow $100,000 for 30 years at a nine percent fixed rate, with a monthly payment of $805. In the first five years, the picture looks like this (Table 16.6):

Table 16.6   The First Five Years of a Mortgage ($805 a Month)

Year	Principal Still Owed	Principal You've Paid	Interest You've Paid	Total Payments You've Made
1	$99,317	$683	$8,972	$9,655
2	98,570	747	8,908	9,655
3	97,752	817	8,838	9,655
4	96,858	894	8,761	9,655
5	95,880	978	6,678	9,655

In other words, after five years of the 30-year loan, you've reduced your $100,000 principal by only $4,120 ($100,000 minus $95,880), but have paid a total interest of $42,157 (the sum of the five numbers in the column headed "Interest You've Paid")! Yet you've been making a monthly payment of $805 all along.

209

The way the math works out, the higher the interest rate, the greater the amount of your early payments that go toward interest. Conversely, the lower the interest rate, the less the amount of early payments that go toward interest.

But as the loan gets older, more and more of your monthly payment will start being applied toward the principal, and less toward the interest. Using the example in Table 16.6, by the time you get to the twenty-third year, about the same amount will go toward the principal and the interest. In your final (thirtieth) year of the mortgage, you will have paid off the original $100,000 loan and paid a whopping $189,658 in interest. Your total payments for principal and interest will be an astronomical $289,658!

Putting the Tax Savings in Your Pocket

The one bright side to the staggering cost of a mortgage is that you can deduct certain items on your personal tax returns. That will effectively reduce the cost of your mortgage. For the deductions you should obtain the help of a professional tax consultant, but the main deductions are these:

➤ The interest costs that you pay per year on the loan.

➤ The points you pay at closing, but only in the year in which the loan is made.

➤ Your (the buyer's) prorated portion of items such as property taxes and other statements that are finalized at closing.

➤ State and local taxes that are associated with the loan.

Using the example from Table 16.6 (a 30-year, $100,000 loan at a 9-percent interest rate), assume you are in the 28 percent federal tax bracket. Table 16.7 shows you what you can deduct from your federal tax returns over the first five years.

**Table 16.7   What Uncle Sam Will Let You Deduct
(28% Tax Bracket)**

Year	Total Annual Payment	Tax Savings Per Year	Your Net Cost After Deduction
1	$9,655	$2,512	$7,143
2	9,655	2,494	7,161
3	9,655	2,475	7,181
4	9,655	2,453	7,202
5	9,655	2,430	7,225

If you also deducted state and local taxes from these numbers, you'd be able to save even more. It gets a little complicated, but again let's assume you're in the 28 percent federal tax bracket. When you factor in state and local taxes of six percent on top of the federal tax deduction, the formula comes out to a total deduction of 32.32 percent.

Your total payment in the first year, for the example in Table 16.7, is $9,655. Of that, $8,972 is interest (see Table 16.6). Multiply 32.32 percent by $8,972 and you arrive at a tax deduction of $2,900 for federal, state, and local taxes in the first year.

The Point Is—Points Add Up!

When they shop mortgages, many home buyers look only at the interest rate, and forget to figure in the points as part of their total cost.

The true annual percentage rate (APR) on a loan should include the points as well as the rate. On the same type of loan, the greater the number of points, the higher the APR. Table 16.8 shows you how the points you pay can affect your APR on a $100,000 fixed-rate loan at nine percent for 15 or 30 years.

Always compare APRs— with the points included— when you shop and compare the costs of mortgages that offer the same interest rate.

Table 16.8 What a 9-Percent Loan Really Costs

Points	APR (15 Years)	APR (30 Years)
5	9.89%	9.58%
4	9.70	9.46
3	9.52	9.34
2	9.35	9.23
1	9.17	9.11

The Least You Need to Know

➤ The two major types of mortgages are fixed-rate and adjustable-rate (ARM).

➤ ARM mortgages generally are a better deal than a fixed-rate mortgage if you don't have the money to cover a big down payment and high closing costs. Government-insured mortgages are also available.

➤ When comparing mortgage deals, make sure you take into account the points, bank fees, and closing costs as well as the interest rate. The Annual Percentage Rate (APR) is a good measuring stick to use in these comparisons.

➤ You may be able to swing a better deal at the bank, thrift, or credit union where you are now doing business.

➤ Make sure your credit is in order at least six months before you apply for a mortgage. Chapter 17 provides more information how to do this.

Inside Those Credit Rating Agencies

In This Chapter

➤ How much personal data the credit agencies already know about you

➤ How to get a copy of your credit report

➤ How agencies "score" your habits and predict your future behavior

➤ How to improve your chances of getting credit and removing errors from your credit record

Like it or not, it's a nosy credit society that you live in. Your ability to borrow money or get a new job can swing on the information contained in your personal credit report. Who has the data? Three giant companies that have the goods on just about every person in the U.S.

People with bad credit? They get stung over and over again because of what's on their credit report. Even those with *good* credit can easily become victims of erroneous information that somehow gets on their report without their knowing it.

More credit applicants get turned down for a loan than get approved. Yet—shockingly—most consumers don't even bother to get a copy of their own credit report to see what's on it. They remain in the dark, never realizing how much negative stuff the credit agencies have dug up on them: the info can range from their date of birth to their income, payment habits, and the people they owe.

This chapter goes inside the shadowy world of credit bureaus, and explains how they "score" your credit history. It tells which mistakes to avoid, as well as how to strengthen your credit file and greatly improve your chances of getting a loan.

Big Brother Is Watching You

You can forget about how "private" you think your personal financial life is. The odds are 450-million-to-1 that if you have a credit card, department store account, savings or checking account, auto loan, student loan or mortgage, there's a computer file on you. Everything is in it—your job, how much money you make, where you've lived, and how you've paid your bills.

A little scary? You bet. Big Brother is watching you like you wouldn't believe. Its computers sit in a company you've maybe never heard of, run by people you've never met. Make that *three* companies instead of one—TRW, Equifax, and Trans Union. They're the three big guns of the credit-agency business, and all three probably have the same info on your life.

They and smaller, regional credit bureaus supply personal credit data about you to any place you go for credit—from credit card companies and auto dealers to, yes, even the company that's considering you for a job. And whenever you apply for credit, those outfits feed your latest personal information into the Big Three's computers.

The Big Three agencies aren't the ones who decide whether you'll get a loan or be hired. They only "compile the data," as they say, and provide it to organizations that determine whether they'll extend you credit. It could be a department store, bank, or credit card issuer. And to confuse the issue, they all evaluate your credit history differently. Little wonder the Big Three are a mystery to the average consumer, who knows zip about how the credit system operates.

REALLY?

Despite the fact that credit agencies have 450 million consumer credit reports on file, last year only 9 million Americans bothered to peer into their own files to see the often gory information on their credit records. Of those, one out of four discovered an error they eventually had corrected, according to the National Center for Financial Education, San Diego, California.

You Wouldn't Believe What They Know About You

Here's what you're up against—those credit agencies look under every rock. They gather information on you from hundreds of thousands companies such as retailers, banks, finance companies, and credit card issuers. In turn, those companies feed monthly updates on consumers back to the Big Three. The info includes, for example: names, old and current addresses, Social Security numbers, birth dates, employment information, and how people pay their bills. They also gather information from public records from state and county courts. But this information is limited to tax liens, legal judgments, bankruptcies, and, in some states, child-support payments.

With a couple of little touches on a computer key, an agency can pull up your credit life story and send it immediately to Megabuck Bank or Bubba's Auto Emporium where you're sweating out a loan. In turn, the information you filled out on your credit application at Megabuck and Bubba's also winds up in the Big Three's computers for the *next* place you apply for a loan. They get you coming and going.

How "Predictable" Are You? The Big Three Think They Know

Credit agencies work with outside mathematical experts to develop what they call "predictive models"—computer programs that try to estimate your future credit behavior based on your previous behavior. Einstein would have trouble understanding these complicated computer whatchamacallits. They involve far-out terms such as "regression analysis" and "neural network"—concepts that are way above the heads of average people.

These programs can predict the probability of someone going bankrupt—three, six, or nine months down the road—or they can determine the likelihood of a person stiffing his or her creditors by never paying bills.

How are these predictions applied? A bank makes a list of the kinds of new customers it's seeking. It goes to a credit bureau and says, "Tell us who has two credit cards and has never been 90 days late on a payment." The bureau prints a list of people who match those criteria. The bank sends a promotional mailing to everyone on the list, offering them credit. The approval rates on these applications are higher than if the bank were to simply mail to everybody in town.

Uncle Sam Protects Job Seekers—Sort Of

Under federal law, if you're turned down for a job on account of your credit report, the employer must notify you of your right to get a copy of your credit report for free from the credit agency. The credit agency must notify you automatically that the employer accessed your credit file if it contains any derogatory public information about you (such as bankruptcies, liens, and judgments).

Your file will show the name and date of any company that nosed its way onto your credit report over the past two years.

In a few states (such as California and Minnesota), employers must notify you before they obtain your employment history in your credit report. The biggest users of employment reports? Companies in sensitive industries such as banking, defense, pharmaceuticals, and others in the medical field.

The Bad Stuff Comes Off—Eventually

Fortunately, under the Fair Credit Reporting Act of 1971, negative information on your report can't hang around forever. By law, the agencies are *supposed to* wipe off any bankruptcy data 10 years after it was entered. They're also *supposed to* erase after seven years any tax liens, lawsuits, judgments or accounts put up for collection.

But don't assume that will happen, or that everything on your report is accurate. The agencies, like every company, are working with the human factor. A data clerk can easily hit the wrong computer key when he or she enters your information. They may have misread the info on your credit application back at Bubba's.

Here's another unpleasant possibility. As has been charged by Congressional committees investigating how the credit reporting services operate, an agency could just plumb forget about eradicating your negative information when it's supposed to.

The "Three C's"—An Old-Fashioned Pipe Dream

There was a time when you could go into a bank, and the banker—who was your friend and neighbor—had known you since you were in pigtails or knickers. He'd okay your loan with no credit check or other hassle. You can kiss those days goodbye. Banking has become big business, and big business today doesn't want to take any risks. You and your habits are now impersonal numbers in a Big Three computer. Oh, sure, banks still insist they lend money the old-fashioned way—on the basis of what they call the "Three C's":

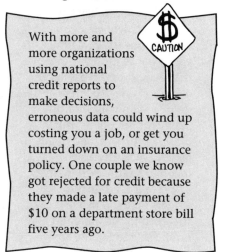

With more and more organizations using national credit reports to make decisions, erroneous data could wind up costing you a job, or get you turned down on an insurance policy. One couple we know got rejected for credit because they made a late payment of $10 on a department store bill five years ago.

➤ **Character**   It may not have anything to do with what kind of person you really are. More than likely, admit the credit agencies, it means how long you've lived at the same address and worked at the same company.

➤ **Capacity**   How much debt can you afford, based on your present income? The lender looks at your living expenses, current financial obligations and the payments that your new loan would require.

➤ **Credit**   How long have you had credit accounts such as credit cards, mortgages, and personal loans? What is the credit limit you're allowed on each one? How close are you to those limits now? Have you made your payments on time?

Nobody's perfect, and lenders know that. But if you've had a car repossessed, or another lender has given up trying to collect on what you owe, the Three C's have probably gone down the tubes in your case.

Your Credit "Score" Is How You're Judged

Remember, it's not the credit agencies that decide aye or nay on your loan applications. It's the outfits where you apply for credit. They all put a different value on the information on your report.

One may look more closely at your income, job, number of years at the same address, and whether you own your own home or rent. Another may be more interested in examining your bank accounts and payment track record. There's no way you're going to find out how they do their thing. You must be prepared for any roll of the dice.

What most credit grantors have in common, though, is that they use a "scoring system" all their own to judge you as a credit risk. That's why, in their back rooms, they call it a "risk score" based on whatever criteria they use. Your total score is made up of up a bunch of little individual scores, one for each thing about you the lender is examining.

For instance, if you've lived at the same address for five years, the lender might score this item as "5." If you've resided at the same place for between two and five years, the score might be "3." And any period less than two years is scored as "0." In other words, it's possible that an axe murderer who's lived in his home longer than you've lived in yours could (technically) score higher on this item than you would.

Other items on your credit report you might be scored on include your current

The thing that creditors examine like a hawk is your debt-to-income ratio. This is the percentage of your average monthly income that goes toward repaying the debts you owe. To arrive at the ratio, add up your monthly payments including your mortgage or rent, and divide it by your monthly gross income. A ratio of more than 35 percent is a signal to lenders that you may be stretched to the limit and may not be able to handle any more debt. Here's an example:

Your monthly income is $3,000, and your monthly debts are $1,000.

Divide $3,000 by $1,000 and you get 33 percent. That's your debt-to-income ratio.

monthly debts versus your monthly income, number of credit accounts, late payments, unpaid accounts put up for collection, tax liens, and the number of inquiries on your credit report.

REALLY? One mistake that many people make when they fill in their annual income on a credit application is forgetting to include the earnings of other people in the same household. If the other incomes were counted, it might raise their risk score and increase their chance of obtaining credit.

The lender adds up the scores for all the items and comes up with a *total* score. If it's high enough, you get the loan; if it isn't, then it's sorry, but so long. Numerically, the range between good and bad in a lender's scoring system can be all over the lot. For example, it could be from 0 to 1,000, or from 375 to 850, depending on the credit grantor. There might be one minimum score that Joe Doaks has to reach to borrow $1,000, and a different minimum for Mrs. Gottrocks who wants to borrow $25,000.

REALLY? Just try to get a bank or any other lender to confide its secret scoring formula to you. It won't... not yet, anyway. But one day it may have to because the Federal Trade Commission has proposed making the secret scoring systems open to the public. That would include how a person's score stacks up against others, and how lenders use a score to approve or reject a credit application.

As of this writing, scores do not appear on anyone's credit report. But a person's score can change over time. How bad can scoring get? One bank employee told us she's seen a huge pile of loan applications on a branch manager's desk on a Friday afternoon—all to be graded by one person arbitrarily, within a few minutes. One applicant, she said, was turned down because he happened to drive a truck instead of a car.

Are You Good, Bad, or Gray?

Lenders have a habit of lumping you into one of three ranges—"good," "bad" and "gray." Its computers make the first cut. The top scores are considered "good," and these customers are automatically approved for a loan. The "gray" scores are for people who score somewhere in the middle of the range. These are personally reviewed on an individual basis. The "bad" group might just as well have leprosy. But occasionally the lender may move a person into the "gray" group to give him or her "an extra chance."

An example of a person who would immediately be lumped in the "bad" category is someone who has had "charge-offs" in the past. *Charge-offs* are loans that creditors eventually have to wipe off their books because they've never been paid. "If we see someone who has had charge-offs greater than $300 in the last four years, we just immediately decline it," explained one credit agency executive. "I don't want anyone in my office spending any more effort on that one."

If you've been habitually 30, 60, or 90 days late in making your payments, you could be hurting your credit record even more. All late payments are bad, but 90 days is worse than 30, as you might guess. Credit card companies are a little looser when you don't pay on time, because after all, those guys *want* you to go past the due date so they can charge you interest on your balance!

It's Thumbs Down in Most Cases

The most closely guarded secret of all? The lenders' *approval ratio*. It's the percentage of applicants who get approved or disapproved for their loans. Sources at the Big Three agencies give this picture:

➤ If a credit card issuer sends a mailing to consumers that says they have "pre-approved" status for credit, the odds are nine out of 10 they'll actually be approved. But if the card company somehow finds out that the person's credit has "deteriorated" lately, it may conclude, "Hey, this guy is not as good as we thought he was." Result? He'll get approved, all right, but the creditor may bust his credit limit down to $200–$500. He also may pay a higher rate of interest on the money he borrows.

➤ The person who just picks up a credit application at a store, then fills it out and mails it in, has a two out of 10 chance of getting approved.

➤ The person who applies for a Gold Credit Card (with a $5,000 credit line and other perks) has a four out of 10 chance of being okayed.

➤ New car loan applicants also have a four out of 10 possibility.

For a plain-vanilla credit card, credit scorers used to look for someone with an annual income of at least $12,000. Now, some have dropped the requirement to as low as $8,000. To obtain a Gold Credit Card, a person needs an income of about $30,000.

Why are the minimums falling? Because of fierce competition for customers. The credit card pie is just *so* big, and more and more outfits want a piece. To cover their higher risks, creditors may charge a higher interest rate (plus special fees) and monitor these new customers once a month. Another reason for easier credit is that the percentage of delinquencies—people who fall behind in their payments—is decreasing.

How to Boost Your Chances of Getting Approved

It's not easy for a lot of people, but the sure way to increase the odds of obtaining credit is to follow these basic rules:

➤ Pay your bills on time.

➤ Pay down the debts you owe.

➤ Don't take on any more credit than you need and can afford.

➤ If, say, you have an auto loan and several credit cards, reduce the number of cards immediately.

➤ Use the credit you have wisely. Don't live up to your credit limit.

➤ Ask the credit agencies for a copy of your report every year or two, so you'll know what kind of picture they have of you.

➤ Correct any errors on the report.

How Credit Inquiries Can Haunt You

Let's say you've been pretty good about paying your bills on time. You earn a nice income, and you've lived at the same address for two years. You can't think of anything that could possibly prevent a lender from giving you credit. No tax liens, no bankruptcies, no nothing.

You carry one credit card, but in the past three months you've applied for two more, and are now in the process of also trying to borrow money to finance Junior's college education. You've also contacted a couple of companies about changing jobs.

Certain inquiries won't show up on your report. Examples include inquiries made by you to monitor your report (or to obtain a copy of it), or inquiries made by companies who want to send you an unsolicited credit offer through the mail.

That makes six new inquiries on your credit report in a very short time. What happens? The two credit card companies check you out at one of the Big Three credit agencies and count four inquiries besides their own. Alarm bells ring in their minds. They figure that all those inquiries mean you're about to plunge into big debt. They look like red flags to a bull. Whammo! You get turned down.

How to Get a Copy of Your Credit Report

For all the reasons we mentioned, you need to get a copy of your report. You can do it easily in a couple of ways. If you're denied credit for any reason, within the next 30 days you can get a *free* copy by contacting any of the Big Three credit agencies. The outfit that denied you the credit must inform you, usually by mail, of the name and address of the credit agency or bureau that supplied the information. What's on your report at one of the Big Three may also be on your reports at the other two credit agencies. But don't count on it. Contact all three. One of the agencies, TRW, has extended the free-report period to 60 days.

If you haven't been turned down for credit, you can buy a copy of your report for an average $8 to $15 by writing to the agencies. TRW will give you a free copy of your report once each calendar year.

How do you do it? First, phone the agencies. When you phone an agency, don't expect to get a live person on the other end. And don't get exasperated. A robot voice will walk you through the instructions of what to do, such as, "Press number 1," "Press number 2," and so on. Stick with it; it's worth the aggravation. Then write a letter to all three credit agencies and keep copies. When you write your letter, be sure to state:

➤ Your full name (don't forget the "Jr." or "III" after your name).

➤ Current and previous addresses, with ZIP codes.

➤ Your spouse's first name if you're married.

➤ Your Social Security number.

➤ Your date of birth.

➤ The name(s) of your business, if you are a small business owner.

When you need to dispute any information on your credit report, remember that *you have a legal right to insert up to 100 words into your file at the credit agency*. Explain your side of the story. State all the facts—the names, numbers, dates, and places concerning what *really* happened. Believe it or not, credit grantors will take your statement into consideration when they check your file because the statement says something about your earnestness and character.

Here are the addresses and phone numbers of the Big Three credit agencies:

TRW
National Consumer Assistance Center
P.O. Box 949
Allen, TX 75002-0949
(800) 682-7654

Equifax
Credit Information Services
P.O. Box 105873
Atlanta, GA 30348
(800) 685-1111

Trans Union Corporation
P.O. Box 390
Springfield, PA 19064-0390
(216) 779-7200

Guard Against Mix-Ups

When Congress was considering the Credit Repair Reform Act of 1994, which unfortunately died on the Senate floor, it found that one in four credit files contained errors. A lot of them undoubtedly were the credit agencies' fault, but there are tons of horror stories created by consumers themselves. You can prevent errors and mix-ups on your credit report by following a few simple tips.

Always use the same name. If your full name is Jeremy C. Bullwhistle III, don't write "J. C. Bullwhistle" or "Jeremy Bullwhistle" (without the "C"). Don't use "Jerry," or your last name without the three Roman numerals after it. The reason for this is you don't want inconsistencies appearing on the report. You could get tagged with the bad credit of Jerry Bullwhistle-the-Credit-Card-Maniac who lives 2,000 miles away. You'd be amazed at how many folks commit that simple mistake, and wind up spending months or years fighting the credit agencies to prove they're the *real* Jeremy Bullwhistle III.

Always use your Social Security number. You've got the only one like it in the world. This will help you prevent your name from being confused with folks with the same name.

Always list your home addresses for the past five years. It will help you in the future if you move.

Protecting Yourself from Fraud

Americans lose more than $2 billion a year to credit-card-fraud artists. You can protect yourself by following these tips, advises TRW:

➤ Sign your new cards as soon as they arrive.

➤ Treat your cards like money. Keep them in a safe place.

➤ Shred anything with your account number on it before throwing it away.

➤ Don't give your card number over the phone unless *you* initiate the call.

➤ Don't write your card number on a postcard, or on the outside of an envelope.

➤ Remember to get your card and receipt immediately after every transaction, and double-check to be sure they're yours.

➤ If your billing statement is incorrect or your credit cards are lost or stolen, notify your card issuers at once.

Beware of "We'll Fix Your Credit" Operators

You come across these bozos in classified ads or even on television. They offer to "fix your credit" by claiming to be able to remove any negative information from your credit report, "even if you have bad credit."

Forget those pitches. Otherwise you'll learn a painful lesson that could cost you hundreds—or thousands—of dollars. The truth is, those "credit-repair clinics" can't do anything for you that you can't do yourself, for free or at a minimum cost.

If the information in your report is correct, by law no one can remove it. You, yourself, can have inaccurate information removed at no charge. Credit agencies will supply you with a simple "dispute form." It's easy to fill out and mail back.

If you have credit problems, such as trying to get creditors off your back, contact Consumer Credit Counseling Services at (800) 338-CCCS for the office location nearest you. For little or no fee, they have helped hundreds of thousands of people just like you.

Helping Hands

Struggling under a heavy personal debt load? Contact the following sources for helpful information on consumer credit and how you can strengthen your credit report:

Bankcard Holders of America
524 Branch Drive
Salem, VA 24153
(703) 389-5445

The Banker's Secret Bulletin
P.O. Box 78
Elizaville, NY 12523
(800) 255-0899

National Center for Financial Education
P.O. Box 34070
San Diego, CA 92163
(415) 567-5290

Consumer Federation of America
1424 16th Street N.W., Suite 604
Washington, D.C. 20036
(202) 387-6121

Maintaining Good Credit

The key to maintaining good credit is to follow a few simple rules:

➤ **Pay your bills on time.** Almost all lenders will look at whether you're on time or late with your bills. Most lenders are lenient and will tolerate a maximum of 30 days late. If you are currently behind on your accounts, catch up before you apply. This is how you can make the grade to get credit. You have to fit the profile of the people who pay their bills on time.

➤ **Don't be too close to your credit limits.** Typically, lenders will compare your credit card balances to the total amount of credit you have available. The more cards you have close to the limit, the more of a risk you are to lenders.

➤ **Cancel any credit cards that you don't use.** If you already have five or six major credit cards (even if they have zero balances), you will have a tough time getting additional credit. Why? Because lenders will think that you already have more than enough.

➤ **Get a copy of your credit report and correct any errors on an annual basis.** As many as 40 percent of all credit reports contain errors, so get out your red pen. Call TRW at (800) 392-1122, Equifax at (800) 685-1111, or Trans Union at (800) 851-2674 for details on how you can get a free copy of your credit report. Note: TRW will give you one free copy of your credit file; after that there's a fee.

➤ **Find out how many inquiries there are on your credit report.** The more inquiries there are, the less likely you are to get the credit you're seeking. For example, every time you apply for a credit card, an inquiry about your credit application is included in your credit report. If too many credit card companies inquire at once, they may be suspicious about your intentions.

Statistics show that people who have recently applied for a lot of credit are less likely to keep up with their payments on a timely basis. If you have five or more inquiries in the past six to eight months, wait a few months before you apply for credit again.

The Least You Need to Know

➤ Most of your financial information—your salary, bank accounts, credit cards, and loan information—is stored in computers at the TRW, Equifax, and Trans Union credit agencies.

➤ When deciding whether or not to approve you for a loan, lenders use items from your credit report to come up with a score that determines how big a credit risk you are. Employers may also use your credit report to verify employment history.

➤ To improve your credit report, pay your bills on time, cut down the number of credit cards you carry, don't live up to your credit limit, and pay off your outstanding debts.

➤ Review your credit report periodically to check it for mistakes. One in four credit files contains errors.

➤ Be sure to dispute any errors on your credit report by inserting up to 100 words on the report to explain your side of the story. Also, show your lender any copies of paid invoices and letters that document your position.

Chapter 18

The Biggest Advantages— and Dangers— of Home Equity Loans

In This Chapter

➤ How home equity loans pay off high-rate bills

➤ Which type of loan is best for you

➤ Tricks and traps your banker won't tell you

➤ How to figure the real cost of your loan

The scenes in the bank ad are gorgeous. One shows a couple relaxing on a faraway tropical beach. Another depicts a guy waving from his sporty Ferrari. A third shows a happy family waving in front of their new home addition. All of these things are made possible through a home equity line of credit.

With a home equity line of credit, you borrow against the amount of money you have in your home, the bank sets the money aside for you in an account you can tap into at any time, and you're supposed to pay the money back somehow. This can be a great way to get a big slug of cash fast for an emergency or to consolidate your debts, but what you've really done is hocked the house—which is probably the single biggest asset you'll ever own. If you fail to make your payments, the bank grabs the farm.

For many unsuspecting people, this is a time bomb that could explode in their faces. This chapter examines the pluses and dangerous minuses of the loan every bank is touting, and warns you of its consequences.

Putting Your Nest Egg on the Line

Pretend you're in this situation: Your home is your #1 asset. You've worked hard to make your house payments, and year by year your house is worth more and more. Why? Well, not only do you own more of your home, but real estate prices have soared because of inflation. So the little abode you bought for $50,000 in the 1970s may be worth $125,000 today.

But you've run up big debts on your credit cards, the kitchen needs remodeling, and Junior starts college in the fall. How can you afford all that? By borrowing against your home.

How a Home Equity Loan Works

You still owe $25,000 on your mortgage, and the appraisers figure that the market value of the house is $125,000. Subtract what you owe from what the house is worth to get your equity—in this case $100,000. Friendly Fred the Banker says he'll lend you up to 80 percent of your equity. Get the calculator out. Wow! That means you can get your hands on as much as $80,000!

Hopefully you wouldn't be foolish enough to borrow that much without a darn good way to make that money grow awfully fast. If you did, the payments on your present mortgage plus the new payments on your home equity loan could strangle you.

What does Fred the Banker require from you before he'll hand over the money? Some collateral, such as a *lien* that gives the bank ownership of your house in case you default. That's right. If you can't pay the bank back, it can grab the home that you busted your hump for all your life. Welcome to the dangerous, fast-growing world of home equity borrowing.

Type A and Type B

Fred will lend you the money one of two ways: a home equity loan or a home equity line of credit. If you take a plain home equity loan, he'll lend you any amount up to $80,000 all at once—provided you meet certain criteria. (This is the same as having a second mortgage on your house.) You borrow a fixed amount for, say, one to seven years, and you pay the money back in fixed monthly installments.

If you take a home equity line of credit, Fred will give you the opportunity to open an account with up to $80,000 that you can access as often as you want for any amount you want. In effect the credit line account works like a giant credit card. You access the amount you need, whenever you need it, simply by writing a check against the account. Typically a home equity line is for five to twenty years. By having access to the money when you need it, you don't have to keep going back to the bank and reapplying for loans.

With either type of home equity loan, you're not only spending your savings, you're also swapping short-term debt for long-term debt.

How the Account Works

A home equity line of credit is a revolving account. As you pay the money back, you replenish the amount you can borrow up to your credit limit. Money goes out, money comes in; that's how the account revolves.

Your monthly payment is generally two percent of the total P&I (principle and interest) you owe. If the amount you borrow (the principle, or P) over a year is $5,000 and your interest rate (I) is 10 percent, the interest is $500. Therefore, the total P&I is $5,500. Two percent of that is $110. That's your monthly payment. But multiply that times 12 months, and the interest you pay is $1,320 per year on the $5,000 you borrowed.

Which Rate Is Better for You: Fixed or Variable?

This decision is critical because the type of interest rate you pay could knock your wallet for a loop. With a fixed rate, you lock in your cost over the full life of the loan. The rate won't ever change, and you'll

The amount you borrow is your principal. The finance charge you pay is your interest. The two together are called your *P&I*.

know your costs in advance. With a variable rate, the rate can go up or down according to whatever "index" the bank ties the rate to. Most home equity lines charge variable rate.

Most banks use their prime rate to determine the variable rate. The prime rate is the loan rate they charge on business loans to their most creditworthy customers. But you're not General Motors, so the bank is going to charge you a higher rate: its prime rate plus something on top of that. Why? They consider you a bigger risk than GM. On average, your rate will be the bank's prime rate plus about two percentage points. But the prime rate keeps dancing up and down, and so will the variable rate you pay on your loan.

Here are some tips to keep in mind when playing the rate game:

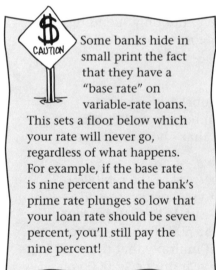

Some banks hide in small print the fact that they have a "base rate" on variable-rate loans. This sets a floor below which your rate will never go, regardless of what happens. For example, if the base rate is nine percent and the bank's prime rate plunges so low that your loan rate should be seven percent, you'll still pay the nine percent!

➤ Often, the more money you borrow, the lower your starting rate.

➤ When interest rates are rising, avoid variable-rate loans or lines at all costs. Get a fixed-rate loan instead. That will tell you your cost from Day One until the loan is paid off. But when rates are falling, you should go with the variable rate.

➤ Also, stay away from variable rates when you borrow for a longer term, such as ten years.

➤ In a rising-rate environment, you can keep your monthly payment budget intact by asking the bank to stretch the number of months to repay the money or by asking the bank to lower the payment—or both. However, remember that the longer you have the loan, the more interest you'll pay.

➤ If you're considering a fixed rate, tell them you want to be able to switch to the future current rate in the event that interest rates start shooting up. For example, Harris Bank in Chicago permits customers to convert to a fixed rate twice during their loan without paying any extra fees.

➤ Most variable rates have a cap (a maximum amount, or ceiling) that the rate can rise to.

The Pros and Cons of Home Equity Loans

Taking out a home equity loan isn't all bad. Consider the following list of advantages to having a home equity loan:

➤ You can save money by paying off the bills you owe at a high interest rate with the money you get from your one loan, which charges a lower interest rate. For example, if you owe $5,000 on credit cards at 18 percent interest and you take out a $5,000 home equity loan at nine percent to pay them off, you've chopped your financing cost in half, from $900 a year to $450 a year.

Here's what big banks and thrifts in seven large U.S. cities were charging on home equity lines of credit, compared with fixed-rate credit cards (according to *Bank Rate Monitor*):

	Home Equity Credit Line	Fixed-rate Credit Card
New York	9.23%	17.80%
Los Angeles	9.74	19.15
San Francisco	9.11	19.65
Philadelphia	9.77	18.11
Detroit	10.50	16.71
Boston	9.50	16.90
Washington, D.C.	8.25	18.00

If you're not sure about your future job security, it might be better to get a home equity loan or line of credit now, while you still qualify. Then if you get laid off, you'll be better able to pay off high-rate credit cards.

➤ Home equity loans (especially the home equity line of credit) give you a financial security blanket for future unforeseen expenses.

➤ You have cash available for home improvement, college tuition, or even a new car. Senior citizens, for example, can tap into the value of their home to pay emergency medical bills.

➤ You can take advantage of the law that allows you to write off as a tax deduction 100 percent of the interest charges on home equity for loans up to $100,000. The interest on car loans and other personal loans is not tax deductible. For example, if you're in the 28 percent tax bracket and get a nine percent loan, your real rate after the tax deduction will be 6.48 percent.

➤ You can pay back only the interest on the loan for several years or until it matures (such as in 10 years). Banks are flexible on this—but there's a built-in booby trap, as you'll discover in this chapter.

Before you dash off to the bank to get your home equity loan, keep in mind that a home equity loan isn't for frivolous folks. It's for disciplined people who will use the money wisely (not for vacations, second honeymoons, or a wild spending spree in Las Vegas). In other words, the rabbit should not go near the lettuce. You should not take out such a loan unless you are 100 percent certain you will be able to repay it. You see, a home equity loan can be a velvet trap. Here's why:

➤ It lowers your equity in the home.

➤ It can be expensive in terms of the total cost over the life of the loan.

➤ If the value of your house depreciates, the amount you owe on the loan stays the same.

➤ The bank can grab your house if you don't pay back the money on time. That's called a foreclosure. In fact, if you used the money to buy a car, they may take the home and not the car, or they might grab both.

Why Banks Love Home Equity Loans

Home equity lines of credit (HELOCs for short) are the banks' darlings of all loans because they're collateralized. The institution has something of value, your house, in case you default. Also, HELOCs are bigger loans than, say, the piddly $3,000 loan on which the bank makes less money. Home equity customers tend to be more upscale than folks with lower incomes who don't own a home.

No wonder every time you turn your head, you see a bank hustling HELOCs. Because competition among the lenders is ferocious, they're wheeling and dealing to get your business. Many outfits are even waiving up-front fees and closing costs on the loans.

They Make It S-o-o-o-o Easy

Banks keep giving you more ways to access the money in your home equity credit line. Besides issuing you a bunch of checks to tap into the cash, some let you use your credit card or let you access the credit line by telephone or an ATM. Why?

Those cunning outfits don't make a dime off you unless you actually use the cash in your account. That's why many of them charge an "inactivity fee" if you don't touch any of the cash within a year's time. The fee could be anywhere from $50 to $150. (When was the last time anyone ever billed you for doing nothing?)

Other banks require that you borrow a minimum such as $300 each time you draw on the line. And some will insist that you take an initial cash advance when you first set up the line to get your debt rolling—a foxy move on the bank's part.

Beware of Low-Ball Teaser Rates

Just about every bank in the land uses artificially low introductory "teaser" rates to get you in the door. For example, Megabuck Bank might feature a giant nine percent rate in a newspaper ad or in the bank's lobby. However, the fine print at the bottom of the ad says, "Nine percent introductory rate is only good for the first six months, after which the rate will revert to Megabuck's prime rate in effect at that time, plus three percentage points." Translation: If you take this loan at nine percent on July 1, next January 1 your real home equity loan rate will jump to 12 percent. Big difference? You bet. The interest cost on a $10,000 loan will go from $900 a year to $1,200.

Never borrow on home equity without finding out how long the rate is good and what the real rate will be after the introductory period.

Balloon Loans: The Ugliest Scenario of All

We can't think of a worse situation than someone falling for a balloon loan. Here's how it works: Jim and Mabel borrow $20,000 via a home equity loan for five years at 10 percent interest. They can't quite come up with $400 a month to repay the loan, so what does the bank offer? A balloon deal.

All Jim and Mabel have to do is pay the interest on the loan every month; they don't have to pay on the principal (the $20,000) until the very end of the five years. Then, BOOM! They must pay the $20,000 all at once—just like a balloon being inflated. But suppose they can't come up with the twenty grand? They could lose their home to the bank. Goodbye American dream!

A balloon loan can explode like a real balloon! On a $20,000 loan at 10 percent interest for five years, the loan will cost you a staggering $20,000 if you only pay back the interest over that period. You'll still owe the $20,000 principal after the five years are up.

Right this moment, millions of consumers who've taken out home equity loans are caught in that trap. The loans are like time bombs waiting to go off. Assuming their credit is still okay five years from now, Jim and Mabel could roll the first loan over into a new loan at the same bank. But that would only cost them more interest on top of the outrageous $20,000 in interest they've already paid.

However, balloon payments aren't a threat if you plan to sell your house before the loan matures. You could pay the loan off with the proceeds from the sale.

Fee-Fi-Fo-Fum... But Mostly Scads of Fees

Fees range all over the lot, regardless of whether you're getting a straight home equity loan (a lump sum all at once) or a home equity line of credit so you can write checks for what you need.

But it all boils down to this: On the straight home equity loan, the fees could run into thousand of dollars for credit checks, appraisal fees, legal fees, title insurance, and closing costs when the loan is finalized. Always ask the bank these three questions before you take out the loan:

1. What are my upfront fees and charges?

2. What is my total financing cost (the interest amount on the loan)?

3. What are my closing costs including points? (A point is 1/100th of the loan amount.)

We know a couple who thought they were breezing through a home equity loan, only to discover that their total fees (not even including the interest) came to $6,000!

On home equity lines of credit, the fees can be a lot less. Because banks are fighting their competition with brass knuckles for new home equity customers, many will waive their fees and closing costs. You'll see their "no-fee" deals in ads. Others will waive an "annual fee" in the first year and start charging you in the second year. A few will even offer you a cash bonus of $100 or $200 (added to your credit line) to get your account.

Figure out exactly how much money you'll really need for your maximum credit line—no more—and check whether interest rates are going up or down. If, for instance, you plan to borrow $5,000 against the line, ask the bank what it will cost you in dollars and cents under each of its formulas.

A fixed-rate home equity line is rare, but if you find one, there could be extra fees and formulas, such as a $75 "finance charge." Or the fee could vary depending on the amount of your credit line and/or the bank's rate formula that's tied to its prime rate. For example, you might get a loan with no fee if your line is more than $20,000 or if you borrow less than $20,000 but agree to a rate of the prime plus two percent. Or you might pay a $200 fee if you choose to pay the prime rate plus 1.5 percent. On variable-rate credit lines, many banks are trading closing costs in exchange for higher margins. For example, you might have the choice of paying no closing costs but paying the prime rate plus two percent, or paying closing costs and the prime plus 1.5 percent.

The Least You Need to Know

➤ Don't borrow what you don't need and can't pay back.

➤ Always read the fine print in the ads and in your contract. If anything is not absolutely clear, ask for a straight answer in plain English.

➤ When you shop, don't be dazzled by gimmick rates and freebies. Consider the total cost of the loan based on how much you borrow, plus the upfront fees and closing costs.

➤ Don't get tricked by low-ball rates. Almost every bank uses that tactic in its advertising.

➤ With a credit line, the bank considers how much money you could wind up owing if you use the whole credit line.

➤ If you only need a small amount of cash for two or three years, home equity probably isn't the answer. You'll be better off with a regular short-term fixed-rate loan.

➤ Get your credit record in order before you apply. Despite the fact that the bank will hold a piece of your house until you repay the loan, it's still going to be nosy about your income, other debts, job, credit payment, record, and so on.

➤ Most important, remember that your house is on the line. It doesn't make sense to drive a new Ferrari if you have no place to park it!

Part 5
Simple Investment Strategies

"Simple Investment Strategies"—sounds like a financial oxymoron, huh?

Finding your way through the investment jungle can be simple… as long as you pay attention and do your homework. You can easily eliminate paying exorbitant fees to Wall Street sharks—and possibly reap better investment rewards—if you concentrate on some of the strategies and secrets revealed in the following chapters.

You don't need to be a financial Einstein to understand (and also roll the dice on) Wall Street. In this Part, you'll learn the pluses and minuses of taking the plunge, the top ten money strategies of the 1990s, and even some investment strategies especially for senior citizens.

Are you ready to begin?

Are You Ready to Roll the Dice on Wall Street?

In This Chapter

➤ How much can you really afford to lose?

➤ The pluses and minuses of taking the plunge

➤ The lowdown on stocks, bonds, mutual funds, futures, and options

---

The odds of rolling the dice on Wall Street and coming up a winner sound easy to most folks. Just see what the most popular investment is, blindly take your broker's advice, and mail off your check—right? Wrong!

When it comes to investing, you have millions of questions, and none of the answers is listed in that last sentence! Should you invest in stocks? Bonds? What about mutual funds? Should you invest for the long haul, or aim for a short-time horizon? Are you willing to accept a lot of risk for an even greater return? And that's just the beginning. This chapter will explain how you can get started making money on Wall Street.

Creating Your Investment Profile

If you don't chart a clear course in your financial affairs, you'll face rough seas ahead. So ahoy, mates—time to create your personal investment profile. Keeping it simple, you can figure out your profile based on your risk tolerance, your return needs, your time horizon, and your tax exposure.

To assess your risk tolerance, ask yourself how much you can afford to lose. This factor is extremely important because of the severe consequences of taking on too much risk. If you understand what your risk tolerance is, you won't have to press the panic button because you've got yourself covered. The rule of thumb: If your investments are keeping you up at night, then sell. No investment, especially a risky one, is worth losing sleep over.

To determine what kind of investor you are, picture the worst-case scenario. Ask yourself how much you can afford to lose in a one-year time frame—and then match it to one of the profiles below.

➤ You're a *conservative investor* if you can sustain losses of no more than 6 percent over a one-year period. That means if you have $1,000 invested and the markets take a tumble, you could withstand losing up to $60 without reaching for the Pepto-Bismol.

➤ You're a *moderate risk investor* if you can withstand losses in your investment portfolio of no more than 15 percent over a one-year time frame.

➤ You're a *high-tolerance-for-risk investor* if you can generally withstand losing between 15 percent to 26 percent of your portfolio in a span of one year. You fly by the seat of your pants and live moment to moment.

Your return needs make up the other half of the equation in the "risk/reward" profile. Once you determine your risk profile, you'll have a general idea of your reward, which is your return. Unfortunately, there is no investment that allows you to have your cake and eat it too. You can't earn a high return and protect 100 percent of your initial investment (your *principal*) without exposing your cash to the ups and downs of the financial markets. That's where the trade-off comes in. If you want to protect your portfolio as much as possible, you won't earn as much in a reward unless you implement some defensive money strategies, which are discussed in Chapter 20.

What are the trade-offs? If you want to protect your initial investment, you'll typically receive a lower return, usually in the form of a lower annual income (such as interest payments you receive from a bond investment). Secondly, there is a trade-off between income and growth. The more certain you are about your annual payment, the less risky the investment is and the lower the potential return in the form of growth.

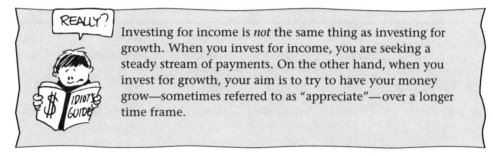

REALLY?

Investing for income is *not* the same thing as investing for growth. When you invest for income, you are seeking a steady stream of payments. On the other hand, when you invest for growth, your aim is to try to have your money grow—sometimes referred to as "appreciate"—over a longer time frame.

Your time horizon directly affects your ability to reduce risk. For example, volatile investments such as stocks—where prices fluctuate greatly over the short term—are considerably smoother over a longer time horizon. That's why diversification is so important—you're not putting all your eggs in one basket. If your time horizon is short, however, you can't be as effectively diversified across all the different types of markets.

Your time horizon begins when you start investing that first buck in your portfolio. If you are investing to save for a child's education, for example, you have already dictated your time horizon: It ends when you withdraw the money. So what defines a short-term, intermediate-term, or long-term time horizon? Industry standards say that if you need the money within one to two years, you have a short-term time horizon. Two to five years constitutes an intermediate-term time horizon. And more than five years is long-term.

Finally, consider your tax exposure. It's difficult to figure out what your tax exposure is because the tax laws are constantly changing. The bottom line in investing is what Uncle Sam says you get as leftovers… or in some cases, what you owe *him*. If you are in a high-income tax bracket, you need to be concerned with tax implications that seem to appear magically when you invest—including some obligations you incur—and that's where timing comes into play. Chapter 24 discusses this in detail.

To get a grip on planning your investment portfolio based on these four factors, look at Table 19.1 to see where you fall.

Table 19.1 Investment Factors at Different Life Stages

	Early Career	Middle Career	Late Career	Early Retirement	Late Retirement
Risk Tolerance	High	High	Moderate	Moderate	Low
Your Return	Growth	Growth	Growth	Growth & Income	Income
Time Horizon	Long	Long	Long	Interm./ Long	Short/ Interm.
Tax Exposure	Lower	Higher	Higher	Lower	Lower

Source: Adapted from *American Association of Individual Investors*, March 1993

The Pluses and Minuses of Taking the Plunge

Making money on Wall Street is all about thinking long-term. By investing in any of Wall Street's products—stocks, bonds, mutual funds, futures, options, and the new derivatives market—you have the potential to reap great rewards. In exchange for these rewards, you do take on risk. The often-quoted legendary trader Bernard Baruch coined a phrase that we're sure is on every investor's mind: "I'm not so concerned about the return on my money as I am about the return *of* my money!"

Of course, every investor wants the highest assured return possible. But returns aren't certain—and neither is the future. But, if you keep the following adage in mind, it will get you started in your investment course:

Seek out investments that pose the greatest amount of return with the least amount of risk.

What you consider to be the greatest amount of return depends on your investment profile. For example, you may favor shorting index futures to gain a quick buck and not care that you could lose all your money. On the flipside, your grandpa loses sleep every time the Federal Reserve tweaks short-term interest rates, so he keeps his money in safe, conservative money market funds. Whatever kind of investor you are, the following tips will help you tackle and reduce your exposure to risks that are associated with investing your money:

➤ **Keep an eye on reports of reduced purchasing-power risk.** Simply, this is how much bang you can get for your buck. A good example is that what you buy for a dollar today will not buy you the same product for a dollar ten years from now.

➤ **Keep your eye on market risk.** (*Market risk* is just being exposed to the ups and downs in the financial markets.) An increase in the amount of risk that the financial markets and our economy experiences will cause any investment to decrease in value.

➤ **Maintain enough liquidity in your investment portfolio.** When an investment is *liquid*, that means you can easily sell it and get your money out of it. If you don't have enough investments that are fairly liquid, you run the risk of not being able to get at your money without a hassle, penalty, or loss. For example, if the market is topsy-turvy, you could be forced to sell your investment at a significant loss if you need the money immediately. If your investment is in real estate, it might be difficult to sell your house because there are no buyers. Therefore, you're stuck—your investment is *illiquid*.

➤ **Monitor any type of inflation reports.** The uncertainty over future inflation rates, called *inflation risk*, can eat into your profit—and, in some cases, your principal! An investment that can't keep up with inflation will not be able to grow, leaving you with little purchasing power. The best indicator of inflation is the Consumer Price Index (CPI).

➤ **Watch for any changes in the business sector.** *Industry risk* is based on how the industry you've invested in is doing as a whole. The certainty of a business' ability to pay income, principal, and other returns due to investors may suffer if the company or the industry as a whole is not doing well. Some of the magazines and financial TV programs listed in Chapter 4 are good resources to monitor changes in the business sector.

Crash Course in Investing in Stocks

Most people think of the stock market when it comes to investing—probably because it has been around the longest. However, here's a kicker: Almost 70 percent of the people who invest in the stock market lose money. Why? Because of fear and greed.

A **security** is any type of investment product, including notes, stocks, and bonds.

The fear is when you are afraid to invest. Investing is somewhat risky, but if you don't invest, you could be missing out on the opportunities of a lifetime in the market. And what about greed? Folks, if you're looking to sink your money into poor-quality stocks on dreams of getting rich overnight, you'll probably pay too much for them and lose your hard-earned savings. Greed is *not* good—sorry Gordon Gekko! What *is* good is *learning as much as you can about your stock investments*—and the best place to begin is right here.

The word *stock* is a shortened form of the phrase *common stock*. Common stock is a security that represents ownership in a company. When you buy stock, you buy *shares*, which represent a proportion of ownership in that company. In order for a company to offer common stock, it has to "go public," which it does when it needs to raise money. This is known as an *initial public offering*. The next time the company wants to raise money, it conducts a *secondary offering*. Once a company is publicly traded, its stock can be bought through most brokerage and discount brokerage firms.

> **REALLY?** Shares are usually sold in *round lots*—groups of 100; less than that is an *odd lot*. To figure out how much ownership you have, simply take the amount of shares you own and divide it by the number of *shares outstanding*—which is the total amount of shares that the company has issued and are currently traded by the public. For example, if you own 100 shares of XYZ Company and there are 1,000,000 shares outstanding, then you own .0001 or 1/1000th of the company. It won't get you the CEO's parking spot, but at least it gives you an idea of how common stock refers to ownership. To find out how many shares are outstanding, you can call a broker for a quote and ask for this information, or you can check the financial pages.

Why invest in stock? The stock market boasts the best returns you can get on your money if you keep it invested over a long time frame. Sure, there are bumps along the way, but if you average all the ups and downs of the stock market over the past 70 years, stocks have grown at an average 10.67 percent rate of return. Remember—there are ups *and* downs! Here's an example that seems too good to be true: Berkshire Hathaway had its stock price multiplied at least *16 times* in just the past decade, for an average return to shareholders of 32 percent a year. If you'd bought 10 shares of Berkshire Hathaway 10 years ago for $12,750, those shares would be worth $198,950 today. Even $1,000 invested in stocks that performed as well as the Standard & Poor 500 from 1971 until 1990 would have grown to $8,727, which tallies to an 11.5 percent average annual return.

Many times investors park their money in stocks to receive dividends. Investors who buy common stock are hoping the company will generate profits so these profits can be distributed to shareholders. Not only can you receive dividends when you invest in stocks, but you have the potential to make a profit when you sell the stock. This profit is known as a **capital gain**. The difference between the price when you buy the stock and when you sell it is known as your *return*. How do you

> **WHAT?** One of the best ways to tell how your investments are doing is to compare them to the **Standard & Poor 500**, which represents a "basket" of the 500 largest blue-chip companies in America. Many portfolio managers use this index, or a **benchmark**, as way to measure their performance.

make a capital gain? *Buy low and sell high!* It's one of Wall Street's oldest and well-proven tricks of the trade.

Finally, the tax benefit comes into play when you invest in stocks. You do not incur a taxable event until you sell the stock. For example, even if you bought 100 shares of XYZ Company stock at $25 a share and it's currently trading at $100 a share, you don't have a profit *until you sell it*. That means you don't have a taxable situation to report to the IRS on your tax return (unless, of course, you receive dividends along the way). Until you do so, it is known as a *paper profit*.

When buying a stock, choose one that is consistent with your investment goals. The three major types of stock are described below:

➤ **Growth stocks** Growth stocks are touted as one of the easiest ways to make money because the companies that issue them are built for growth. You can define a growth stock company as one that maintains faster-than-average gains in earnings and profits over the last few years and its future looks similar. The only difference within this category is that there are large growth stocks, medium-sized growth stocks, and small-sized growth stocks. Each type depends on company sales. Some examples of growth stocks include Xerox, Abbott Laboratories, McDonalds, and Eastman Kodak. Keep in mind that growth stocks tend to have higher p/e ratios than other stocks!

Just as growth stocks can increase in value, they can also sink in value. To minimize the risk involved with these volatile stocks, invest in large growth stocks and hold them as part of the long-term section of your investment portfolio. Some growth stocks offer some pretty decent dividends, too.

REALLY?

When you are searching for a growth stock as a potential investment, check out the company's p/e ratio, which is its *price/earnings ratio*. This tells you whether the stock is overvalued or overpriced. As of December 31, 1994, the *average* p/e ratio on Wall Street is around 16. Obviously, the higher the p/e ratio, the more the stock has a potential to be overpriced. It is calculated simply by taking the price of the stock and dividing it by its earning per share. All brokers and other investment professionals should have this information. *Value Line Investment Survey*, which details company financials, is a great resource for this type of information.

➤ **Income stocks**   If making a steady income off your investments is more important to you than earning a large capital gain some-time down the road, consider investing in income (dividend-paying) stocks. Examples of these stocks include electric, gas, and telephone companies. Although income stocks tend to be less volatile than growth stocks (and don't have as much price appreciation at times), a stock with solid dividend increases can pay more over time than if you were to invest in bonds.

➤ **Growth and income stocks**   With these stocks, you can benefit from the price appreciation and also collect income through dividend payments. Some examples of growth and income stocks include DuPont, Emerson Electric, and Dun & Bradstreet. Growth and income stocks at times may not be able to capitulate on as much of a growth rate as some pure growth stocks.

Other types of stocks are available. These include *cyclical* stocks, which are considered to "ride the economic highway" because the companies involved depend on the state of the economy. *Initial public offerings* are another opportunity, though they can often be a bit risky because the company is a new publicly traded stock. There are also *penny stocks*, which trade for $5 a share or less.

The ideal situation would be to enter the stock market when it's rising and exit when it's falling, but it ain't that easy. All too often, small investors bail out after the market has started to fall and jump in after it has started to rise. Because the stock market movements are jerky, investors, particularly new ones, should always plan

To realize a profit from cyclical stocks, you must time your buys and sells carefully (or you can diversify your portfolio to help smooth out the ride). *Buy* cyclical stocks when their well has just about run dry but their situation can't get any worse (buy low), and *sell* cyclical stocks when they are enjoying record profits and everything seems hunky-dory (sell high).

on investing in stocks for the long-term—no jumping in and out. The bottom line? Unless you have a crystal ball and can predict the future of the market, investing in good, solid growth stocks will typically win hands-down over the long haul.

> REALLY?
>
> There are about a zillion financial newsletters offering stock recommendations and theories from gurus about the financial markets. The Select Information Exchange, (212) 247-7123, gives you a list of more than 50 different financial newsletters to choose from. They offer a package of 20 trial subscriptions for only $11.95. If you want more information about stocks that trade for $5 or less, check out *The Cheap Investor*, a newsletter published by Bill Matthews, who tracks this specific market of stocks. For more information, call (708) 830-5666 for subscription information. Additionally, if you're having trouble picking out a newsletter, contact the "newsletter of newsletters:" the *Hulbert Financial Digest*.

My Name Is Bond, U.S. Bond

Just like companies issue stock to raise money, companies can also raise money by issuing bonds. Stock, as you know, represents ownership in a company. Bonds, on the other hand, represent an IOU from the company to you. As a bond investor, you are *lending* your money to the corporation or government. This "loan" requires the bond issuer to pay you the amount borrowed plus interest over a stated period of time. Bond investments are also known as fixed-income investments because they typically pay interest to bondholders on a semi-annual basis. This interest is considered income, hence the name.

The following sections explain common bond jargon and the types of bonds available. Before you read on, however, learn the cardinal rule of investing in bonds:

Interest rates and bond prices move in directions opposite to each other.

Understanding Bond Jargon

When you invest in bonds, make sure you know the following:

➤ The *maturity date*, which is a fixed date when the amount of money borrowed by the company must be paid back to you. Although there is a stated maturity date, you don't have to hold it until maturity. You have a right to sell it whenever you want. (Hint: What you want to do is sell it for a profit—remember, "Buy low and sell high?")

➤ The amount of the original investment is the *face value* or the *par value*. This amount is equal to the amount of money you agreed to lend to the borrower/company. You can, however, buy bonds that are more than the face value—known as a *premium*—or less than a face value—known as a *discount*.

➤ In exchange for these companies borrowing your money, they promise to pay you back your *principal* plus interest. This interest is based on the bond's *coupon rate*, which is either a fixed rate that pays you the same amount of interest every year—typically every six months—or a floating rate, which fluctuates and is based on some pre-determined index.

You can always buy a bond and wait until maturity to get your money back. Or you can buy a bond and hope to sell it at a price higher than the one at which you bought it, even *before* its maturity date. This is practicing the art of buying low and selling high.

You see, even though bonds have a face value, they also have a *current market value,* which fluctuates. What determines the current market value? The current level of interest rates. Suppose you owned tens of thousands of dollars' worth of 30-year government bonds that were issued in the early 1980s with coupon rates averaging 13 percent—some even as high as 15 percent—that matured in 2010. These specific bonds are still earning that coupon rate/interest today, which makes them pretty attractive, considering the average coupon rate on long-term Treasury securities was between 7 to 7.83 percent as of December 31, 1994.

Because you own these attractive bonds that pay high rates of interest, other investors (like us) would be willing to pay you a higher price for those bonds. Why? Because right now (February 1995) we can only go out into the market and get 7.5 percent for the same type of bond. We'll sacrifice our dollars now to get that higher coupon rate.

Whether you practice the strategy of waiting until maturity or selling your bond before maturity out in the market, you should be aware of the *current yield* of a bond. The current yield is the return (expressed as a percentage) that the bond would earn in the current marketplace. To calculate this percentage, you divide the total market value of the bond by the annual interest payment, and multiply that total by 100.

Let's plug in some numbers. Suppose you bought a bond with a $1,000 face value and a 10 percent coupon rate at a price of 90. This means that you paid 90 percent of the face value of the bond. Because the bond has a face value of $1,000, the current market value is equal to $900 in this example. ($900 is the current market value. Depending on the direction of interest rates, this current value may be different *tomorrow*.) The annual interest paid on this bond is equal to the coupon rate multiplied by the face value, which would be $100 in this case (10% × $1,000). Your finished equation would be ($100 ÷ 900) × 100, which equals a current yield of 11.11 percent. The current market value depends on what interest rates are and the overall bond market.

If you decide to hold onto your bond until maturity, you should concern yourself with another type of yield: the *yield to maturity (YTM)*. This is a measure of the total return you can expect to earn if you hold the bond until maturity. It's difficult to calculate, but you should ask your broker what it is before you invest your money. In a nutshell, it takes compound interest into account!

Uncle Sam and Friends: Bond Types

When the government borrows money, it borrows from *you*, the investor. You invest your money in the debt instruments of the U.S. government, which are known as *Treasury bills*, *Treasury notes*, and *Treasury bonds*.

Each of these debt instruments has a reputation of being a safe investment because it is backed by the full faith and credit of the U.S. government. No other bond investment (with the exception of Ginnie-Mae securities, which are bonds issued by a government agency that pools mortgages together) can make this claim. In exchange for the degree of safety, Treasury investors receive lower interest rates than those on comparable bonds of different issuers.

Treasury bills are considered a discount security because of how they are issued. T-bills don't pay any interest. You purchase the security at a discount from its face value and at maturity you receive the full face value. The difference between the discount price you paid and what you receive at maturity is the interest payment. Treasury notes and bonds are different: They are considered coupon securities, pay interest semi-annually, and pay the face value at maturity. The interest you receive is federally taxable but exempt from state and local taxes.

Typically, the longer the time till maturity, the higher the coupon rate you will receive. Why? Because in exchange for having the use of your money for a longer period of time, the borrower is willing to pay you a higher rate. Here's how the length of maturities stack up for each Treasury security:

➤ **Treasury bills** are bought in maturity dates of three month, six month, and 1-year maturities. They are sold by the Treasury department at weekly auctions to all types of purchasers. Three and six-month T-bills are auctioned off every Monday, and 1-year T-bills are auctioned off every month. Minimum investment is $10,000.

➤ **Treasury notes**, typically issued in two- and five-year increments, are auctioned during the third week of every month. Minimum investment for two- and three-year T-notes is $5,000 although additional increments can be added.

➤ **Treasury bonds** have the longest maturities: 10 years on up. T-bonds are auctioned in February, May, August, and November. Minimum investment is $1,000.

Here's a quick rundown of the other types of bonds:

➤ **Municipal bonds.** The interest payments you receive on these government bonds are exempt from federal taxes. In fact, in some states, they're also exempt from state and local taxes.

➤ **Government agency bonds.** Even though these bond securities are issued by a government agency, they are NOT backed by the full faith and credit of the U.S. Government—just the issuing agency—and carry a "moral obligation." Depending on the agency, most minimum denominations are as high as $25,000 per bond. The three best-known agencies are Freddie Mac, Ginnie Mae, and Fannie Mae. Each was created to pool together a large quantity of mortgages and produce *mortgage-backed securities*. How do they do this? They purchase them from banks and savings and loans. These mortgage-backed securities offer higher yields (and thus more credit risk) than Treasuries. Even though these agencies are borrowing money from investors with the promise to pay them back on the maturity date plus interest, the interest income you receive can fluctuate.

Although tax-free bonds sound like the best deal for everyone, people in a tax bracket of 28 and 33 percent or more have the most to gain from this investment. If you're in a lower tax bracket, you could make more from corporate bonds. To evaluate the numbers for yourself, check out Chapter 24, "Tackling Taxes."

➤ **Zero-coupon bonds.** This type of bond gets its name because they are issued with no coupon rate at all. Zero-coupon bonds are issued by the Treasury department (Treasury zeros), corporations, municipalities, and government agencies. You buy these bonds at a deep discount from their face value. You make money off the increase in the bond price as it approaches maturity. Keep in mind, however, that even though you don't receive any semi-annual interest payments, you *are* taxed on these interest payments at all levels. Zero-coupon bonds are a great investment vehicle for planning long-term financial commitments, such as retirement and a child's college education expenses. (Check out Chapter 26 for details!)

➤ **Corporate bonds.** The biggest attraction of corporate bonds is the higher yields they offer—you may find they offer two more percentage points than a Treasury security of the same term. Of course, more risk is involved because they are not backed by the full faith and credit of the U.S. government. Minimum denominations? $1,000 face value per bond on up.

For the best review of the different types of bonds, read *The Complete Idiot's Guide to Making Money on Wall Street*—a definite must for investors!

➤ **Junk bonds.** A junk bond is simply a corporate bond that offers a higher yield. Technically, junk bonds pay such high rates of interest that the corporation may not earn enough money—either through sales or bottom-line profits—to cover the interest payments investors should receive every six months. That's why they're often called *high-yield bonds*. Note that you should be wary of credit risk. Follow the ratings given by S&P and Moody's, often quoted in sources like *The Wall Street Journal*. Junk bonds come from issuers who are less credit-worthy. There is a danger they could not repay the principal and interest during tough economic times.

Getting Started with Mutual Funds

Mutual funds allow investors to pool their money into a large fund organized by investment professionals. Investors own shares that represent stocks and bonds in several different companies. The number of shares you own depends on how much money you put in. The more you invest, the more shares you can buy. You don't need a trillion dollars to get started, either. Some mutual fund companies allow you to begin with as little as $25 a month. Plus, you can have access to your money all the time. And you can even invest in mutual funds that don't charge *any* sales charges. Mutual funds also tend to be less risky because they build on the idea of diversification.

If a mutual fund salesperson approaches you to invest in a company's mutual funds, ask what's in it for them. Does he or she receive a commission? Make sure you check out the company's performance history, going back five to ten years if possible.

Mutual funds come in two basic flavors. *Load funds* are those that charge you a sales commission. (Keep in mind, however, that just because a load is being charged does *not* mean you'll earn a better return.) *No-load funds* do not charge their shareholders any sales commissions, but other expenses are sometimes assessed, such as management fees or advertising expenses.

Table 19.2 shows a payoff comparison on a $1,000 investment in a no-load versus a load mutual fund. Assume a 12 percent return on a no-load fund versus a fund with an 8.5 percent load. As the table demonstrates, no-loads are usually the best way to go.

Table 19.2 No-Load Versus Load

Timing	No-load	Load	Difference
Investment less load	$1,000	$915	$85
Value at one year	$1,120	$1,025	$95
Value at five years	$1,762	$1,613	$149
Value at ten years	$3,106	$2,842	$264
Value at twenty years	**$9,646**	**$8,826**	**$820**

Source: Taken from *The Complete Idiot's Guide to Making Money on Wall Street*

When a No-Load Isn't a No-load

You know that if you buy a mutual fund through a broker, you will pay a commission—a load. You can buy a mutual fund directly from the company and not pay a load—a good, cost-effective move. But, some no-load mutual funds are not *pure* no-load funds; they can hit your pocketbook with some fees and charges. Some of these not-so-obvious fees are:

➤ *12b-1 fees* (also known as *12b-1 plans*) are charges that cover marketing and promotional costs. These fees range anywhere from .25 percent to 1 percent of the fund's total assets each year.

➤ *Expense ratios.* Typically expressed as a percentage of total investment, which shareholders pay for mutual fund operating expenses.

➤ *Fees for reinvesting your dividends.* These fees can really wallop your wallet. Make sure you ask your shareholder rep if this type of fee is involved. You want to avoid funds that charge it.

➤ *Management fees.* This pays for the portfolio manager job of managing the fund. Typical management fee expenses run about .5 percent.

➤ *Back-end load funds* have been hyped as no-load funds but are *not.* Even though all your money goes to work for you in the beginning when you invest, you get nicked with a "penalty load" if you withdraw your money before a certain time. The longer you keep your money invested in the fund, the less of a back-end load is assessed.

Because no-load doesn't always mean no-*fee*, you must be careful. Total cost of fees is deducted from the fund's earnings. One mutual fund company that touts its funds as no-load charges its shareholders up to 1.5 percent of their investments to open an account, stating it's a "portfolio reimbursement fee." Table 19.3 lists some other sneaky fees and the funds that go with them.

Table 19.3 Funds and Fees

Name of Fee	Amount	Funds Assessing Fee
Transaction	1 to 3% of investment	Five Vanguard Funds*
Portfolio transaction	.25% of investment	Vanguard Index Total Stock Market
Account opening/ close-out	$5 to $75	Would you believe 29 funds total?
Portfolio reimbursement	1.5% of investment	Four DFA funds (foreign funds)

* Vanguard's Emerging Markets portfolio charges 2 percent when you buy into the fund and 1 percent when you sell. Four other Vanguard funds—International Equity Pacific, Extended Market, Small Cap, and International Equity Index—each charge 1 percent up front.

One final note: All this talk about no-load fees may make you believe a broker who tries to tell you that the marketing costs and other expenses associated with the fund are "really" what keep no-loads from being no-loads. Teach the lug something new: explain that *no-load means there are no sales commissions.* And then steer clear of the sales pitch. You can do your own homework and save hundreds of dollars
in commissions!

Mutual Fund Selection Secrets

Keep the following factors in mind when selecting a mutual fund:

➤ **Select no-load funds whose objectives coincide with your own.** Are you looking for growth? Income? Or both? You can narrow your mutual fund search by matching the investment objective of mutual funds available to your own investment objectives. For example, if you are a Nervous Nellie who can't sleep a wink because of the ups and downs in the stock market, don't plunk down all your money in an emerging market fund that invests solely in Third World countries.

➤ **Look for mutual funds that can provide at least a 3- to-5-year track record.** You should be able to select your mutual funds based on performance history. Five-year track records will tell you how well (or poorly) the fund did in a variety of environments— when interest rates were high or low, when the stock market was up or down, and when our economy was in an inflationary period or a recession. For a quick review of economic cycles, look at Chapter 12.

➤ **You don't have to limit yourself to just one type of mutual fund.** Even though a mutual fund offers diversification, you can invest in more than one. Fifty? Well, forget it. The experts would label that as mutual fund overkill. You can diversify your mutual fund portfolio by choosing a growth fund, an income fund, an international fund, and perhaps a bond fund. If you divide your money among three or four different types of stock funds, you'll always have some money invested in the most profitable sector of the market.

➤ **Buying last year's biggest winner is foolish.** Don't even think about it. Maybe the portfolio manager got lucky. Instead, stick with a fund that is a steady performer instead of moving in and out of funds trying to catch the waves.

➤ **Enroll in an automatic investment plan with at least one of your mutual funds.** This program's awareness is increasing in the world of the wee investor. As little as $30 a month can be electronically debited and transferred from your bank account to your mutual fund account. Because you are doing this on a regular basis, you can take advantage of any dips in the share price. This is known as *dollar-cost averaging*.

Where to Go for More Info

If you're in the market to invest in mutual funds, several sources of performance information are available. Only, with more than four-thousand mutual funds to choose from, how can you cut through the murk?

One option is to check out *Morningstar Mutual Funds*, a twice-monthly newsletter published by Morningstar, Inc. It is considered to

For those cyber-space junkies out there, America Online makes available Morning-star's information on the mutual funds it covers.

be the most informative and user-friendly survey of mutual fund performance, covering almost 1300 funds total. *Morningstar* rates each fund with a star rating system on a scale of 0 to 5; five stars is the highest honor given to a mutual fund. Each fund receives a star (or no stars) depending on a combination of past performance and the risks involved. The newsletter is available on a three-month trial basis for $55—and it's free at your local library reference desk. A dozen newsletters are published by Morningstar, so to find one that fits what you're looking for, call toll-free anywhere in the U.S. (800) 876-5005 or write to Morningstar, Inc., 225 W. Wacker Drive, Chicago, IL 60606.

CDA Weisenberger is a rating service that tracks performance on almost 4,600 mutual funds in its reports *The Mutual Fund Report* and *The Mutual Fund Update*. These reports are updated monthly and are available in a newsletter report format or in a software package. Call (800) 232-2285 or write to CDA Weisenberger, 1355 Piccard Drive, Rockville, MD 20850 for more information.

The *Value Line Mutual Fund Investment Survey* also tracks performance information on two thousand mutual funds, providing in-depth coverage and analyst's opinions on the equity of each and fixed-income mutual funds for subscribers. This report is also available in your local library, but if you would like more information about subscription rates, call (800) 284-7607.

Standard & Poor/Lipper Mutual Fund Profiles is a quarterly survey, evaluating past performance on the 800 largest load and no-load mutual funds. The cost is $132 for an annual subscription (that's four reports), and additional subscription information is available if you call (212) 208-8000.

One Last Word About Loads

Just when you thought you knew the difference between a load and a no-load fund, a new twist to the load fund industry develops.

Load funds, as you know, average a 4 percent sales fee. But, depending on what load fund it is, the 4 percent load may not be charged at the same time. Many times, when you buy a load fund—and we're not recommending that you necessarily do so—the fund company offers Class A, Class B, and Class C shares. As if the industry wasn't complicated enough!

Class A shares are front-end loads—meaning when you invest $1,000 in a 4 percent load fund, your $40 is automatically taken out before it's invested. The sales fee was charged at the beginning—the "front"—of your investment. Class B shares assess a 1 percent annual charge to your account—that's its sales fee. Class C shares are back-end loads, so the load is charged when you sell.

The bottom line? Stick with no-load funds for the least costly investment strategy.

Futures and Options for High Rollers

When you invest in futures and options, you must be prepared for a bumpy ride. The futures and options market is not for the amateur investor. You can make a lot of money in these financial markets, but you could also lose more than your shirt.

Betting on the Futures

The best way to describe what futures are is to look on the shelves or in the freezer of your neighborhood grocery store. Orange juice, wheat, sugar, and corn, to name a few, make up the products that investors "bet" on in the futures market.

Unlike stock, bonds, and mutual funds, there is no ownership or IOUs—just exponential rewards if you win big—but you have to know how to play the game. A *future* is simply a contract in which a "preselling" of the commodity is taking place at an agreed-upon price today for delivery in the future. Each delivery date is different because they are pre-set by the financial futures exchange. The months in which the contracts expire are known as the *spot months*.

The people who do not own the underlying commodity, but rather, bet on the rise and fall in the commodity prices, are known as

Investing in commodity funds takes a big chunk out of your initial investment because of the high commissions that these portfolio managers earn. But that's not all; additional fees—sometimes as high as 6 percent of managed assets—are assessed. That's on top of high commissions, sometimes as much as 10 percent. This type of investment is for high rollers who have the money to invest and don't mind the ups and downs of the futures market.

speculators. As a speculator, you try to achieve a profit from the ups and downs in the price of the contract. Speculators invest in futures contracts either to buy goods they do not want or to sell goods they have no intention of delivering. If you own the underlying commodity (like a farmer who owns his wheat crop and is trying to sell it) you are known as a *hedger*. The floor traders at the exchange are known as *scalpers*.

Even though you are not obligated to come up with a lot of start-up money to invest—usually about 5 to 10 percent of the contract's value—it doesn't make the futures market any less risky. In fact, if your contract is dropping in value, you may have to put up additional money to keep your position—definitely not an investment for the beginner!

If you're interested in the futures market but don't want to risk as much money, you may want to invest in mutual funds that invest in commodities. These are called *commodity funds* or *futures pools*, and there have been some surprising profits in these. The performance of these pools varies widely from fund to fund and from year to year. Usually, they will do well when the markets move sharply upward or downward and the pools are invested on the side that will profit.

If you want more information about the different commodity funds available to you, contact the newsletter that tracks the commodity funds industry: *Managed Account Reports*. For a sample copy, call (212) 213-6202.

Know Your Options

If you want to protect your investments, consider dabbling in the options market. Options, like futures, have an expiration date and can help protect your portfolio. *Call options* allow investors the right—but not the obligation—to buy the underlying security (typically stock) at a set price (the strike price) for a particular period of time. *Put options*, on the other hand, give you the right—yet not the obligation—to sell the underlying security at a set price for a particular period of time.

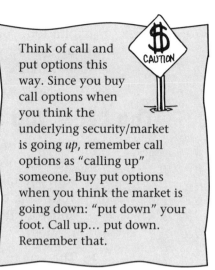

Think of call and put options this way. Since you buy call options when you think the underlying security/market is going *up*, remember call options as "calling up" someone. Buy put options when you think the market is going down: "put down" your foot. Call up... put down. Remember that.

Many times put options are used if you are feeling bearish and expect to profit from falling stock prices or to protect your investment portfolio, kind of like insurance. Let's say you own 100 shares of XYZ Company stock. You hear rumors that third-quarter earnings reports are not expected to be all that great, so you're worried about the stock price taking a hit because of the news. Instead of selling all your shares (because, of course, you are investing for *long-term* price appreciation, no matter what bumps happen along the way) you can purchase insurance. The price drop is just short-term, so you don't want to sell your stock, but you still need to protect your shares against any decline.

To protect your position, you could cushion the blow in case XYZ company stock price drops. Here's how. Assume you bought XYZ Company stock at $25 a share a few years ago. The current price is $36, but you've noticed it starting to pull back a bit. Instead of selling your shares, you can buy a put option (*not* a call option) because it will give you the right to *sell* 100 shares of XYZ stock at whatever the strike price is—no matter what the current trading price is.

Plug in some numbers. If you bought an XYZ put option with a strike price of 30 for $200 (quoted as $2)—which is the *premium*—and the XYZ stock price falls to 30 or below, you have two choices:

➤ You have the right to *exercise* (sell) your option by selling your shares of your underlying XYZ stock for $30 a share, no matter what the current stock price is.

➤ You can hold onto your underlying stock and "close the position"—meaning, sell your put option. If you did this, you would make a profit because your put option would be *in-the-money*. It has to hit the price of 30 and keep going down for you to be *in-the-money*. If, however, the option never dropped to 30 before expiration, your option would expire worthless. Your loss? The total amount you paid for the option, which is the premium. But it's insurance, so consider yourself protected!

The Least You Need to Know

➤ If you want to make money on Wall Street, first you have to know what your investment profile is. Make sure you take into consideration your risk tolerance, your financial goals (and dreams!), your tax exposure, and your time horizon (which is when you need the money).

➤ The way to make money in investing is to buy low and sell high.

➤ You can make a good return off growth stocks if you invest for the long term.

➤ Interest rates and bond prices move in opposite directions.

➤ Mutual funds usually involve less risk because your investments are diversified. Make sure you look for a no-load fund that doesn't involve a lot of extra fees.

➤ Futures and options are not for the faint of heart.

Chapter 20

Ten Smart Money Moves You Should Make NOW

In This Chapter

➤ Pay yourself first

➤ Making money the old-fashioned way

➤ Don't just buy—diversify!

If you're a fan of late-night television, you've probably heard of David Letterman's "Top Ten List." Our list isn't as kooky, but it will help you make your money work as hard for you as you do for it. This chapter takes the knowledge you've gleaned from previous chapters and helps you turn the top ten strategies into the money-making secrets of your life.

1. Pay Yourself First

In Part 1 of this book, you learned how to make the decision to manage your money more effectively, get out of debt, and set up a personal financial plan that will enable you to reach your financial goals. So what is the common denominator among the three?

You!

You are learning about personal financial planning and investing for yourself—not your neighbor, your Uncle Moe, or your Great-Aunt Bertha. You are adapting new—and smart!—financial habits that will help you reach your financial goals. But the most important habit is to pay yourself first.

Treat yourself as if you were a monthly bill. Call it the "Pay Yourself First" category. By doing so, you begin to practice the art of self-discipline. By earmarking your personal "bill," you are creating your financial future without even realizing it.

There is one requirement: Do it before Friday night out with the boys, your daughter's Girl Scout dues, or monthly health club dues. Pay yourself every time you get paid. This money doesn't have to be a lot—even $10 a paycheck will do it. Ten dollars a week is forty dollars a month. Forty dollars a month for twelve months is $480. Take this money, whatever the amount, and invest it. You have a number of options available to you, as you learned in Chapter 19.

2. Shop Around for Your Bank

Why include a Top Ten Tip about banking? Because banking is an integral part of your overall financial plan. Because banking in the 90s is plagued with exorbitant fees and charges, a smart money move is to shop around for your bank.

It sounds as easy as pie, but few people realize how much money they're paying these rich cats in blue suits. Shop around! Heck, you kick a few tires when you buy a new car—and that's not even an investment (it almost never goes *up* in value)! Why pay a bank an extra charge if you're a left-handed welder or if you wear your hair in a bun? Okay, we're exaggerating. But these tips will help you reduce some of your expenses, and that will enable you to put more of your money to work for you in your investment game plan. For more information about the banking industry, have another look at Part 2.

Keep these points in mind when shopping for a bank:

➤ Look for free checking. It shouldn't have a monthly maintenance fee; there should be no penalty fee if you drop below a certain balance, and no transaction fee—no matter how many checks you write.

➤ Don't go with a bank that charges "foreign" ATM transaction fees. (Not those in Versailles, France, but those at a rival teller across the street.)

➤ Skip the bank that hits your account with an activity fee. Some of us aren't big check writers. Instead, if you write fewer than three checks per month, opt for a Money Market Account. More interest!

➤ Look for low bounced-check fees. This is a killer. Even if you don't bounce any checks, there are times when you may deposit some-one *else's* check and it will bounce—and *you'll* get hit with the $22 charge!

3. Do Your Homework

Ask anybody for advice—believe us, they'll give it to you. Everyone loves to hear himself talk, especially if it's about a hot investment he made a bundle on. Asking for advice is okay, but you can't bet the farm on it. What you can do is your homework. That includes subscribing to a few investment newsletters that offer advice from some Wall Street professionals.

But there's a problem. There are a ZILLION newsletters out there with editors touting their latest recommendations—and not all of them work. So how can you tell the best from the rest? In Chapter 4, we paved the way through the money jungle to get you started. One recommendation was to follow *The Hulbert Digest*, a monthly compilation of the good, the bad, and the ugly in the newsletter business. But now it's time for a more advanced strategy that will enable you to save a few bucks and sample, sample, sample!

Contact Select Information Exchange at (212) 247-7124; for only $11.95 you get a package of *twenty* different financial newsletters. Once you choose which newsletters you want, call the newsletter company and ask for *next month's* issue as a sample or free copy. If they won't provide one, see how much their trial subscription costs.

Also, review the financial TV programs and magazines listed in Chapter 4 as additional resources for research.

4. Dollar-Cost Average Your Way to Wealth

This is how you make money the old-fashioned way. Slowly. Dollar-cost averaging is a smart investment strategy. All you do is make fixed regular investments in a stock or any type of mutual fund—even if the market is rising or falling. This strategy works in your favor no matter what the market does.

When you dollar-cost average, you have a variety of choices—including all different types of mutual funds and stocks, such as in a dividend reinvestment program. No matter which investments you choose to dollar-cost average your way into, make sure you choose your investment on the basis of your financial goals, your risk-comfort level, and your age.

For example, when you buy shares in an equity mutual fund and the price rises, you buy fewer shares. When the price falls, however, you buy *more* shares. Plus, over the long haul, the average cost of your share will be less than the average price or market price when you sell.

You can start with $100. One hundred dollars a month, invested over a 12-month period, is $1,200. Easy enough. But oh, how it can grow. You'll be amazed at how $200 a month can grow, too. If you want to see how dollar-cost averaging is practiced, look at Table 20.1.

Table 20.1   How to Get There from Here

Time of Investment	Amount of Investment	Price Per Share	How Much Do I Own?
January 15	$200	$10	20.00
February 15	$200	$12.50	36.00
March 15	$200	$14	50.29
April 15	$200	$13	65.67
May 15	$200	$13	81.05
June 15	$200	$ 9	103.27
July 15	$200	$10	123.27
August 15	$200	$11.25	141.05

Time of Investment	Amount of Investment	Price Per Share	How Much Do I Own?
September 15	$200	$13.50	155.86
October 15	$200	$15	169.19
November 15	$200	$14.50	182.98
December 15	$200	$14	197.27
Total number of shares:		197.27	
Total Investment:		$2,400.00	
Total Value of Portfolio:		$2,761.78	
Net Profit:		$ 361.78	

And that's just for one year! It's never too late to start an investment program by dollar-cost averaging. And it works! If you dollar-cost averaged your way to wealth by investing in the Dow Jones Industrial Average beginning at its highest peak in 1929 (before the Crash) and purchased at the *highest* price every year until the mid-1960s, you would still be rewarded more than *300 percent* on your money.

5. Don't Just Buy—Diversify!

By allocating your money into several different investments, you reduce your risk. Think of it this way: If you put one dozen eggs into one basket, and a few in another, and so on, and then you drop one basket, only a few are cracked and the others are intact.

To see how this theory works with investing, pretend you have $10,000 to invest. You've done your homework and have come up with a beauty of an investment: a company stock that created the gadget that takes the salt out of the ocean. You found they have great management, their good-debt-versus-bad-debt ratio is healthy, and historical performance numbers are appealing. You sink all of your $10,000 into this stock and wait for it to take off.

And boy, does it! Two years later, the stock has increased by 50 percent. You have roughly $16,000—including reinvested dividends. And then tragedy strikes. The company president jumps ship, the money they lent to that small country off the coast of Chile *won't* be repaid, and earnings estimates are seven times below Wall Street's expectations. The stock drops 25 percent in value in one day, and another 25 percent the next. Your eggs are smashed to pieces!

That's where the beauty of diversification comes in. Financial research shows that if you own 20 to 25 stocks, you won't get burned by one bad investment.

Let's use another example. If you take that $10,000 and split it up among several types of equity mutual funds (growth or aggressive growth), an international equity mutual fund, and maybe a short-term bond fund, you will reduce your risk, especially if one fund zigs while the others zag. This is practicing the art of diversification!

6. Invest as Much as You Can in a Retirement Account

This may be the biggest, most overlooked secret. Of all the retirement programs available to Americans, only 60 percent of Americans admit to contributing to some type of retirement savings program. Why?

Because they want instant gratification. Save money for the future? B-O-R-I-N-G. Put an extra $100 bucks in a savings account to earn 23 cents? Big deal. Credit cards, however, have cured short-term boredom, enticing men and women to charge now and pay later. Unfortunately, this bad habit dissuades us from socking away any money for the future because we're trying to climb out of debt today.

Turn your thoughts of instant gratification upside down by knowing that money inside a retirement account—such as a 401(k) plan, a company pension plan, or an IRA—grows and compounds *without* getting hit by Uncle Sam. The only time you pay taxes is when you take the money out, which is when you're typically in a lower income-tax bracket anyway.

The benefits? If you save $2,000 a year at six percent for 30 years in a regular savings account, you'll have close to $120,900 after paying taxes. However, if you sheltered your $2,000 each year in your IRA at six percent, your savings increases to almost $168,000 because of the tax-deferred feature.

7. Build a Portfolio of Mutual Funds

Investing in more than one mutual fund is a great way to diversify your portfolio. But the question always remains: How many mutual funds is too many? Like a nervous five-year-old taking swimming lessons for the very first time, just getting your feet wet is a better beginning than jumping straight into the deep end.

Getting your feet wet doesn't necessarily mean putting all of your money in low-risk mutual funds. That strategy would not be practicing diversification, and you wouldn't be lowering your risk. Low-risk funds may have a lot in cash periodically, which may not be what you want when you diversify. You lower your risk by mixing stock funds, bond funds, U.S. and overseas funds, and money market funds. Diversification offers the idea that a gain in one fund offsets losses in another. In financial mumbo jumbo, you should create a portfolio of funds that have a low "core correlation" with one another.

The first step is to look at your whole investment picture; decide what you're trying to achieve. Make these goals reachable—not astronomical. Next, set parameters to determine how much money you can afford to lose and how much money you plan on keeping "liquid" (safe). This will help you decide how risk-tolerant you are. Sorry, folks, but a lot of the players in the mutual fund industry don't do enough to inform or protect the investor against the risks associated with fund investing. Your goal is to look for the highest return with the lowest risk.

Of course, the higher the reward, the greater the risks. A good way to follow mutual funds to see how they rate on risk is to read *Morningstar Mutual Funds* (800/876-5005); a three-month trial subscription is $55, but it is probably available in your local library. Experts tell us that people should be educated about risk. If you think you're going to lose 100 percent of your money and stick it in a money market fund that earns *less* than inflation, that's just as bad as investing in a fund with a 20 percent fluctuation rate!

Your age will also determine your selection of mutual funds. If you're fairly young, you can be more aggressive in your investment approach. Keep 70 to 80 percent in aggressive investments, such as growth and aggressive-growth mutual funds. Pre-retirees should still maintain a portion of their mutual fund portfolio in growth investments, though they should pull back to allocation percentages around 40 percent. Balance the remaining 60 percent between safer investments—for example, a small percent in money market and some in growth and income funds.

> The last thing a retired person should be doing is experimenting, especially with growth funds. Only 20 percent should be allocated to that category. You can balance the remaining amount with 20 to 30 percent in growth and income funds and the rest in income funds and money market funds.

8. Consider DRIPs

A DRIP stands for *dividend reinvestment program*. Its theory is that if you drop a little bit of money on a steady, consistent basis into stocks—paying little to no commissions—you'll benefit from dollar cost averaging through a DRIP program.

DRIPs build wealth slowly through accumulating small shares of a stock, enabling you to bypass a stockbroker and high commissions. If the company does charge a fee, it's quite nominal. In fact, around 100 of the 1,200 companies that offer DRIPs offer investors the advantage of purchasing company stock at discounts of three percent to 10 percent below the current market price of the stock.

It only takes a few bucks to get you started and as little as $10 for *optional cash payments*, which allow you to purchase additional shares. What if the stock is trading at $60 and you want to send in $30? No problem. You will receive a fraction of a share—in this case, half a share. These fractional shares continue to build, along with your future OCPs, and you receive that fractional part of the dividend.

Typically, you must be a shareholder of record (you must own at least one share) to enroll in a DRIP. This share must be registered in your name, not the brokerage firm's name, and the certificate must be sent to you. Once you receive the certificate, contact the shareholder services department at the company that offers the DRIP program—not all companies do— to enroll.

Buy this one share at a deep discount brokerage firm so you can save almost 70 percent in commission and avoid full-service brokers.

To find out which companies offer DRIPs—and those companies that are now joining the No-Load Stock sector, which allows investors the opportunity to go *directly* to the company, no initial share certificate needed—subscribe to the bible of the DRIP industry, *The Drip Investor*. For more information, call (219) 931-6480.

9. If You Don't Need the Full-Service, Use a Discount Broker

Full-service brokers will charge you up to $4 just for sending you a trade confirmation. Makes the increase in postal rates look miniscule by comparison, doesn't it? Like banks, full-service brokers may charge you an inactivity fee of close to $50 if you do not generate at least $100 in commissions in one year. And—get this—account holders can get penalized with a $50 maintenance fee just for having the account. That's like paying someone $50 a year just so they can hold onto *your* money. No way, José!

Instead of the full-service broker, opt for a discount broker. You still get research reports—but no advice. And no ghastly fees, either! The dynamic trio of full-service brokerage firms are Quick & Reilly (800/672-7220), Charles Schwab & Company (800/435-5000), and Fidelity Investments (800/544-8888).

10. Go Global... But Watch the Risks

We live in a global economy. Many of the products we buy are imported. Many U.S. companies have more than half of their revenue generated from overseas sales. Socking away a portion of your investment dollars—no matter how old you are—to invest in world financial markets is a common investment strategy in the '90s, and it can be *very* rewarding. But there are some short-term *and* long-term ups and downs. Citing a short-term example, in 1993, international mutual fund investors celebrated an average 40 percent return. But there are also some major blows that world financial markets have dealt to investors. In the 1970s, many funds invested in Mexico lost 75 percent of their value.

Allocating a portion of your investment portfolio to international (non-U.S. companies) or global (both overseas and U.S. companies) investing is a smart move, as long as you do two things:

➤ Understand the biggest risk involved with international and global investing: currency risk.

➤ Maintain a long-term time frame for your international and global investments (at least five years).

It used to be that the all the world's currency exchange rates were tied to the U.S. dollar. But that was eliminated in the early 1970s, which created currency risk if you were to invest or exchange your money for local currency abroad. Currency risk is simply the risk involved when you convert foreign currency back into dollars or into other currencies. The reason this is risky is because the rate at which the currency is calculated (converted) is determined by current state of world economies. If France is in a recession, their francs may be worth more (or less) in U.S. dollars, depending on how our economy is doing and vice-versa.

For example, if you're an American tourist in Japan, you will quickly learn that the number of Japanese yen you get for $1,000 may be different tomorrow than it is today. That's because the currency fluctuates in value, and when put into the conversion process, your end result (how much yen you get for your American dollars) will change.

But that doesn't mean you should keep all of your money in the good ol' USA. It would be a mistake to avoid investing abroad, since so many investments, such as mutual funds, have made it so easy to do so. You should, however, still monitor your international and global investments, and add international or global funds (because of the diversification) to a portfolio of U.S. stock and bond funds. This strategy helps reduce how much money the entire portfolio will lose in today's global economy. So before you park your pesos overseas, make sure you do your homework!

Also, stashing your cash in foreign markets is a long-term process. That's why if you want to iron out the volatility you should plan for the long haul. Ask yourself how long you can leave that money there. If you need it right away, stick your money into a less aggressive investment. Overseas investing is not for short-term investors.

The Least You Need to Know

➤ *Pay yourself first!* Before any other financial obligation, allocate a small portion to an investment for yourself and your financial future.

➤ Investing in several different investment products is a good way to reduce your risk. This is called *diversifying your portfolio*. Just make sure the investments coincide with your objectives.

➤ Stay informed about your investments. That means doing your homework!

➤ Investing in retirement accounts will help you plan for tomorrow. Plus, it's a smart financial strategy because tomorrow will be here before you know it. Just do it!

WHOOOOO!!!

Chapter 21

Investment Strategies for Seniors

In This Chapter

➤ Learn when you do—and don't—need Social Security benefits

➤ Income strategies you should start thinking about now

➤ Getting a lift from special banking services for seniors

➤ The clout you get with AARP

Imagine being 65 years old and living on $22,000, with almost a third coming from Social Security benefits. Many of you might spout off, "Oh, that's not going to happen to me!"—yet it's a very real statistic for the 13 million seniors who live on that type of fixed income. So ask yourself: Can you live on that?

Seniors—and those who one day will be (which is all of us!)—need to arm themselves with some sound money strategies for retirement years. Even if you're only 25 years old, learning these money tricks for seniors *now* can help shape your financial tomorrows.

This chapter goes beyond the traditional money strategy for seniors: Certificates of Deposit. Seniors are so used to investing in super-safe CDs that anything that doesn't work or look like a CD scares them. But if they want more income, they've got to allocate a portion of their investment planning to something a little more complicated than a super-safe CD. This doesn't mean it's not safe—it just has different characteristics. This chapter will give you some super-smart financial strategies for seniors—and for those who one day will be seniors!

Social Security Secrets

It's no secret: rumors of the depletion of the Social Security fund in about 20 to 30 years are nothing new. But government funding could change. Whether Social Security is here or not, don't consider benefits to be your only means of paying for your living expenses. Studies indicate that average-wage earners can expect Social Security benefits to replace 42 percent of their income—and those are today's figures. What about tomorrow?

> REALLY?
>
> As you work and pay FICA taxes, you earn Social Security credits. The number of credits needed for retirement benefits depends on your date of birth. If you were born January 2, 1929 or later, you need a total of 40 credits. In 1995, workers earn one credit for each $630 in wages, or four credits for earnings of more than $2,520. Extra credits, however, do not increase your benefits.

To learn the secrets of the Social Security system—and to make the most of your benefits—be informed, but don't let Social Security be the end to your means. Following are a few tips that will help you get the most out of your Social Security benefits when the time comes.

Secret #1: No Matter How Old You Are, Get an Idea of What Your Retirement Benefits Are NOW

Call the Social Security Administration's toll-free line (800/772-1213) and ask for an *Earnings and Benefit Estimate Statement*. The SSA will send you a form asking you how much you earned last year, your estimated earnings for this year, the age you plan to retire, and your estimated future annual earnings.

Based on this information, you'll get a complete earnings history, along with estimates of your benefits for retirement at age 62, 65, or 70. It includes estimates of disability or survivor's benefits and lists total Social Security taxes you have already paid.

Secret #2: Verify Your Social Security Record Every Three Years

Make sure all the taxes you have paid are credited to your account. Errors identified early are easier to correct. If you happen to run across an error, have your past tax returns and pay stubs available for proof.

Secret #3: Delay Retirement and You'll Increase Your Social Security Benefits

Age 65 is considered to be full-retirement age for receiving full benefits. Benefits are reduced if you retire sooner and collect them; they are increased if you delay retirement. You can start collecting benefits at age 62, but check out Table 21.1, which shows how it pays off to retire later.

Table 21.1 How Early Retirement Reduces Your Benefits (For Retired Workers Born Before 1938)

Retirement Age	% Reduction in Benefits	Benefit if Full Benefit Is		
		$600	$850	$1,100
65	0%	$600	$850	$1,100
64 1/2	3 1/3%	$580	$822	$1,063
64	6 2/3%	$560	$793	$1,027
63 1/2	10%	$540	$765	$ 990
63	13 1/3%	$520	$737	$ 953
62 1/2	16 2/3%	$500	$708	$ 917
62	20%	$480	$680	$ 880

It may pay to wait if you…

➤ have sufficient financial resources and do not need Social Security benefits to meet living expenses.

➤ earn so much from your income that it triggers a tax on your Social Security benefits.

➤ earn so much from your income that you will lose benefits due to an earnings limit.

You may be better off using your savings or investments for living expenses. By spending your savings, you'll have less interest income to push benefits into the taxable range. Plus, waiting to collect Social Security will mean bigger benefit checks in the future. The following scenarios may help you understand how to determine when the best time is to start collecting your Social Security benefits.

Scenario #1: Milton, age 64, was forced to take early retirement. Currently, he receives $1,800 a month in pension benefits and about $650 a month from his well-established investment portfolio; his asset allocation is spread among stocks, bonds, and CDs. Plus, his home and car are all paid for. Even though he's 64, he hasn't applied for Social Security. If the total $2,450 he receives in monthly income covers his living expenses, he's done a smart thing—delayed his Social Security benefits today as a way to possibly increase his future benefits.

What he could do: He's doing the right thing. He should, however, contact the Social Security office to receive a copy of his estimated benefits now and when he turns 65.

Scenario #2: Norman and Merna, ages 64 and 62, are approaching retirement and are toying with applying for benefits. Norman has had commission-only sales jobs all of his working life, and,unfortunately, has no retirement benefits from any of his jobs. Merna works part-time and also has no retirement benefits. Their combined salaries are almost $55,000, and they have worked hard at accumulating almost $100,000 in their IRA.

What they could do: Even though Norman is approaching 65, his salary alone almost makes up the total $55,000—wiping out Social Security benefits. No reason for him to apply yet. What about Merna? Because she works part-time, she could file now because she is eligible to receive a year's worth of benefits.

Scenario #3: Sheila just turned 62, and wants to know if she should take her early retirement. She's married to Lester, who retired at age 63 from his job. Currently they both receive pension benefits of $2,200 a month, Social Security benefits (from Lester) of $700 a month, and about $1,500 a month in investment income from their retirement nest-egg. As his wife, she could start collecting benefits on the basis of on her husband's work record (there are special spousal rules—check with the SSA). They don't really need the extra income, but the couple hundred extra bucks per month would allow them to play a lot more Bingo games and take dance lessons at the local Y.

What they could do: Because she's only 62, Sheila would be better off waiting until she turns 65. Why? Because the extra money per month would put them over the income limit and subject a substantial percent of their Social Security benefits to taxes.

Whatever your situation, understanding the quirks and rules involved with applying for Social Security benefits will only make the system work for you. After all, you'll be working for it for quite a long time, right?

The $64,000 Question: How Can Seniors Earn More Income?

Average-wage earners can expect Social Security benefits to replace only 42 percent of their monthly income, according to the Social Security Administration. (Maximum-wage earners can expect benefits to replace 28 percent of their income.) So where can you get the remaining 58 percent if you're an average-wage earner?

Don't count on bonuses, commissions, stock options, severance pay, or even vacation pay. These all chalk up to income that will count toward the Social Security earnings limit—which can eventually reduce your Social Security benefits. That's why the following income sources are so important—they don't count toward the earnings limit.

Typically, pensions from jobs where you paid Social Security taxes will not affect your benefits. However, pensions from government jobs may reduce your benefits. If you are a government employee/retiree, check to see which rules apply to your situation. Call the Social Security Administration at (800) 772-1213.

➤ Pensions and retirement funds

➤ Investments (unless you are in the brokerage business)

➤ Individual Retirement Accounts (IRAs)

➤ Social Security and other types of government benefits

➤ Annuities and some tax-exempt trust funds

➤ Rental properties

➤ Gifts or inheritances and lottery winnings

➤ Money received from a reverse mortgage plan

So even if you've built up a sizeable IRA and take distributions from it as a source of income, you don't have to fret about not getting your full Social Security benefits. The following sections explain ways you can boost your income.

REALLY?

If you decide to supplement your Social Security benefits by working, your benefits can be reduced. The *earnings limits*, as of January 1, 1995, are:

Under age 65:	$8,160	For every $2 over that amount, $1 is held for benefits.
Age 65–69:	$11,280	For every $3 over the limit, $1 is held for benefits.
Age 70+:		You can earn an unlimited amount of extra wages with no reduction in benefits.

The rule of thumb is that if you are between age 65 and 69, $1 is deducted from your Social Security benefits for every $3 you earn above the earnings limit.

Boosting Your Income

Similar to the concept of a home equity loan or line of credit, the *reverse mortgage* allows seniors over the age of 62 to withdraw money that doesn't have to be repaid unless you sell the house and move or you die (different rules apply, depending on which state you live in). What's the catch? Well, you must fully own the home or have only a small mortgage balance left over.

How much can you get? That depends on your age, the current market value of your home, current interest rates, and the program you choose. Plus, you can use the money for whatever your heart desires. What you do is withdraw monthly checks while you still live in your home and hold the title to it.

Sounds inviting, huh? Take the equity built up in your home and turn it into a steady stream of income! It's not a newfangled idea. Here's how reverse mortgages work. Borrowers typically draw between 30 and 80 percent of their home equity in the form of a schedule of fixed monthly payments or a line of credit. The borrower agrees to repay the balance if he or she moves.

Because many lenders base life expectancies on outrageous calculations, be careful of the fees and interest charges so they don't leave you high and dry.

What to do: Question the loan terms to make sure they equal the life-expectancy rates they use. This way you probably won't use all the equity in your house before you move or pass away.

So what about repayment if you move or die? It is secured by a first trust deed on your home. The lender is then repaid from the proceeds of the sale.

There are three types of FHA-insured reverse mortgages you can choose from:

➤ **The Line of Credit Plan**   In this type of reverse mortgage, you can take out money at any time. It is the most flexible because you sign up for a line of credit. As you get older, the line of credit increases.

➤ **The Term Plan**   Here, you decide how many years of payments you want to receive. The shorter the term, the higher the payments. When the term is over, your monthly payments cease. When the term is up, you don't have to repay the "loan" until you sell the home or you die and your heirs repay it out of your home equity.

➤ **The Tenure Plan**   You will receive a fixed monthly "loan" amount for as long as you live in that same house, until you die. This house must be considered your principal residence.

But reverse mortgages don't come for free, folks. Up-front costs include closing costs, plus a "fee" from one to two percent of the home's market value. Wait—there's more. Insurance premiums tack on about 2 percent of the home's value, plus an added .5 percent that's added to the interest rate on your loan. Sure, you can finance all of this, but to really see if it's worth it, have your lender work it out *in simple English* on paper. The following is an example of how a reverse mortgage might work.

You own your house, which was just appraised at $150,000. Since you need additional monthly income, you decide to take out a reverse mortgage on the equity in your home. If you have a $150,000 home, you'd pay two percentage points (or $3,000) in insurance fees, another two percentage points ($3,000) in an origination fee, and another $1,500 for appraisals and closing costs.

Home value	$150,000
Insurance fees	$3,000
Origination fee	$3,000
Appraisals and closing costs	$1,500
Total amount to close the "loan"	$6,500

To get more information about reverse mortgage loans, contact one of the following organizations:

➤ Phone the FHA at (800) 732-6643 to find federally insured lenders in your area.

➤ Send $1 to NCHEC Locator, 1210 E. College, #300, Marshall, MN 56528.

➤ AARP, 601 E Street NW, Washington, D.C, 20049, publishes "Homemade Money" for people considering reverse mortgage plans.

Investment Secrets

Many seniors have found their incomes cut in half as a result of savings yields dropping. In 1989, for example, the one-year CD average was 9.51 percent. By 1994, that one-year CD yielded 3.08 percent. Think of it this way: for every dime in interest you used to receive from your CD, you'd get only about three cents of that in 1994. This was a major financial blow to seniors who counted on that money every month. The result? Struggling seniors considered even riskier investments to earn higher yields and make up for the loss in monthly income. You know what happens when you try to earn a better return—you have to take on more risk. And for those fixed-income folks, that can be scary. Here are a few suggested strategies seniors can try without having to struggle.

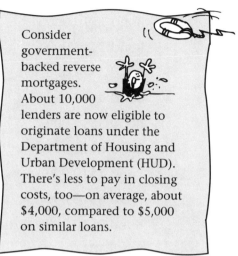

Consider government-backed reverse mortgages. About 10,000 lenders are now eligible to originate loans under the Department of Housing and Urban Development (HUD). There's less to pay in closing costs, too—on average, about $4,000, compared to $5,000 on similar loans.

Reverse mortgages are a great tax-planning tool if your estate is worth more than $600,000. By having a reverse mortgage, you could shrink your assets below the $600,000 threshold and avoid paying high federal estate-tax rates of up to 55 percent. (You'll find more estate planning strategies in Chapter 28.)

Secret #1: Ladder a Bond Portfolio

Let's say you have $100,000 to invest. You divide that money into ten parts. Take one-tenth of your money ($10,000) and invest it in a 10-year bond (or even municipal bonds or CDs). The next one-tenth of your money will be invested in a nine-year bond, the next one-tenth into an eight-year bond, and so on. Continue until your $100,000 is fully invested, which would be all the way down to a one-year bond. The idea is to hold all these bonds until maturity and then roll them over, once matured, into another ten-year bond. Here's what it looks like on paper:

Bond 1 $10,000	1-year Treasury bill matures next year
Bond 2 $10,000	2-year Treasury note matures in 1997
Bond 3 $10,000	3-year Treasury note matures in 1998
Bond 4 $10,000	4-year Treasury note matures in 1999
Bond 5 $10,000	5-year Treasury note matures in 2000
Bond 6 $10,000	6-year Treasury note matures in 2001
Bond 7 $10,000	7-year Treasury note matures in 2002
Bond 8 $10,000	8-year Treasury note matures in 2003
Bond 9 $10,000	9-year Treasury note matures in 2004
Bond 10 $10,000	10-year Treasury bond matures in 2005

This financial planning strategy allows you to increase your yields without taking on too much risk. You increase your yields because extending maturities allows you to take advantage of the higher rates paid on longer-term securities.

Secret #2: Invest in Utility Companies

Rather than put their earnings back into the company, many utility and telecommunications companies will pay high dividends to shareholders. Sometimes, if a company has had a particularly profitable year, extra dividends are paid. It works both ways, however; some utility companies are cutting dividends due to the impact of interest rate increases. You can invest in these sectors through stocks, or through mutual funds that maintain these types of companies in their portfolios. Examples of this latter approach include Fidelity Utilities Income Fund, (800) 544-8888 with a three-year annualized return of 8.26 percent; and Invesco Strategic Utilities, (800) 525-8085, which posts a three-year annualized return of 8.87 percent.

To keep your money super-safe, consider laddering Treasury securities; they're backed by the full faith and credit of the U.S. government.

Sometimes high-paying utility stocks are better than bonds. The semi-annual interest that bonds pay is fixed until the bond matures. When you own a stock, the dividends you receive can increase year after year. The bond might provide a higher current yield, but a good-quality utility stock can pay better over time if there's a solid record of dividends.

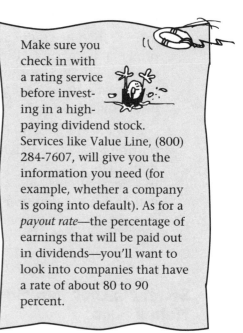

Make sure you check in with a rating service before investing in a high-paying dividend stock. Services like Value Line, (800) 284-7607, will give you the information you need (for example, whether a company is going into default). As for a *payout rate*—the percentage of earnings that will be paid out in dividends—you'll want to look into companies that have a rate of about 80 to 90 percent.

Not so fast, Charlie. Risks involved with utility investments must be factored in, especially in a rising-rate environment. Why?

Utility stocks are subject to swings in interest rates because utility companies tend to borrow a lot of money. If interest rates rise, their cost of borrowing goes up, which hurts profits... and ultimately dividends. How does that affect you and your pocketbook? Because of the drop in profits, the stock price may drop—and dividends will be cut. So make sure you re-read Chapter 12 and keep up with the latest interest rate cycle!

Secret #3: Create a Split-funded Annuity

Investing in an annuity is one of the top ten ways to "get there from here" when it comes to retirement planning because it takes advantage of tax-deferred compounding. Annuities are easy to understand; they're no-load mutual funds or fixed-rate CDs wrapped up inside an insurance product. There is no limit to the amount you can invest, and you are never required to take your money out—unlike an Individual Retirement Account. For a quick refresher on no-load mutual funds, refer to Chapter 19.

This conservative strategy uses two kinds of annuities: immediate and deferred. *Immediate* annuities pay you a monthly check for life, which is based on the amount of money you put into the plan, interest rates, and your age. In fact, the monthly check you receive is more than what you would get from a bank CD because in addition to your interest income you're also receiving a portion of your principal. Your principal is *not* subject to income tax; only the interest income is taxable. A *deferred* annuity lets your cash grow—it "defers" your money until a later point in time—and your interest compounds tax-deferred until you decide how you want to withdraw your money.

For example, suppose you split your $100,000 investment in half, putting $50,000 in a deferred annuity and the remaining $50,000 in an immediate annuity. The $50,000 deferred annuity sits there and grows in a tax-sheltered environment, compounding for 10 or 20 years—you decide the timeframe. The second half—the $50,000 immediate annuity—is letting you receive monthly checks at a stated interest rate. It pays out all of your original investment and interest earnings for that certain period of time.

Secret #4: Look into Municipal-bond or Corporate-bond Mutual Funds

If you are looking for higher yields—depending on your tax bracket—check out corporate-bond or municipal-bond funds; they may be the way to go.

Bond mutual funds work just like stock mutual funds; your money is pooled together with that of all the other shareholders. The way you make money on these types of funds is on the interest dividends paid every month—which most bond funds do—or by receiving capital gains at the end of the year if the portfolio manager sold bonds during the year at a profit (remember, buy low and sell high!).

The main idea to keep in mind when choosing a corporate-bond fund is to note the *quality rating* of the bonds in which the fund is allowed to invest. The higher the yield, the lower the quality.

Choose a corporate-bond fund that has AAA-rated holdings to ensure quality.

Municipal-bond funds work the same way—make sure you base your choice of fund on the quality of the bond holdings—but they're not for everybody. Typically, the higher the tax bracket you're in, the more advantageous a municipal-bond investment would be. You would need to figure out your *taxable equivalent yield*. Don't panic—it's not that hard to figure out. All you do is find your marginal tax rate. For example, if you're in the 28-percent tax bracket, take 100 minus 28 to get your denominator (your marginal tax rate). The answer is 72. Next, take the municipal-bond yield (return) and divide it by your denominator. If you were interested in investing in a muni-bond with a yield of six percent, you would find your taxable equivalent yield using the following calculation:

Municipal-bond yield return (six percent) divided by denominator (100 minus 72, the marginal tax rate) equals the taxable equivalent yield. In this case it would be 8.33 percent.

This means you would have to earn at least 8.33 percent on a taxable bond (like a corporate bond) in order to end up with the same amount after taxes that you'd have if you invested in a municipal bond.

Secret #5: Look into a Growth and Income Stock Mutual Fund

This type of mutual fund buys blue-chip stocks, so there's a lot of room for long-term growth potential. If you're looking for yield, however, you still receive income through the "equity-income" stocks that pay higher dividends. Here you have the best of both worlds: long-term growth *and* dividend income. Plus, there is less risk involved here than there would be with an aggressive growth fund—you still receive inflation protection, too.

REALLY?

According to the National Institute of Health, a study indicates that 24 percent of people 85 and older need help managing their money. In fact, almost 10 percent of all senior citizens need help performing basic, everyday financial tasks. To help the mature market handle financial affairs, a new breed of money-handling services is evolving.

Paymaster, in Washington, D.C. at (800) 234-4454, will pay your telephone bill, set up payment plans with collection agencies, and assist paying doctor bills. The service charge includes a one-time $52.50 enrollment fee and then $52.50 for every hour that Paymaster works on your case. Paymaster usually spends an average 45 to 60 minutes on each client per month. The billing is similar to the way an attorney would bill a client; Paymaster keeps track of all the people who work on your bills and logs the transactions. It will show when a check was cut to the power company or telephone company. It will list the amount of time spent on each function.

Last but Not Least, the Clout You Get with AARP

Once you hit age 50—even if you're not retired yet—you are eligible to join the American Association of Retired Persons, known as AARP. All you need to do to join is call (310) 496-2277 for a membership application. Here's a basic list of the perks you get with AARP, according to the association.

Insurance Benefits   As an AARP member, you can insure everything from your health to your car, your home, and even a mobile home at pretty good discounts.

➤ Group health insurance plans cover hospital stay and even some expenses not fully covered by Medicare. Call (800) 523-5800.

➤ Life insurance has a sweetener: no physical exam is required. Call (800) 795-9990.

➤ Auto insurance offers full 12-month rate protection and lifetime renewability. Call (800) 541-3717.

➤ Members who need homeowner's insurance can call (800) 932-9922 for details.

➤ You can even get coverage for your mobile home. Call (800) 752-2441.

Pharmacy Service   AARP members have the "shop-at-home" convenience on medical prescriptions, over-the-counter medications, and other health and beauty aids. The association reports average annual savings of 10 to 15 percent over regular pharmacy prices, especially if you buy generic-name drugs. Plus, you don't even have to be an AARP member to get price quotes or prescriptions from the AARP pharmacy. Call (800) 456-2226 to get more information.

Investment Program   Offered from Scudder, the $11.1 billion mutual fund family of funds, the AARP Investment program is designed for AARP members only. A total of eight no-load funds are designed with the following objectives: income, tax-free income, capital growth, and safety of principal. Call (800) 253-2277 ext. 6911.

Motor Club   Amoco's Motor Club is available to AARP members at a discount that varies from state to state. Toll-free emergency help is available 24 hours a day—including towing and emergency roadside service. Call (800) 334-3300.

Purchase Privilege Program   This includes discounted travel packages, rental cars, and hotel accommodations. Discounted cruises, city packages, and foreign travel programs are offered to AARP members at a typical discount of 15 percent to 20 percent off travel fares and rental car rates. Examples include Gray Line bus tours around the U.S. and Canada, food and beverage discounts available at some hotels, and 15 percent off regular room rates at hotels such as Best Western, Courtyard by Marriott, and La Quinta Inns. For more information about discounted tour packages, call (800) 927-0111 or the toll-free number of the hotel where you plan to stay. Make sure you have your name and AARP member number ready in order to participate.

AARP VISA Credit Card   You can sign up for a Gold or conventional card issued from Bank One, which offers extended warranty, purchase protection, and travel accident insurance. (Before you enroll, make sure you shop credit cards because of the high annual percentage rates. Your membership dues might not make up for what you get slapped with as interest if you don't pay down your credit card balances, but it may help those of you who need to begin establishing a credit report.) Call (310) 496-2277 for further information.

The Least You Need To Know

➤ Know what benefits you are entitled to by contacting the Social Security Administration.

➤ Don't draw on Social Security until you absolutely need to. Waiting will increase your benefits.

➤ A reverse mortgage can be a good way to increase your income without reducing your Social Security benefits.

➤ Potentially high-return investments that don't involve a lot of risk include: utility stocks, annuities, growth and income funds, and quality municipal-bond and corporate-bond funds.

➤ You can save money by taking advantage of special financial services and miscellaneous discounts that are available to seniors.

➤ Joining AARP can save you money on insurance, travel, prescriptions, and much more.

Part 6
Money Issues You Don't Have to Deal with Every Day

Because most of us work for a living—whether you're a bricklayer, an accountant, a mother of two, or the President of the United States—we all have financial responsibilities: rent or a mortgage, car payments, clothing expenses, groceries… you name it. The list seems endless.

Many of us get so caught up in the day-to-day grind of work that we often overlook another responsibility: protecting ourselves and our families financially. Financial responsibility goes beyond making sure the telephone bill gets paid each month. It requires you to think a bit harder about how you can help you and your family in the event of a financial emergency, take advantage of your employee benefits at work, protect your health and wealth through insurance, and tackle taxes. As luck would have it, you're going to learn all about those very issues in this Part.

Chapter 22

Money on the Job

In This Chapter

➤ The best perk you'll ever receive from your boss

➤ Dipping into your 401(k)? Watch your fingers!

➤ How to squeeze more out of your paycheck

➤ Emergency plan if you're fired

You have the world at your feet. Two different prospective employers you interviewed with last week offer you positions in their company. Here's the lowdown.

Job Offer #1: You have your own office with a view that faces Lake Michigan. Your boss doesn't expect you to clock worktime hours more than 9 to 5. You have two executive assistants, a company car, $65,000 in income, and weekends off. You're allowed 10 sick days a year, two weeks vacation. They offer you a reimbursement feature for your health-care costs and there's no retirement savings program.

Job Offer #2: Your office faces north—no window. You have a secretary, a parking space (no company car), $64,000 a year in income, 2 sick days a year, and 1 week vacation for the first year (which increases to two weeks after 12 months). You have access to a major medical plan, a 401(k), an employee-stock-purchase plan and a pension.

Which do you choose? The lake view? No way. You get the gold star if you chose Job Offer #2. Why? Because of the opportunity to earn 50 to 100 percent on your money. This chapter will explain all the opportunities that you can receive working 9 to 5.

Working 9 to 5—It IS a Way to Make a Living!

You have access to one of the most convenient and important investment resources—right at your employer's doorstep. It's your employer's *retirement plan*, which is one of the most important asset-building tools available to consumers. Once you participate in your employer's retirement savings program, you avoid one of the biggest mistakes too many people are making: doing nothing.

The younger you start, the better—the more time your money has to grow, and the less you might have to save overall. Look at a couple of examples:

Sylvia gets her first job at age 21. Over the next eight years, she accumulates a bit more than $10,000. Eight years later, she gets married, has two children, and decides to put her career on hold. She stops investing and lets her money ride, earning around eight percent (compounded monthly) on her $10,000 until she retires at age 65. She has accumulated $176,448.

Myron doesn't invest a penny until he's about 29 years old. On his 29th birthday, he decide to stash $70 a month into an investment account that earns the same amount as Sylvia's: eight percent. He does that for 36 years, all the way to age 65, contributing a total of $30,240. His total accumulation? $174,771.

Who's better off? They both have relatively the same amount of money by age 65. But Sylvia's initial wad of dough was only $10,000. Myron contributed *three times* that amount—$30,240. Why is this? *Because Sylvia started earlier and had more time for her money to grow.*

Even though Americans socked away more than $4 *trillion* into some type of company-sponsored retirement program, such as a 401(k) or a pension or other type of defined benefit plan, there is solid evidence that young Americans are not saving enough. Of all the employees that have access to a retirement savings program, only 60 percent contribute. They're really behind the eight ball.

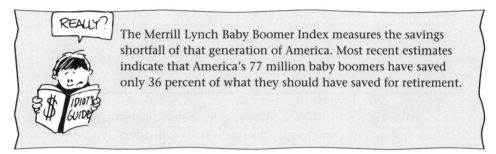

REALLY?

The Merrill Lynch Baby Boomer Index measures the savings shortfall of that generation of America. Most recent estimates indicate that America's 77 million baby boomers have saved only 36 percent of what they should have saved for retirement.

Why the problem? Because many people are living moment to moment and can't think about the future. Others don't want money taken out of their check because "they need it NOW." Ya know what? These people who can't afford the deduction now won't be able to afford retirement. Still others do not contribute because they just don't understand how the dang thing works.

Another culprit is that many people *are* savers, and a company retirement program sends chills down the spines of Americans who couldn't stand the thought of losing money by investing. Saving is something you used to do when you were a kid, often dropping coins into a piggy bank. Sure, you can save today. A prime example is the emergency fund you should save in a SAFE place (such as a money market fund), that will cover three to six months' worth of living expenses.

Contributing to a retirement plan practices the strategy of tax-deferred investing. Stocks, bonds, and mutual funds are purchased within a qualified investment plan, such as a 401(k) and pension plans (which you'll learn more about in this chapter).

By deferring your income taxes, you can increase your investment returns. For example, look at Table 22.1 for comparison, assuming a $2,000/year investment at an average nine percent return in a tax-deferred versus taxable account.

Table 22.1 Advantages of Deferring Taxes

Years	Investment Dollars in a Tax-deferred Account	Investment Dollars in a Taxable Account
10	$ 33,150	$ 28,725
15	$ 64,200	$ 51,500
20	$112,000	$ 83,100
25	$184,700	$125,100
30	$298,000	$184,600

Investing is a different story: you create goals and work toward those goals. True, whenever you invest in a product, there is a potential of risk. If you look at the facts, however, you can see how investing in a company-sponsored program is the best investment deal in America today. For example, here's how much you can save by sheltering your contributions from taxes. If you contribute $2,000 a year in your company's plan and your account earns a modest six percent a year for 30 years, you'll have about $168,000—which would be $48,000 *more* than if your $2,000 investment went into a taxable account.

The Fabulous 401(k)

A 401(k) plan—which was dubbed for the section of the tax code it represents—allows you to make contributions on a pre-tax basis. The money is taken out of your check and invested in several different options, all of which you choose. The money grows tax-deferred until you take it out.

The upside of a 401(k) is that you decide which investments you want to put your money in (unlike other company retirement plans, such as a pension). Your investment choices in a 401(k) plan are strictly up to you. Typically you'll have a choice between a Money Market Account, a general growth or equity stock fund, a fixed-income choice, and an investment in your company's stock. Any money you contribute is yours, even if you leave the company, and you can roll it over into a tax-deferred IRA when you leave the company (more about this in Chapter 27 on retirement). The biggest allure, however, is that you don't pay taxes on the money you contribute.

So what exactly is a 401(k)? It's sometimes known as a *salary reduction plan* because when you enroll your employer deducts a percentage of your salary— usually between two and 10 percent, the percentage is up to you—and deposits the funds in your plan account. The money is deducted from your paycheck before being taxed federally, state, locally and even before Social Security takes its chunk. So, the earnings you report (your wages/salary) to the IRS on your income tax return is lessened by the amount of your contribution.

If you have at least 10 years until you retire, invest your 401(k) for growth instead of stockpiling your money into the Money Market Account.

What a perk, huh? Many times the money you set aside is matched by your employer. For example, some plans will pay 50 percent for every dollar that you contribute; others may even match your contribution 100 percent. Meaning, for every dollar you put in, your company matches your contribution and contributes a dollar to your retirement account in the plan. Where else can you earn 100 percent on your money like that?

The IRS does limit how much you can contribute annually, although this figure increases each year with inflation. Currently, the limit for 401(k) plans is about $9,200. Now, that figure is not for *all* employees; typically the more money you make, the less you can contribute—it's known as "rank-and-file"—and rules vary. Make sure your employer spells this out for you.

So what's all this *vesting* talk? It's not a clothing phenomenon, rather it tells you how much of your employer's matched contributions and earnings in a retirement plan you can take with you if you leave your job, get laid off, get fired, or retire. You can keep all of *your* prior contributions and earnings, but your company's vesting schedule will determine how much of the company's money you can keep. Vesting schedules differ among employers, so check with your boss to make sure what the company rules are.

Dip into Your 401(k)? Sure, but Watch Your Fingers

You can borrow against your 401(k). But is it worth it? Many 401(k) programs offer this option to its contributors. All you do is borrow from your tax-deferred savings program and pay interest into your own account. Kind of like "paying yourself back" plus interest. What a great loan customer.

The rates are low—about a point lower than what banks charge on secured personal loans, but the hidden costs are high. The largest hidden cost is the lost opportunities of the earnings you might have gained on your tax-deferred savings. Consider it like transferring the money from one pocket to another; the money you borrow is not collecting any interest or increasing in capital growth. But, if you need the money, it is a source you can count on.

The loan must be repaid quarterly and within five years, unless you're using it to buy a house, usually your principal residence. The vacation home in Bermuda is not an exception. If it is your principal residence, you may have up to 30 years to repay, often through payroll deductions. If you borrow from your 401(k), follow these rules:

➤ There are hardship rules you will have to follow—and it's usually up to the company to decide—such as uninsured medical costs. If it's to buy the flaming red Maserati, forget it.

➤ Try not to leave the company with a loan outstanding. Why? Because the balance will be subtracted before you receive your 401(k) funds. What does this matter? Enter Uncle Sam, who says if you don't pay back the loan within the 60-day grace period, you have to roll the funds over into another qualified plan or an Individual Retirement Account (IRA), or he'll take a chunk out. The IRS considers it an early withdrawal, and will hit you with a 10-percent penalty as well as income tax.

➤ If you take a leave of absence from work, see if you can still make your loan payments. Even though most companies will allow you a grace period of one year, once you return, your loan payments are raised in order to meet the five-year time frame requirement.

The drawback of a 401(k)? The dollar amount you contribute each year is subject to a limit set by your employer as a percentage of your salary. The other drawback is that it's completely voluntary. You don't have to participate and many people don't, for various reasons. The biggest one is that they don't understand what a 401(k) is. You shouldn't necessarily be *forced* to invest, but take a look at why you should.

If you contribute $2,000 a year every year for thirty years into a 401(k) (which is a company-sponsored plan) instead of a taxable account, you will have accumulated almost $50,000 *more* in the 401(k) than a taxable account in the same amount of time. And that's not even including the matching contributions your company makes.

If your company doesn't offer a 401(k), lobby for it.

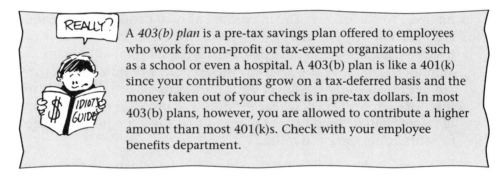

REALLY? A *403(b) plan* is a pre-tax savings plan offered to employees who work for non-profit or tax-exempt organizations such as a school or even a hospital. A 403(b) plan is like a 401(k) since your contributions grow on a tax-deferred basis and the money taken out of your check is in pre-tax dollars. In most 403(b) plans, however, you are allowed to contribute a higher amount than most 401(k)s. Check with your employee benefits department.

Take Advantage of Other Company Plans

Most large companies offer traditional pension plans, known as a *defined benefit plan*, but about 30 percent fewer companies are offering such plans to employees these days. Instead, they're shifting the burden of saving for retirement onto you, the employee, through the 401(k) plan. Make sure you understand all the benefits you are garnering under your company's plan. Most large companies have an employee benefits officer who should be able to explain to you in street language how their plan works.

A *defined benefit plan* guarantees that you receive a fixed monthly sum at retirement and for the rest of your life. That's why it's called *defined*; the benefit you'll receive at retirement is defined in advance. Typically, it is based on the average of the last five years' salary, the number of years of employment, and your age at retirement. You don't

If you have a defined benefit plan, check whether the plan is insured by the Pension Benefit Guaranty Corporation. The PBGC guarantees to cover retired workers and the "vested portion" of current employees.

make any contributions—the employer makes them each year so that when you reach retirement age there will be enough money in the plan to pay your lifetime benefits.

If your company offers a *defined contribution plan*, you'll have more flexibility than a traditional pension plan (*defined benefit plan*)—but not as much as a 401(k). There are two types of defined contribution plans: a money purchase plan and a profit-sharing plan.

So how does a *money purchase plan* work? You must usually work at your job for at least one year to participate. The maximum annual deductible contribution is 25 percent of your salary or $30,000, whichever is less. The reason it's called a money purchase plan is that the retirement benefits amount to whatever the assets in the account will purchase at the time you retire. The only employer obligation is to make a defined contribution for each worker each year regardless of profits. These plans are different than defined benefit plans in that there are no guaranteed benefits at the time you retire.

A *profit-sharing plan*, on the other hand, obligates the company to contribute part of its profits each year, if any, into each worker's account. However, the company can change the rate of contributions, based on profits, or eliminate them in any year. Monthly benefits are whatever the money you have in your account will buy when you retire. You still contribute to this type of account: 15 percent of your salary or $22,500, whichever is less.

Your contributions are made with pre-tax dollars to defined contribution plans, and the money grows tax-deferred, which is a great advantage. Look at Table 22.2 to see how much your pre-tax contributions can grow over five years if you save $3,000 a year for five years and your employer matches 50 cents on the dollar. This table also assumes a 10 percent average annual rate of return.

Table 22.2 How Pre-Tax Contributions Can Grow

	401(k)	Taxable Account
Amount contributed:	$15,000	$15,000
Less your taxes: 30%	0	$4,500
Invested amount, plus employer's match:	$22,500	$10,500
Total amount, assuming 10% average return:	$30,220	$12,920

No matter what type of plan is available to you, make sure you ask your employee benefits officer the following questions:

1. How are my retirement benefits computed?

2. How long will it take until I'm *vested*? (That's how long it will take for plan contributions made by the company to be owned by you.) By law, your pension benefits must be fully vested in a maximum of seven years.

Squeezing More Out of Your Paycheck

Don't have time to trek down to your local bank to buy savings bonds? Look no further than your paycheck. Most major companies offer you a chance to purchase Series EE savings bonds through automatic payroll deductions. Although the money is not deducted on a pre-tax basis, these deductions are a great way of breaking the "see-it-buy-it" mentality because the money is deducted automatically from your check. Plus, you can use the opportunity as an avenue to stash your "safe" money—money that you can't afford to lose.

You can have the deductions taken out weekly, monthly, or quarterly. Since savings bonds are purchased at a discount from face value (a $100 face value bond has a purchase price of $50), they're a great way to invest your safe money for the future. Over the years, the value of the bond will increase as the interest accrues.

If you want to know what your savings bonds are worth today, call (800) US-BONDS to find out.

One woman who works for a major brokerage firm in Chicago tells us she has $50 deducted from each paycheck to buy $100 savings bonds each month. "They're for my two-year-old daughter's future," Pam tells us. Good thinking, Pam. In just one year, you'll have invested $600 for $1,200 face value worth of bonds for your daughter's future. (Tip: You can use these as a way to pay for her college education and possibly *not* pay taxes on the interest you'll receive. More on this in Chapter 26 about college planning.)

Here's one more tip for getting the most out of your paycheck. Have your check directly deposited. This sounds so simple, but many consumers aren't doing this. They should take advantage of this paperless transition. No bank lines or traffic to wait in. Plus, direct deposit guarantees immediate access to your cash at most banks and thrifts. As you learned in Chapter 6 about checking accounts, it can take several days for your deposited check to clear. Why wait?

Besides the added convenience, you can make a little extra money off direct deposit with this little strategy: Have your paycheck directly deposited into a Money Market Account to earn the better rate of interest than a savings or checking account. You'll earn interest on payday since your check was directly deposited. When you need money, write a check to yourself and deposit it in your non-interest-bearing checking account to pay the bills.

You're F-I-R-E-D

Before the pink slip arrives, make sure you have an emergency fund. About three to six months' worth of living expenses is the rule. Keep this money in a money market fund that has a check-writing feature. This way, as you're adding to your emergency fund, you can take advantage of the higher rates. *Do not keep this money in a checking account.*

Unless you live under a rock, you probably aware of all of the layoffs that have taken place in Corporate America in the past decade. Whether or not it is due to technology or companies tightening their belts isn't the point. The point is what *you* should do if it happens to you. You have an overwhelming amount of decisions to make. This section will help answer some questions about what to do with all the financial issues you face.

Does your company provide continued health insurance coverage in the event you leave voluntarily or involuntarily? Many companies offer you an option to continue health insurance coverage at the same rate the company pays for a maximum of 18 months. After that, you're on your own.

What will happen to your pension or 401(k) benefits? When you're let go and have contributed to a 401(k) plan, you may have to take all of your contributions in a *lump sum distribution*. That's a wad of dough that you need to make some quick decisions about within the next 60 days. You can:

➤ Roll it over into a new IRA *deposited directly from your employer into an IRA* and keep up the tax-deferred savings you've established. By doing so, you won't get hit by Uncle Sam's 10-percent tax penalty, which is on top of the income tax penalty you'll pay if you keep the money—BUT if you take hold of the check, then the company must withhold 20 percent for income taxes. However, you're only allowed one IRA rollover per year.

➤ Roll it over into your *new* employer's plan, if you've secured another job. It's a simple transfer with no tax penalties.

➤ Keep the money growing tax-deferred in your company's 401(k) plan. While it may sound like a good choice so you can still take advantage of tax-deferral feature, ask yourself this: Why keep your money with the company that just laid you off?

You're better off rolling the money over into an IRA if you can, especially if the company's pension plan is not funded to full capacity—a problem many corporations have been facing over the past decade.

You don't have as much flexibility with your pension benefits, unless you're being offered early retirement. You will have to meet with your employee benefits department to determine what is allowed according to their plan. During this meeting, find out how much of your benefits you own, known as being *vested*. You can roll that money into an IRA, or you may have to leave it with the company until you retire. Get the specifics from the benefits department.

Do you have access to outplacement counselors through your company? If so, take them up on it!

Finally, are you going to receive any type of severance? Two weeks is pretty standard, and employers can pay you in a lump sum or over a period of a few weeks. You can take the lump sum, but know that you'll face a bigger tax bill next April if you receive the money at the end of the year. The decision is up to you. If you are going to receive a severance, why not lobby for more? The worst thing that could happen is that they say no.

The Least You Need to Know

➤ Take advantage of your employer's retirement plan, whether it's a 401(k) or something else. It's one of the best investments you can make. If you're not sure how it works, sit down with your company's benefits specialist and get him or her to explain it to you.

➤ If you really need the money, you can borrow from your retirement fund. Although you'll get a lower interest rate than what you would at the bank, you're also costing yourself future earnings on the fund when you do this.

➤ If your company offers it, take the payroll deduction to invest in savings bonds. You'll thank yourself later. Also, have your paycheck directly deposited into your bank account. You'll save yourself some time and earn an extra day's worth of interest if you have it deposited in an interest-earning account.

➤ If the worst happens and you're fired or laid off, make sure you find out whether you can continue your health insurance, what happens with your 401(k) and pension, and whether you will get any severance pay.

Covering Your Assets: Insurance and You

Many folks believe that paying a lot of money on insurance premiums is like flushing your money down the toilet—that is, until tragedy strikes. Then those expensive insurance premiums seem like the best thing since the invention of the paper clip.

You need to insure your health and protect your wealth. And the more you have to protect, the more you'll spend on insurance. Typical insurance policies include homeowner's insurance to protect your home, automobile insurance to help in case of an accident (whether or not it's your fault!), life insurance to help your loved ones financially when you die, and disability insurance to cover you if you aren't able to perform your current job.

This chapter defines which types of insurance you need. In addition, it will help you get the best buy for your insurance dollars and show you how to shield yourself from unexpected disasters.

Making Sense of Insurance Mumbo-Jumbo

Your insurance needs are determined by which of these categories you fall under: single, married couple with no kids, married couple with kids, or married couple with adult children (empty-nesters). The following list explains the insurance needs for each category:

➤ **Singles**   You can skip the life insurance, but you'll need auto insurance (make sure you get comprehensive coverage if you have an outstanding car loan) and renter's insurance (unless you own your home). Disability insurance is also a good idea; you can usually get this through your employer.

➤ **Married without children**   Look into term life insurance, particularly if one spouse does not work or you own a home. Auto insurance is a must, as is homeowner's or renter's insurance. Get disability insurance through your employer, but look into a supplemental policy if your employer's coverage is not enough.

➤ **Married with children**   When children enter the picture, the necessity for insurance coverage increases. For one thing, you definitely need life insurance. Term life insurance is the best bet if you are in this age range. As you get older, the premiums may rise, so you'll need to reevaluate your situation and perhaps choose another policy. Your car insurance coverage may remain the same, with one addition. If you have children who can drive, see how much a multi-car discount policy would be. You may be able to save as much as 25 percent on your total premiums.

Disability insurance is more important when you have children. Choose a policy that is guaranteed renewable, and lock into a guaranteed annual premium that cannot be increased and is noncancelable until you turn 65. Add a cost-of-living adjustment clause to your policy for an extra premium. This will raise your disability payments based on an index tied to the Consumer Price Index (CPI).

Finally, get complete coverage on your homeowner's insurance. Make sure you know what your policy does and does not cover, and purchase additional coverage if necessary.

➤ **Empty nesters** The kids are gone and you have the house back to yourselves—Hallelujah! All previous insurance needs remain the same, although you may need insurance to cover any debts— such as death/funeral expenses and estate taxes, which are usually cared for by a good life insurance policy. Keep in mind the following exceptions:

Automobile coverage Senior citizens usually get 20 percent discounts on auto insurance. Remember to get rid of your multi-car discount now that the children are on their own.

Homeowner's insurance Re-evaluate your existing policy and what it covers. If you've sold the house and moved into a smaller place, you'll need less coverage— which means lower annual premium costs.

Long-term care insurance People with substantial resources they don't want to lose need this type of coverage. Average annual premium costs are $1,100 a year. Make sure that there's an inflation-protection rider, that the policy is renewable for life, and that there is a short elimination period, such as 20 to 60 days. For more tips on shopping for long-term care insurance, contact the National Association of Insurance Commissioners, Attn: Publications Dept., 120 W. 12th Street, Suite 1100, Kansas City, MO 64105-1925. Ask for their free booklet, "A Shopper's Guide to Long-Term Care Insurance."

If you are married, it's better to purchase a second-to-die insurance policy. This covers you and your spouse, but pays off in the death of the second person. This strategy saves you money two ways. First, instead of purchasing two independent insurance policies and paying two premiums, the insureds pay only one lower premium on both of their lives. Second, the unlimited marital deduction means you would pay no estate tax on the death of the first spouse. The total cost of a $1 million second-to-die policy can save you more than 66 percent over the cost of purchasing two separate $500,000 policies.

Life insurance   Purchase a cash value life insurance policy to pay your estate taxes in the event of your death, especially if you have more than the $600,000 exemption that Uncle Sam allows. Why? Keeping term insurance becomes too expensive as you get older. Plus, in a cash value insurance policy, the cash inside the policy builds up and may be used in the future to pay premiums or help pay estate taxes. This isn't true of term insurance.

The rest of this chapter explains the ins and outs of the different types of insurance.

Insuring Home Sweet Home

No matter where you live or whether you rent or own, you need some sort of insurance to cover your belongings. The following paragraphs explain what kind of insurance you need depending on your living arrangements.

If you rent your home, you need to have a renter's insurance policy. Renter's insurance is available through most insurance agents. The form is known as an HO-4 form and covers any damage to your personal property and any structural damage to the building caused by tenants.

The amount you will pay on your renter's insurance policy can be on a monthly, semi-annual, or annual basis. No matter what the term, the amount you pay is known as a premium, and the amount of your premium depends on where you live. Do you live in a good neighborhood or a bad one? Is there a 24-hour doorman? Is the apartment unoccupied for more than two hours per day? Another factor is whether you have taken out other insurance policies (such as car insurance) with the insurance agent. If you haven't, your premium will be higher. Typical premiums average around $150 per year.

If you are a condo- or co-op owner, you will need an HO-6 policy. Similar to a renter's insurance policy, this policy covers risks and damage to your personal property. Building property is covered for 10 percent of contents (such as cabinets and wall fixtures). Make sure you check with your insurance agent about anything that is not covered.

If you own your home, you should already have homeowner's insurance. Mortgage lenders require that you have property insurance before you buy a new home. If you are in the market for a new home and are getting homeowner's insurance for the first time, you should understand the basic forms of homeowner's coverage.

Types of Coverage

If you want to get the right type of coverage for your home, compare the following types of homeowner's insurance. The items that are listed as types of coverage are known as *perils*, as in "all the things that could go wrong." In the industry, it is known as a *standard peril policy*. The more coverage you acquire, the higher your insurance premiums will be. It is up to you to decide if you want to pay more in insurance premiums and have more coverage. However, if you try to cut corners on your homeowner's insurance policy to save a few bucks and tragedy strikes, you will be sorry.

HO-1 covers the 11 most common perils: glass breakage, fire or lightning, smoke damage, explosion, riots, damage caused by vehicles, damage caused by aircraft, theft, property loss, vandalism, and windstorm/hurricane/hail.

HO-2 covers HO-1 perils plus roof collapse from snow, heavy sleet, or ice; damage from hot or frozen water pipes; heat or air conditioning explosion; damage caused by falling objects; damage caused by electrical surges to appliances (except televisions); and collapse of any part of your home.

HO-3 is a special form that covers HO-1 and HO-2 and other risks to an older home, except floods, wars, and earthquakes. You do pay a premium for having replacement cost.

HO-4 is a policy that varies from insurance company to company; check with your insurance agent to see what an HO-4 homeowner's policy covers.

HO-5 includes replacement cost, and personal property is covered for 75 percent of home—as opposed to HO-3, where 70 percent is covered. To qualify for this type of coverage, your home must have been built after 1950 and must be in decent condition. It's required that you have a smoke detector, a dead bolt lock, and a hand-held fire extinguisher. If you don't have these items, you *cannot* get an HO-5 policy. You will pay more in premiums for this type of policy, but it does provide the most extensive coverage (including HO-1 and HO-2 disasters).

HO-6 policies, as previously described, are for condo and co-op owners only.

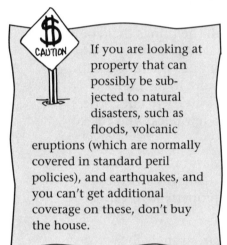

If you are looking at property that can possibly be subjected to natural disasters, such as floods, volcanic eruptions (which are normally covered in standard peril policies), and earthquakes, and you can't get additional coverage on these, don't buy the house.

Now that you know what is covered, let's find out what is not covered. For example, the HO-3 policy does not cover flood damage, but you can purchase separate flood insurance. However, you do have to qualify for this insurance by meeting the federal zoning standards, so check with your insurance agent to determine if you even need this type of coverage. The National Flood Insurance Program "backs" this type of insurance, but be aware that flood coverage is limited. It does not provide coverage for valuables stored below the ground level in your basement—except for major appliances, such as a freezer or washer and dryer.

REALLY?

Earthquake insurance is expensive for Californians. It carries an extremely high deductible—between nine and 10 percent of the coverage. This means if you are trying to insure a $250,000 home with a 10 percent deductible, you'll pay the first $25,000 of repairs before your insurance coverage kicks in.

Saving Money on Homeowner's Insurance

There's no escaping it—you must have homeowners insurance to buy a house. What you can escape are the extra costs that most folks end up paying because they haven't done their homework. Here are a few financial secrets that will help trim the fat:

➤ **Raise your deductible amounts.** If you're willing to accept a $1,000 deductible, you can save almost 15 percent on your premiums.

➤ **Take protective measures.** Installing a burglar alarm, dead bolts, or a smoke detector, purchasing a hand-held fire extinguisher, and/or having a non-smoking household protects your home and lowers your premiums.

➤ **Get replacement cost insurance.** Most insurance policies plan to give you the *actual cash value* of your personal property in the event of loss or damage. Folks, it's not worth it. If you buy a $3,500 leather couch today, five years from now it will be worth only $1,500 (because it's used). If you have a fire when that couch is five years old, the insurance company will pay you $1,500. Just try to find the same type of couch for $1,500. It's not likely. However, if you have replacement cost insurance, the insurance company is required to pay you whatever it costs to purchase a new replacement item.

➤ **Purchase your homeowner's insurance from the same insurance company that insures your automobile.** Purchasing both policies from the same agent or company may qualify you for a discount.

➤ **Pay your homeowner's insurance annually.** Although most insurance policies have annual, semi-annual, and monthly terms, you will save a few dollars if you pay it on an annual basis. For example, a renter's insurance policy with a $160 per year annual premium may cost you $87 on a semi-annual basis. This comes out to be an extra $14 out of your pocket.

➤ **Make a home video of your property and all of its contents.** By doing so, you ensure—and insure—that your claims will be paid.

➤ **Familiarize yourself with the additional coverages and exceptions noted on your policy.** For example, if your policy allows you to have additional coverage on credit card losses, don't take it. Why? Because most standard credit card companies limit you to a $50 loss per card. That's just wasting money. Read the fine print!

Car Coverage

The liability involved when you are in a car accident is phenomenal, which is why automobile insurance costs so much. You need to know what is required in your state and what's worth paying for. Comparing the differences between the two can save you a few dollars. The following sections cover what types of coverage are available and give you some money saving strategies.

Types of Coverage

Liability coverage is required in almost every state and is split into two parts: bodily injury liability and property damage liability. Bodily injury liability provides insurance against lawsuits. Most states require a minimum of $25,000 per person and $50,000 per accident. If you want to protect your assets in the event of a lawsuit, you'll need as much as $300,000 worth of coverage. Property damage liability covers damage done by your car to other people's cars and property. The standard minimum for this is $10,000.

If you're a victim of a hit-and-run accident, you'll need uninsured motorist coverage. Uninsured motorist coverage allows you to collect lost wages and payments for any medical expenses that result from an accident with an uninsured motorist. Do *not* skip over this type of insurance, especially since an increasingly high number of drivers have dropped their insurance coverage because of high premiums. And you should especially include this if you don't already have a comprehensive medical plan and long-term disability insurance.

REALLY?

Uninsured motorist coverage should not be confused with underinsured motorist coverage, which is the part of your policy that pays after the other driver's coverage has been used up.

You must also have comprehensive coverage if you have an outstanding car loan (which many of us do). Comprehensive coverage covers theft and damage to the car from riots, fire, flood, falling trees, and theft.

Collision coverage, which pays for damage to your car if you're in an accident or replaces a vehicle that is a total loss, is optional unless you have a loan on your car. If you do have a loan, this type of coverage is usually required by the lender.

As your car gets older, consider dropping your collision coverage. Why? Because the cost of collision coverage may be more than what your car is actually worth. By doing so, you can save almost one-third of your insurance costs.

Medical payments coverage and personal injury protection (PIP) covers medical, hospital, and funeral bills that result from an automobile accident—no matter who is at fault. PIP goes one step further and covers any lost wages. If you have a good medical plan and/or disability insurance policy, you may want to pass on these types of coverages since they can be expensive.

Saving Some Moolah

When you apply for automobile insurance, you always want to look for the best rate possible, but that's not always so easy. Insurers take into account certain considerations when they give you quotes on auto insurance. Keep these financial tidbits in mind to help cut costs on auto insurance:

➤ **Comparison shop.** You don't always have to go to your friendly insurance agent down the street. In fact, if you do your homework, you'll find that the price of similar auto coverage can vary as much as 80 percent from insurer to insurer. Check with the largest national insurers, which could potentially save you a few bucks if you buy directly from them.

➤ **Drive safely and defensively.** This tip is just common sense, but the fewer traffic violations and accidents you have under your belt, the lower your premiums will be. Maintain a good driving record!

➤ **Don't buy the latest "fad" or "hot" car.** In 1994, the vehicle stolen most often was the 1994 Chevy Blazer, which is why the average annual premium to insure this automobile is higher than the average premium for a not-so-trendy car.

➤ **Buy a car that will handle well if you are ever in an accident.** Ask the car sales rep how much of the car is damaged during an accident and whether or not it holds up well in an accident. For example, if you buy a car that falls apart in a fender bender, your insurance premiums will be much higher than if you buy a car that is a bit more resilient in an accident. In addition, find out how expensive any repairs may be. The more expensive it is to repair, the higher your premiums will be.

➤ **Raise your deductible and pay premiums annually.** Carrying a higher deductible will decrease your insurance premiums. For example, say you're a 30-year-old single female living in Chicago, driving a 1995 Pontiac Grand Am, and carrying full coverage on your car. You could pay $634 in semi-annual (every six months) premiums on a $250 deductible, or you could pay $584 in semi-annual premiums with a $500 deductible. You can reduce your premiums even further by paying on an annual basis.

The DOs and DON'Ts of Buying Life Insurance

Life insurance is a bugaboo in mainstream America because not many people understand it. It's really quite simple, though. Most folks buy life insurance to provide benefits for their survivors in case they die before "their time."

As you do for car insurance, you pay premiums when you buy life insurance. Your annual premiums are based on your age, your health, how much money your insurance company can earn by investing the money you give them (your premiums) until you die, and the expenses the insurance company incurs for mailings and commissions for its agents. Whew!

What makes life insurance a difficult concept to grasp is choosing which kind will best suit your personal needs. The most common reason to purchase life insurance is to support your family members who depend on your income in the event that you die prematurely.

316

Life insurance can also prove helpful by providing immediate cash to pay estate taxes when you die or to repay business loans (if you are an owner of a business and you die prematurely).

Although life insurance can be confusing, figuring out the differences in insurance policies doesn't require a secret decoder ring. You just need to find out if you need life insurance and, if so, how much you need.

Do you need life insurance? The rule of thumb is that if you're young and single and have no one else depending on your income, you don't need it. Even if you're married, if both of you are working, you probably don't need life insurance. But if there are family members who depend upon your income, you definitely do.

How much insurance you need depends on how old you are and how well your family can live without your income. To determine this, consider the following factors:

➤ Your family would need immediate cash to cover death-related expenses. This would cover uninsured medical costs, funeral expenses, debts, taxes, and estate-settlement fees. Many insurance agents recommend at least $5,000.

➤ Tack on six to 12 months of your family's lost net income because of your death (to take immediate economic pressure off of your family).

➤ Calculate your family's expenses on an annual basis (you learned out how to do this on a monthly basis in Chapter 2). What percent of these expenses are covered by your income? The mortgage still has to be paid and Junior's college tuition bill is still due. Also, how much will these expenses grow over the next five to eight years?

➤ Contact the Social Security Administration at (800) 772-1213 to see if your spouse and children are entitled to *survivors' benefits*. However, if your surviving spouse earns more than $20,000 a year, he or she is not entitled to any survivors' benefits coverage. If your family is eligible, have them determine what percentage of your current income the benefits cover. Why? Because if the survivors' benefits replace 30 percent of your income, you would have to purchase 30 percent less in life insurance benefits. Got it?

Without any mind-bending calculations, here's a basic rule of thumb for purchasing life insurance, according to a Citibank report. After the death of its principal income producer, a family requires 75 percent of its former after-tax income to maintain its standard of living. It must have at least 60 percent to get along at all. If you want to figure out your after-tax income without the help of a CPA, simply multiply your gross income by 60 percent if you earn a high income, 70 percent if you earn a moderate living, and 80 percent if you have a low income. Otherwise, if you want to simply figure out a rough estimate, just make it five to eight times your current wages. It comes out to about the same amount as Citibank's calculation.

Finally, you need to decide what kind of life insurance you need. Yuck! Because this could be the American public's most-despised question, we're going to make it easy on you and help you save a few bucks along the way. There are two very basic types of life insurance coverage: term insurance and cash value insurance. Term insurance is usually the best bet for all but the very wealthy. Whichever type of life insurance you decide to buy, keep the following things in mind:

➤ **Check out the insurance company's financial stability.** Even though term insurance policies always get paid—even if the insurance company goes belly up—those of you who are weak-kneed when it comes to your money should check on the health of the insurance company. Contact Weiss Research at (800) 289-9222 for more information. Other sources are A.M. Best (908/439-2200); Duff & Phelp's (312/368-3157); Moody's Investor Service (212/553-0300); and Standard & Poor (212/208-1527). These services will provide you with the financial strength of the insurance company and give you an explanation of how it grades each company. Of course, you want the highest rated companies possible, with grades of A++ and A+.

➤ **Buy your life insurance from a fee-only financial planner or a "direct-purchase."** You can save up to 40—sometimes 50—percent on an insurance agent's commissions if you go to a discount insurance broker. Better yet, if you purchase a policy directly from an insurance company, you can avoid the middleman altogether. Whichever type of life insurance you're purchasing, contact USAA at (800) 531-8000 for more information. Ameritas also provides low-cost cash value insurance policies to the public. Contact them toll-free at (800) 552-3553.

318

In addition, if you're not sure about your policy, contact the National Insurance Consumer Organization (NICO) for information about how they can evaluate your proposed insurance policy (typically, the performance per $1,000 of coverage). Write to them at 121 N. Payne Street, Alexandria, VA 22314.

➤ **If you build up a sizeable net worth, consider life insurance as an option to pay estate taxes.** As you'll see in Chapter 28 about estate planning, life insurance can help alleviate the sting for wealthy people who owe Uncle Sam a lot in estate taxes. Make sure you review your situation with an estate planning attorney (not your insurance agent) to figure out what options are available to you.

Term Insurance 101

Term insurance is usually the least expensive form of insurance coverage and is very affordable when you're young. As you get older, your risk of dying increases, so the cost of term insurance goes up. This risk is known as the *mortality rate.*

As with most other insurance coverages, you pay premiums annually, semiannually, or quarterly for term insurance. For this premium, you receive a predetermined amount of life insurance protection. If you are the insured spouse and you die during the term you are insured, your beneficiaries will collect. If not, all of the premiums are gone since there is no cash buildup in the policy, as there is in other types of life insurance policies that promote savings features (and hefty commissions). You will probably be required to take a physical examination to qualify for term insurance.

REALLY? Young women who are non-smokers tend to pay the least amount in premiums for term insurance. Because the cost of term insurance does not depend solely on age (where the younger you are, the lower your premiums are), and women live longer than men, women will pay less—especially if they don't light up.

Term insurance is very inexpensive, which is why it's a popular life insurance policy. However, it only provides for death protection—there's no build-up of the money you pay in premiums.

When you buy term insurance, you can buy it with level (same) premiums for one year, called *annual renewable term* (ART), and renewable until age 90. Other term policies and specified time periods are typically five, 10, 15, or 20 years. At the end of these time periods, the term insurance is renewable at sharply higher premium levels because you are older and statistically more likely to die during this time period.

Some people refer to term insurance as "renting coverage" because the only way your insurance policy pays out is if you die during this period. The payouts are offered in a lump sum payment or a steady stream of payments to your beneficiaries.

Make sure your policy offers a *guaranteed renewability feature*, so you don't have to take a medical test to continue coverage for another term, especially as you get older. Also, if you have an annual renewable term policy, you can convert it to a whole-life policy—without a medical exam. This is called *guaranteed conversion*, and allows you to convert from rising-premium term insurance to a fixed-premium whole life (cash value policy, which you'll learn about later in this chapter) policy. Here's a tip: If you think you may do this sometime down the road, make sure your term insurance policy is convertible into a whole life policy without another medical examination. There's an additional cost for this provision, but as you get older you'll end up saving more in premiums by doing so and avoiding the medical examination.

Here are some things to keep in mind when looking at a term insurance policy.

➤ **Make sure the illustrations that your insurance agent gives you illustrate the rates you will pay and show the maximum guaranteed rate they can require you to pay.** There is a state law that regulates the maximum guarantees. But remember, policy illustrations are not guarantees—even if they're in black and white. Term premiums are subject to change based on mortality and the insurance company's finances.

➤ **Compare a *level premium term* policy to an annual renewable term (which increases after each term).** You know that premiums on ordinary ART policies increase in cost every year, right?

Well, some companies offer a form of *level premium term*, in which they project that the annual premium will remain the same for 5, 10, or 20 years. At the end of the specified time period, your policy may kick back into a policy that has increasing premiums every year, or remain level for five years and *then* kick back into increasing premiums. Ask your agent if the premiums are projected or guaranteed. Insurance companies are not obligated to meet projected premiums—even if they are in the illustrations they give you.

➤ **Don't always settle for a short-term level term policy.** Why? Because the premiums may skyrocket after the short-term is over. Again, because this is the life insurance industry, it depends on the policy. Make sure the agent explains all details in black and white.

➤ **Choose a guaranteed annual renewable term to avoid medical exams.** This ensures that you do not have to have a new medical exam every year to renew your term policy. Avoid those policies, which are known as *reentry term*.

If you would like quotes on term insurance, contact one of the following quote services. There is no obligation to purchase term insurance, but make sure they can handle the transaction in your state if you do buy a policy.

TermQuote (800/444-8376) maintains a database of 70 companies and will search to find the lowest cost term insurance policy based on your specifications, your age, and health condition.

SelectQuote (800/343-1985) tracks term insurance prices nationwide.

INSurance INFOrmation (800/472-5800) provides only advice—they do not sell insurance—but will find the lowest cost term insurance policy for you and can even reevaluate your existing policy.

Insurance Quote Services (800/972-1104) sends a free booklet "Simple Guide to Insurance Savings," in addition to providing a quote service on low-cost term insurance. They will do a simple analysis on your life insurance needs based on your criteria and personal situation.

Cash Value Insurance

Sometimes known as *permanent insurance*, cash value insurance generally covers longer-term needs because term insurance becomes too expensive as you get older. But beware: Cash value insurance only makes sense for a few people and generates a lot of commissions for the insurance agent... unless you buy low-load or no-load insurance.

Cash value insurance combines life insurance plus a savings "account." Most of the money you pay in premiums goes toward life insurance, and a few bucks are deposited into this "account" that is supposed to grow in value over time. Sounds like a winner, huh?

Wrong. The biggest hit your account takes in the early years you're building it is the commission that your insurance agent earns, which is shown to you in the illustration he or she shows you. What most folks don't know is that the commission is built right into the premium you pay for the insurance. It may take years until the true return (what the insurance company promised you) on your account is equal to what it's supposed to be. To find out how much and what portion of your premium is going into your account, ask your insurance agent to show you the *surrender value* on the piece of paper (usually a ledger) he has. If the amount in the first few years is ZILCH, that's what your little account is getting.

All of the cash value insurance policies offer a tax-deferred savings feature to the insurance protection component of the policy. It is merely a death benefit plus an investment fund.

Interestingly enough, both term and cash value policies come in two varieties: participating and nonparticipating. Why all this gobbledygook? It seems confusing, but pay attention and you'll know more about how to make life insurance *work for you* than anyone you know!

Participating insurance entitles you to receive dividends (kind of like stock dividends) from the policy. These dividends are considered a refund of the portion of the premium that the insurance company did not pay in death benefits or administrative expenses over the previous year. This means that if the insurance company is collecting all of these premiums and no one died or administrative costs for the year were low, all the policy holders would get a "refund" in the form of dividends.

So what do you do with these dividends? You can take them as cash—and, of course, pay taxes to the IRS because the dividends are considered income. You can reinvest your dividends and *reduce* the future premiums you have to pay. Or, you can buy additional "paid-up" (more) insurance. The choice is yours.

Nonparticipating policies pay no dividends, so there's nothing to reinvest. Instead, your premiums are fixed when you buy a policy at a set amount. True, these premiums on a nonparticipating policy will be less than those on a participating policy, but nonparticipating policies *do not* offer the perks of reinvesting your dividends for future growth... or whatever your choice.

Be careful; some insurance company illustrations show that dividends from a paid-up policy can cover the premiums for a new policy, and they *don't*. Instead, the new policies will really borrow against the death benefit (like a loan) in order to pay the premiums. Watch out for the fine print!

Because cash value insurance policies are not straightforward (it would make life too easy if they were), here's a rundown of the terms you can expect to hear about from an insurance agent:

➤ **Whole Life**   Your premium stays the same every year, and your death benefit is fixed. Since the amount of the premium is much more than what you would need to pay death benefits in the early years, the extra money is "deposited" into your "account" (inside the policy), which earns and grows tax-deferred. You can choose from two types of whole life policies. In the first, you pay the same level premiums into your old age—where you can borrow against the policy to get some extra cash in your retirement years. In the second, you pay premiums for a fixed number of years only; after that, the cash value in your "account" pays for the premiums. This is known as *vanishing premiums*. But be careful. If you don't have enough cash value built up to pay for those future premiums, your policy will be the thing that vanishes! And then you're stuck with kicking in more money. Whole life premiums are often invested in long-term bonds and mortgages.

➤ **Universal Life**   Unlike a standard whole life insurance policy, universal life offers you flexibility because it allows you the decision of changing the premium payments or the amount of the death benefit, as long as certain minimums are met. (Sometimes, if you don't meet the minimums or you violate the rules, your tax liability may skyrocket if you borrow or withdraw the money.) *You* decide how to design your policy. You can pay hefty premiums, build up a lot of tax-deferred cash value in your account, and then later change your mind that you want your cash value to pay for your premiums. Or, you can opt for lower death benefits and a larger cash buildup or a smaller cash buildup and higher death benefits. It's up to you. You can even take a cash withdrawal and lower the death benefit. There's no interest expense if you do this, but even if you pay back the withdrawal, this permanently lowers the death benefit. Typically, there's enough cash value earnings to cover the cost of the insurance. Universal life premiums are invested in and reflect the current short-term rates available in the money market.

➤ **Variable Life**   Even though the annual premiums are fixed, the cash value of your account doesn't earn a fixed rate of return. The growth of your account in the policy depends on what investment choices you make. Generally, the investment choices are mutual funds managed by the insurance company. You have the option of shifting your money around. Note that the death benefit also rises and falls based on the performance, but it will never drop below the original amount of insurance coverage you specified on your contract.

➤ **Single-Premium Life**   The person who would benefit from this type of policy is someone who is older, has a lump sum of cash to invest on a tax-deferred basis that meets with IRS guidelines, and wants insurance benefits for his or her beneficiaries. These policies can earn a fixed rate of interest (like those in a whole life or universal life), or you can choose your own investment (as in a variable life policy).

Whatever you do, don't look upon a cash value insurance policy as retirement savings or your first means to accumulate growth on a tax-deferred basis. Even if your insurance agent tells you that your cash value account is compounding on a tax-deferred basis, that

If you plan to keep this variable life policy for a long time, invest the cash value portion of your policy in a growth stock mutual fund to take advantage of long-term market performance.

shouldn't be the reason to buy a cash value policy. If you're seeking tax-deferred growth, you should be participating in a company's 401(k) or an individual retirement account.

Insure Your Paycheck!

Have you ever thought about what would happen if you were suddenly unable to perform the work that provides your income? You should. According to the Health Insurance Association of America, if you are between the ages of 35 and 65, your chances of dying are equal to your chances of being unable to work for three months or more because of a disability through illness or injury. It is stressful enough trying to deal with an injury or illness that you don't want to have to worry about whether you're going to receive your salary while you're off work.

Your earning power is the most valuable asset that you will ever own—not your home, your car, or even your antique furniture. If you own your home, you probably have homeowner's insurance in case of loss or damage, and automobile insurance protects you and your family in case of a car accident. So why not insure your paycheck, too?

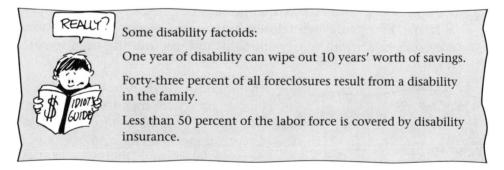

REALLY? Some disability factoids:

One year of disability can wipe out 10 years' worth of savings.

Forty-three percent of all foreclosures result from a disability in the family.

Less than 50 percent of the labor force is covered by disability insurance.

If you're like most folks, you probably have some type of access to a company-sponsored disability plan. Most companies extend a form of paid sick leave or actual disability payments in case you are unable to work for a long time period under the plan. According to these plans, in order for you to receive benefits, many companies require you to be totally disabled. Other companies have both short-term and long-term disability plans. Ask your employer what provisions the company provides for both short- and long-term disability. The industry standard is 26 weeks for short-term disability, and you must qualify for most long-term disability plans. On average, an employer will pay the premiums for its employees' short-term disability insurance policy. For a long-term disability policy, it is standard for the employer and the employee to split the cost of the premium.

> REALLY?
>
> If you are paying part of the premium on disability insurance and your employer is paying the remainder, the benefits you receive are taxable equal to the amount of the premium your employer pays. For example, let's say your annual premium on your disability insurance policy is $1,200. You pay a third of your annual premium ($400), and your employer pays the other two-thirds ($800). If you were to become disabled and start collecting benefits, the portion of the premium that your employer paid would be considered taxable income. You would owe ordinary income taxes on your monthly benefits check.

Make sure you find out as much as you can about your company's disability plan. One woman we know did her homework before she went in for surgery. She was able to take a short-term disability leave for eight weeks and received 60 percent of her salary while recuperating at home. Many folks who don't do their homework go back to work a lot sooner without recovering fully and risk injuring themselves further.

Check your company's terms carefully. One clause to watch out for is whether your company offers residual benefits. If it does not, your company will not pay you the difference between the income you are able to earn after your disability and the original amount of your guaranteed monthly payments.

If your company does not sponsor a plan, you can purchase your own individual policy. However, you have to have a job to receive disability insurance—no ifs, ands, or buts. But only you can determine which type of disability policy is best. Your goal should be to maximize your coverage without paying for any unnecessary benefits.

Annual individual policy premiums range anywhere from $800 to $1,800, sometimes a lot more, depending on the bells and whistles you add to the policy. You will need enough coverage to provide between 60 and 70 percent of your gross earned income. Sit down and figure out what your living expenses would be if you were disabled for three to six months... or more. Keep in mind you'll have to cover the mortgage or rent, automobile expenses, food, clothing, and utilities. Plus, you will incur additional expenses: medicine, doctor visits, and possibly nursing care.

Keep these other factors in mind if you're considering buying disability insurance:

➤ **If you have a risky job, you will pay a higher premium for disability insurance.** The cost of disability insurance is determined by your job and the amount of income you want. If you are in a hazardous occupation class (for example, if you are a firefighter, carpenter, or construction worker), you might not be able to receive long-term disability at any cost, unless it's through a company or a union.

➤ **Stay in good health and maintain a good credit report.** You will be required to take a medical exam to qualify for disability insurance. Plus, the insurance company looks into your credit history. If you have a poor credit history or have recently filed for bankruptcy, an insurance company might not cover you.

If you are not eligible for disability insurance, start doing your own "self-insure" program. You still need to protect yourself, especially if you are in a risky occupation. Start your own nest egg by putting your own monthly premiums aside into safe investments.

➤ **Start your policy as soon as you can.** Why? The younger you are, the less your annual premiums will be.

➤ **Set a long elimination period.** This is the period of time before the benefits start. What you can do is match your emergency fund to this time period. Your premiums may be reduced by nearly 10 percent.

➤ **Avoid policies that pay only if you are totally disabled.** Instead, look for a policy that covers the "own occupation." This guarantees that you will receive the full guaranteed disability payment, no matter what other work you do, as long as you are not able to return to your original occupation.

➤ **Make sure your policy is noncancelable as long as you keep paying the premiums.** Also make sure it has a guaranteed annual premium that can never be increased. Also crucial is a waiver of premiums clause, which states that you don't have to pay any more premiums once you become disabled.

➤ **Shop around.** Want the best price? Get quotes from three different insurance agents. Then contact USAA Life Insurance Company (which sells directly to consumers) toll-free at (800) 531-8000 and compare prices.

➤ **See what Social Security has to offer.** Through Social Security you will receive disability income if you are completely disabled for five months and the disability is expected to last for at least one year or your lifetime.

Insurance Products You DON'T Need

You want to cover your life, health, and wealth, right? That's why you're reading this chapter: to protect yourself and your loved ones. Unfortunately, many companies are jumping on the insurance bandwagon to take advantage of consumers, making them think they need these superfluous policies. Not so. Here's a list of what to avoid.

Credit life and credit disability policies   Sold by credit card companies, such as VISA and MasterCard, these policies will pay a small monthly income in case of liability or a small benefit in case you die with an outstanding loan. Skip this coverage and purchase disability insurance instead.

Extended warranties   Never purchase an extended warranty on anything—a television, VCR, or even an automobile. If something breaks down, it's likely that it would cost less to pay for it out of your own pocket.

Flight insurance   This type of insurance is based on fears and misconceptions. Instead of protecting yourself with flight insurance in case you die while flying, choose a good life insurance policy that protects you wherever you are—even if you're at 31,000 feet.

Dental insurance   Many employers offer this type of coverage through company-sponsored health insurance plans. Take advantage of it. If your employer does not offer this, the routine cleanings cost much less than your annual premiums would.

Life insurance for your children   Touted on late-night television, this form of insurance boasts inexpensive monthly premiums to provide coverage for your children. It's not necessary at all, and it can be quite expensive. Besides, what parents would spend the benefits from a life insurance policy on their children if something terrible happened?

The Least You Need to Know

➤ Renter's insurance is inexpensive and can help you replace your belongings in case of fire, theft, or other disaster.

➤ Homeowner's insurance is required by mortgage lenders. It's usually best to get as much coverage as you can afford. You can save money on premiums by raising your deductible, paying your premium annually, and using the same insurance company for your home and car.

➤ Car insurance is required by law in most states. You can save money on your premiums by being a safe driver, driving a reliable car, and shopping around.

➤ There are two types of life insurance: term and cash-value. Term insurance is a better deal unless you're older or wealthy.

➤ Long-term disabilities that leave you unable to work can result in financial disaster. Take advantage of any disability insurance available through your employer and consider buying supplemental insurance if necessary.

Chapter 24

Tackling Taxes

In This Chapter

➤ Avoiding common tax mistakes

➤ Strategies to keep tax liabilities to a (legal) minimum

➤ Finding a good tax pro

Tax planning doesn't just concern the wealthy. The money you save in taxes creates more investment dollars that can be put to work for you and your family if you start your tax planning now. Plus, prepping for April's tax season ahead of the typical last-minute schedule will help you get your records in order for when you really need them.

Being smart about your taxes is more than just correctly using a black pen instead of a pencil on your tax return. Your investment strategies impact your tax situation—and vice versa. How? You'll see how in this chapter, and you'll find out how to avoid common problems people make when it comes to tax planning. Because tax planning isn't always the easiest task to complete, this chapter also reviews the best ways to find a competent tax professional who can help you.

Avoiding the Ten Most Common Tax Mistakes

Mistake 1: Failing to keep good records. Getting organized is imperative. At some point, most people have the motivation to sort out their tax records, but they seem to drop the ball several months later. If you are one of those consumers whose sock drawer is stuffed with unopened envelopes holding your mutual fund statements and past IRS tax-returns, kick the habit. It's time to clean house.

You have several options for maintaining good records, including tax software programs for your computer and your basic file folder for file statements. Tax preparation software packages for your computer can save you time and money. You just have to answer a few questions, and the software program plugs the information into the appropriate tax form. In addition, most tax-software packages print and file your returns automatically. Such software programs include Andrew Tobias' TaxCut, $29.95 (203/255-1441); TurboTax, $39.95 (800/964-1040); and Personal Tax Edge Software, $19.00 (800/223-6925).

Simply Tax (developed by 4Home Productions), which retails for $69.99, not only helps you answer questions about your income but also gives tax advice from the *Ernst & Young Tax-Saving Strategies Guide* (John Wiley & Sons). Simply Tax also includes an automatic deduction finder that reviews your return for commonly overlooked deductions or credits.

Mistake 2: Not withholding the right amount of taxes. Estimated tax payment and underpayment penalty rules have eased somewhat for Americans, but that does not give you the green light to ignore the rules. Because interest rates increased in 1994 and are poised for an upswing in 1995, penalties will be more expensive for those who underpay. On the other hand, if you're anticipating a tax refund, all that means is that you've overpaid the government. You could have put that "extra" money to work for you in an investment instead of loaning it to Uncle Sam.

If you make estimated tax payments (as do many self-employed individuals or people who earn a whopping taxable income from investments outside a tax-deferred account), you should constantly monitor your tax-paying situation. The best way is to get Form 1040-ES, Estimated Tax for Individuals, from the Internal Revenue Service by calling (800) TAX-FORM. Your goal should be to not overpay but not underpay: try to get as close to the mark as possible.

Mistake 3: Getting help when it's too late. This mistake is so common it's not even funny. It's like trying to prevent a cavity that has already made its way into your molar—there's no way to do it. Because many of your personal finance and investment decisions will affect your tax plan, get *preventive* help before it's too late.

Once you assess your personal financial picture and investment game plan, you'll need to consistently monitor it, especially as you build your wealth and accumulate a higher net worth. In the section "Finding a Tax Pro" later in this chapter, you'll read which types of tax pros can help you no matter what your circumstances are.

Mistake 4: Not contributing to a tax-deferred investment program. Up to certain limits, Individual Retirement Accounts (IRAs), 401(k)s, and other popular tax-deferred retirement plans allow you to reduce your taxable income by the amount of your contribution. Even if you only receive a partial or no tax deduction, investing your money in a mutual fund within your IRA takes advantage of the power of tax-deferred compounding.

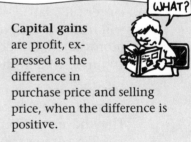

Capital gains are profit, expressed as the difference in purchase price and selling price, when the difference is positive.

Here's the magic of tax-deferred compounding at work. If for 30 years you invest $2,000 a year in a mutual fund in your IRA instead of in a taxable account, assuming a nine percent annual return, you will have accumulated almost $300,000 in your IRA. In contrast, you would have accumulated only $184,000 in a taxable account in the same amount of time. The capital gains and dividend distributions made would be tax-deferred for the entire 30 years. So just do it!

Mistake 5: Not replacing personal debt with mortgage debt to the extent possible. It's a smart tax planning strategy if you do this, especially since interest expense on mortgage loans is 100 percent tax-deductible. Interest expense on personal debt, such as credit cards or personal loans, is *not* tax deductible at all. If possible, and where applicable, you may wish to consider a home equity loan to pay off your personal debt. The interest on a home equity loan is 100 percent tax deductible, and you can get rid of your personal debt, too!

Mistake 6: Forgetting to check last year's income tax return for important items. For example, if you have $10,000 worth of gains in one tax year and $10,000 worth of losses, you can net the losses again the gains, and not have any taxable income from your investments. However, if your ordinary income (from your wages or salary) is $30,000 and you had $10,000 worth of losses (and no gains), you could only apply a total of $3,000 to your ordinary income to reduce your taxable income. The mistake people make is forgetting to carry forward the remaining loss amount on next year's return. Under current IRS rules, the remaining amount over $3,000 (in $3,000 increments) can be applied to the *following year's* tax bill.

Mistake 7: Not taking a profit because you're afraid to have an capital gain. When you buy low and sell high, you earn a profit, which is a capital gain. And, depending on your income tax bracket, you are subject to pay capital gains of 15 percent or 28 percent under current IRS law. Of course, review the tax implications a capital gain will have on your investment portfolio—and tax return—with your tax professional, but don't shy away from taking a gain. After all, why are you investing in the first place? To *lose* money? We hope not.

Mistake 8: Choosing the wrong filing status. Usually newly married couples have this problem—not knowing which filing status to choose. They have two options: married filing jointly and married filing singly. The IRS advises confused newlyweds (and other married folks) to complete returns based on both situations and, based on the bottom-line outcome (whether you owe a little, a lot, or expect a refund), make your decision then. Nine times out of ten you'll "save" more in taxes by filing jointly.

Mistake 9: Anticipating a large refund. If you regularly look forward to receiving a huge income tax refund, know this: You're having too much in taxes withheld from your paycheck and, in effect, giving an interest-free loan to the IRS. Changing the number of allowances you claim on a W-4 form will increase your take-home pay.

Mistake 10: Forgetting to attach the right copy to your tax returns. Sounds silly, but it happens. Attach all the "Copy Bs" of your W-2 forms to your return in order to avoid future correspondence with the IRS. And, above all, make copies of all your returns and correspondence... just in case!

Investments and Taxes

Whenever you invest your moolah, you have tax consequences to consider. For example, when you buy low and sell high, you earn a profit, which is a capital gain. And, depending on your income tax bracket, if it's a sizeable gain it can really make a difference in your bottom-line return figures.

How can you determine if you should invest your money in an investment vehicle that stresses capital gains (which is a profit that you pay a maximum 28 percent tax on) or income (usually in the form of interest payments or dividends that are taxed at your income tax rate)? The decision depends on your investment objective but also creates different tax consequences.

Here's an example. Let's say you are in a higher tax bracket and invest more of your money in taxable bond funds. You get a pretty steady income stream through interest payments (remember, bonds pay interest, as you learned in Chapter 19). These interest payments are taxed at *your* income tax rate. If you are taking out any cash distributions, that is a taxable event and subject to your tax bracket.

On the other hand, if you are investing in an investment that stresses capital gains (profit), it's a different story. For example, if you are investing in growth funds (no dividend income, rather long-term appreciation), any capital gains you realize are taxed at a maximum rate of 28 percent—a rate much less than taxable income brackets for high-income individuals.

The general rule of thumb is not to necessarily base your investment decisions solely on tax implications. If that were the case, many investors would never sell their investments! Your investment strategy is more important than a tax strategy. If you think market prices are dropping, you should take your profits and pay your taxes. A capital gain is always better than a capital loss!

Two of the Biggest Tax Blunders Ever

When folks hear "tax-free" or "tax-exempt," they jump for joy. The allure of tax-free investing is appealing, but it's not for everybody.

Many times, investors put their money in tax-exempt investments, such as municipal bonds, for the wrong reasons. Investors jump at the chance to boast of receiving tax-free income. But many of these municipal-bond funds tend to have lower yields than comparable taxable mutual funds for investors in lower tax brackets. If you are in a higher tax bracket, investing in municipal-bond funds is worth checking out because the income distributions you receive are exempt from federal tax. (Remember that the capital gains payouts are taxed.)

The best way to determine whether a fund's tax-free yield is competitive with the yield of a similar taxable fund is to find your taxable equivalent yield. If you want to calculate your taxable equivalent yield, take your marginal tax rate (your tax bracket) and subtract it from 100. For example, if you were in the 28 percent tax bracket, subtract 28 from 100 to get your denominator, which is 72. Therefore, if you were deciding whether to invest in a tax-exempt or a taxable fund, you would take 5.25 percent (the tax-exempt municipal bond return rate) and divide it by 72 to get your taxable equivalent yield, which is 7.29 percent. That means you would have to earn at least 7.29 percent on a taxable bond fund to end up with the same amount you would have left over after taxes if you were to invest in a tax-exempt bond fund.

Table 24.1 does the math for you so you can easily determine whether a municipal-bond fund is a worthwhile investment for you. Compare the taxable equivalent yield for municipal bonds listed under your tax bracket with the rates listed for non tax-exempt treasury-only and corporate-bond funds to see which provides the highest yield. As you can see in Table 24.1, the lower the tax bracket, the less incentive there is to invest in tax-exempt mutual funds.

Table 24.1 Tax-Free or Not Tax-Free?

		Your Tax Bracket			
Investment	Return	39.6%	33%	28%	15%
Municipal-Bond Fund	5.25%	8.69%	7.83%	7.29%	6.17%
Treasury-Only Bond Fund	6.00%	6.00%	6.00%	6.00%	6.00%
Corporate-Bond Fund	7.50%	7.50%	7.50%	7.50%	7.50%

Another blunder is when folks forget to swap or exchange investments to take a tax-loss and offset any other capital gains. If you sell an investment for a profit, you must pay captain gains tax on that profit. Depending on your level of income, you are taxed on the gain at either 15 percent or 28 percent, which is the maximum tax rate on capital gains.

If you sell an investment at a loss, you can get a tax benefit, too. For example, if you have exchange privileges with your mutual fund family, consider using it in the event you are going to take a loss. Why? First, if you exchange shares of one mutual fund for shares of another mutual fund, it is considered a sale and a new purchase. If the sale of the first mutual fund constitutes a loss, you can use that amount to offset any other capital gains you have realized. This is considered a tax swap. Although your investment position is the same, you've saved on taxes. If you want to repurchase the shares in the same fund, you must wait 31 days before doing so according to IRS rules, in order to take the tax loss on the initial sale. If you don't wait the 31 days, it is known as a "wash sale," and you don't get to claim the loss. All capital gains and losses are reported on Schedule D of your tax return.

REALLY?

You can deduct up to $3,000 in losses from capital gains, thereby reducing your capital gains taxes. If you have no gains to offset your losses, you can deduct up to $3,000 from your ordinary income. Any additional amount can be carried forward to future years.

Finding a Tax Pro

Congress keeps talking about simplifying the tax code, yet it doesn't seem to get any easier. If you don't understand the tax system, you probably pay more in taxes than necessary. A good tax professional will cut through the muck and identify tax-reduction strategies that will help reduce your tax bill, possibly increase your deductions, and decrease the likelihood of an audit (which can be triggered by any mistakes you make).

Hiring a professional isn't cheap, but you can save a few bucks if you know what to look for. Keep the following tips in mind before you hire anybody:

➤ **Don't hire the first tax adviser you find.** You don't buy the first house you look at, so apply the same theory here. You will be telling this person the most intimate financial details of your life. Make sure you interview at least five tax professionals face-to-face before you make your final decision. If the person is a true professional, he or she should spend quality time with you, ask a lot of questions, and above all, listen to you.

➤ **Ask the tax adviser about his or her credentials.** The recent crackdown on unscrupulous tax preparers in September 1994 has created stricter guidelines for tax preparers who file electronically. This effort screened out preparers with criminal records and severe financial problems who were claiming false refunds on clients' electronic returns. Preparers with access to IRS computers must be at least 21 years old and be a U.S. citizen or permanent resident alien. Credentials for all other types of tax preparers are listed in the appropriate section below.

➤ **Understand how the adviser gets paid.** There are flat fees, hourly fees, and fees based on a percentage of your return. The method of compensation is important because it can sway an adviser to recommend one course of action over another. By knowing the adviser's motivation, you can guard against any self-serving advice.

The Lowdown on CPAs

You will need a CPA if your tax situation is complex. For example, if you are self-employed, run a small business, or have a high salary and claim many deductions, a CPA can not only help you prepare your return but help you plan your taxes throughout the year. She looks at your entire financial picture and how each of your financial decisions (whether it's unloading a poor performing stock or buying real estate for income) will impact your tax situation over the long haul. In addition, she can save you thousands of dollars in taxes by helping you conduct your financial affairs in a way that minimizes the government's tax bite.

Just because a CPA specializes in accounting issues doesn't mean he or she files tax returns. Make sure you find out if the CPA does before you shell out any dough.

Follow these guidelines when using a CPA:

➤ **Get a letter of engagement from the CPA.** This will list in detail what the CPA will do for you and what she will charge. Since a CPA charges more than any other tax preparer, the letter should state whether you are charged on an hourly basis or as a flat fee per return. You should also get an estimate of the time the CPA will spend on your return. If the CPA works on an hourly basis, ask her to guess how long it will take to do your tax preparations and complete your returns. However, if your CPA gives you a flat fee, see what other types of services are included in this fee, such as tax planning advice or whether she will attend an audit.

➤ **Don't simply dump your box of receipts and tell the CPA, "It's up to you to figure this all out."** One way to minimize their fees is to provide accurate records. You'll end up paying bucks deluxe if you're disorganized.

➤ **Find out how many tax returns the CPA works on each year.** If it's fewer than 300, consider him a candidate. If he prepares any more than that, he's probably sacrificing quality. Also, see what percentage of your CPA's clients had to file extensions last year. If it's more than 20 percent, the CPA is probably swimming in (and behind on) paperwork.

➤ **Find a CPA in your area by contacting the AICPA.** This is the professional organization for CPAs, and you can reach it at (800) 862-4272.

Try an Enrolled Agent

Enrolled agents are the biggest secret in the world of tax preparation. They are tax experts who worked for the IRS at least five years as auditors or who have passed a strict two-day test of federal tax law. If you don't mind that an enrolled agent doesn't have "CPA" listed after his name on the letterhead, an enrolled agent can be just as good—for much less money. Enrolled agents are experts in all areas of tax preparation; some even specialize in a few areas of the law. Make sure you determine an agent's specialty before you hire him. The best way to find an enrolled agent near you is to contact the National Association of Enrolled Agents (NAEA) at (800) 424-4339. They will send you a list of three agents in your area.

The Truth About Tax Attorneys

Tax attorneys know the ins and outs of federal tax law, but they do not prepare tax returns. Their role is to offer tax advice to your CPA or enrolled agent if you are in a complicated legal tax jam.

Hire a tax attorney if—and only if—you find yourself in a major legal jam resolving tax issues, such as a serious tax dispute with the IRS that can only be resolved in Tax Court. You may also need a tax attorney when you are working on the details of your estate plan and how it will affect your tax situation. Keep in mind, however, that these professionals are expensive! You will pay a price for their legal advice. Tax attorneys charge as much as several hundred dollars per hour, sometimes more if they represent you in court. Their fees may be deductible, but it's not guaranteed.

If a legal problem arises and your CPA cannot recommend a competent tax attorney, call the American Bar Association at (312) 988-5000 or find one listed in the *Martindale-Hubbell Law Directory*, which lists lawyers by state and specialty.

Certified Financial Planner: A Jack-of-All-Trades

Imagine someone who knows your entire financial picture *and* can prepare your tax return. Sound like a financial dream come true? A certified financial planner (CFP) can create a budget for you, help you build an investment portfolio, and assist you with retirement and estate planning and tax preparation. Since CFPs must be licensed by the International Boards of Standards and Practices for Certified Financial Planners (IBCFP), look for their accreditation. There are a lot of financial planners out there masquerading as professionals; unless they have the acronym, don't deal with them.

You do not want to be troubled by a nagging concern that your CFP is recommending products because of the commissions they generate instead of for their appropriateness of your situation. Make sure you get a written estimate of any fees you must pay, and make sure he or she is certified by the IRS to help you with your tax returns.

CFPs do *not* have the same credentials as a CPA. People who choose CFPs to help with their tax preparation often do so because they know their whole financial picture.

CFPs are compensated in one of three ways: on a commission-only, fee-only, or commission and fee basis. The least expensive of the three for you (if you plan to maintain a working relationship with this person) is fee-only. For tax preparation, the most common form of payment will be fee-only. Fee-only planners do not get a dime for any type of investment recommendations they make, which is one of the reasons this condition works out best for most folks. When you find a fee-only planner, she should give you a no-cost, no-frills initial consultation to assess your financial condition. Based on this information, the CFP will give you an estimated fee that is set in advance. Typical rates average $75 an hour, depending on the complexities involved.

To find a qualified CFP in your area, contact the Institute of Certified Financial Planners (ICFP) at (800) 282-7526.

H&R Block and the Like

Places like H&R Block or Jackson Hewitt Associates process millions of tax returns each year and file electronically, which speeds up your refund if you are expecting one. In addition, some chains offer an instant refund, which is actually a loan that is paid back when your refund arrives from the IRS.

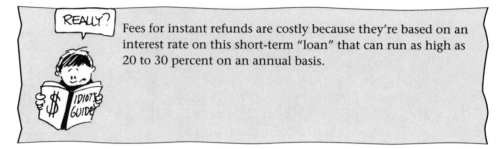

REALLY?

Fees for instant refunds are costly because they're based on an interest rate on this short-term "loan" that can run as high as 20 to 30 percent on an annual basis.

If you don't have a complicated tax situation, check out a national tax preparation chain. They are convenient, and they help you on a first-come, first-serve basis. However, keep in mind that you probably won't establish a long-term relationship with your tax preparer as you would with other tax professionals. The best way to find a national chain near you is to look in the Yellow Pages.

Going It Alone

Even if you have a CPA do your taxes, you should know *every* single detail that goes into your income tax return! If you prepare your own tax return, you know the ins and outs and can monitor your tax situation. Just make sure you keep up with any major changes in federal tax laws.

If you do go it alone, the IRS can actually help you. Although the IRS won't fill out your return, it will help you do so free of charge. All IRS offices hold tax preparation clinics, distribute free IRS publications, and answer tax questions over the phone. To contact them toll-free, call (800) 829-1040. There are some free books and publications that can help you, such as Publication 17, *Your Federal Income Tax*, which is published by the IRS to help individual tax-return preparation.

The Least You Need to Know

➤ The key to having a less stressful tax time is to keep your tax-related documents organized. Tax-preparation software can help you do this.

➤ Investing in IRAs and 401(k)s is a great way to reduce your tax liability.

➤ Before you invest in stocks, bonds, or mutual funds, make sure you assess what effect those investments will have on your tax situation. However, don't base your decision solely on the tax consequence.

➤ Tax attorneys and CPAs are only necessary if your tax situation is complex. Less expensive sources of help include enrolled agents, certified financial planners, and tax preparation chains such as H & R Block.

➤ The cheapest way to handle your taxes is to do them yourself. The IRS can help; they provide tax booklets, clinics, and over-the-phone advice. Call (800) 829-1040 for more information.

Part 7
Getting Ready for the Year 2000

The year 2000 seems so far away. But it's not. Less than five years from now, we will be in a new century. There will be new rules, new hairdos, and new types of investments products. One thing won't change, no matter what century it is: how you plan for the future. You can create your future tomorrows by what you do today.

In this Part, you'll learn how to manage your money online (and you don't need to be a computer nerd!), how to start saving for your child's college education, and how to plan for your golden years. Start planning today—the future will be here before you know it. So why not create it?

Chapter 25

So How Come Your PC Doesn't Have a Modem?

In This Chapter

➤ The '90s way to managing your money

➤ How to do your banking from an armchair

➤ Top financial software packages

Just when you thought all the kids have gone to sleep, you hear cries of "I've got it!" and "That was so-o-o easy!" coming from the den. Your 14-year-old is still up, playing on the family computer. You know, the 486DX-50 with 340 MB hard drive and eight megs of RAM the children begged and squealed for during the 10 weeks before Christmas.

You're hip—you know that "edu-tainment" is in. So you ask your child if he's having fun with the Megablaster Tri-color-rama battle field game on the CD-ROM. Your child gives you one of those "Get real" stares, turns to you and says, "Nope. I just balanced your checkbook, paid off your credit line at the bank, and reconciled your VISA account. Wanna update your stock portfolio?" he queries. "I got the modem all set up on COM port 2."

"Geez," you say, as all the pride of learning the difference between the floppy drive and hard drive flushed right out of your toes. Welcome to managing your money in the 21st century. This chapter presents to you the different types of financial software packages and online services available without making you feel like a speed bump on the information superhighway.

Connecting Your PC to the Information Superhighway

In today's electronic world, it makes a lot of sense to stay connected, and technology has provided the world with a number of choices. The onslaught of online services has allowed many Americans the opportunity to ride the information superhighway. But just what *is* an online service?

It's a form of communication in the '90s. Online services provide information to the masses with their extensive databases. If you subscribe to an online service, you can access their information with your computer, a modem (which needs a telephone line to "dial into" the database), and the appropriate software.

Here are a few of the top contenders:

➤ **America Online** Of the three main online services (CompuServe and PRODIGY being the other two), America Online offers a greater selection of personal finance forums. You can obtain historical performance information on mutual funds tracked by *Morningstar*, keep up with the latest financial news in *Investor's Business Daily* and *Business Week*, and post your money questions to the folks at the *American Association of Individual Investors*. And that's just for starters. America Online reduced its hourly fee to $2.95 in January of 1995 and gives five free hours each month to subscribers. For more information, call (800) 827-3338.

➤ **CompuServe** You can monitor the latest financial market information and update a personalized stock portfolio as part of CompuServe's basic services. Additionally, FundWatch Online by *Money* magazine and Loan Analyzer—an online mortgage calculator—are available. You do have to pay extra for some of CompuServe's extended financial services. The monthly fee is $9.95 for the Standard Pricing Plan. For more information, call (800) 848-8199.

348

➤ **PRODIGY**   For $9.95 a month, PRODIGY allows you to ask questions to many financial experts—one of them being an author of this book! You can also post questions to tax experts and other Wall Street gurus. For more information, call 1-(800)-PRODIGY.

➤ **Women's Wire**   Basically designed for women, this online service gives subscribers the opportunity to post questions to its financial forum "Women & Investing." The forum is mostly educational, covering topics such as how to get started in investing to learning how to protect your wealth. The online service is $9.95 a month. For more information, call (415) 378-6500.

➤ **Dow Jones News/Retrieval Service**   This service gives price quotes, historical data (not many online services do), and news on individual stocks and the economy.

In fact, if you'd like to send us your money questions, you can e-mail us at *moneyanswr@aol.com*, which is our e-mail address. We can't guarantee to answer all of your questions, but we would love to hear from you!

For those seniors who want to go online, "SeniorNet" was introduced in early 1995 to help seniors learn the ropes of the information superhighway. America Online offers a reduction in its monthly charge to participate in its online services.

Home Banking Basics

Move over ATM. The PC is gaining on you. Millions of consumers have access to the banking industry's latest advertising gimmick to keep your deposits: home banking online. It goes beyond the concept of an automatic teller machine handling transactions. You can pay bills and balance your checking account all with the help of your personal computer and a modem.

High-tech interactive banking is not new. Several large financial institutions, such as Chase Manhattan Bank, tried offering online banking software to consumers ten years ago—but they had no luck. Consumers didn't want it because it was too impersonal a way to do business. Now, a natural progression into Buck Rogers-mania banking

If you want more information about all types of online services, pick up a copy of *The Complete Idiot's Guide to Modems and Online Services* by Sherry Kinkoph (a definite must-read!). Also available is *The Woman's Guide to Online Services*, (June 1995) written by Judith Broadhurst, which provides *both* men and women the rundown on all of online services available. In an easy-to-read format, the book gives real-life anecdotal information about channel-surfing the information superhighway and how you can find what you're looking for.

is taking place. That's why banks are boosting their technology spending. In 1994, $16.3 *billion* dollars was spent on increasing technological advances in the banking industry. Forecasts for 1995 run as high as $17.4 billion and $18.6 billion in 1996.

And computer giants are raking in the bucks. Intuit markets the hot financial software program Quicken, which is the "critically acclaimed" number one personal finance software available. Chase Manhattan Bank advertised its Microsoft Money-based software to its customers so well that more than 5,000 people have signed up for the service. First National Bank of Chicago and Michigan National Bank are marketing the software to their customers, too. Citibank offers a similar program, with the choice of a screen phone or computer software. PRODIGY, one of the nation's largest online services, has teamed up with 17 banks to transfer money and pay bills.

Home banking (or online banking) is easy to use. You need a computer, the financial software (depending on the bank, when appropriate), and a modem to do it—that's it. Each home banking software differs slightly. For example, an online service called CheckFree lets people do most of their banking from their home computers; its users just can't withdraw any cash from their accounts.

Typically, you can pay utility bills, make a mortgage payment, and even pay your insurance premiums. Costs for each source varies, so check with your financial institution to see if it offers a home banking feature!

The advantage to home banking is obvious: you can easily do your banking—from balancing your checkbook to paying your mortgage—from home. No need to jump in the car and fight traffic to get to the bank before it closes. Plus, you can do your banking whenever *you* want. You are not limited to lobby hours. On the other hand, it can be time-consuming to enter all of your financial information.

The results of all of this home banking activity? The percent of transactions made at bank branches, such as depositing your paycheck with a live teller, is falling. Fast. By 1997, only 44 percent of all transactions will be made at the bank location. That's down from 51 percent in 1994.

The positive side of online banking is also a negative. Since people are likely to see electronic banking as being more like a debit card rather than a credit card, they may change their "buy-now-pay-later" attitude. But because a debit card deducts money from your account immediately, online users may feel vulnerable and fear giving up control of their money to a computer. If your bank offers an online banking program, make sure you understand all of the features and whether or not additional charges are assessed.

Software Packages That Won't Make You Feel Like an Idiot

You are learning how to manage your money for a reason: to get organized and create financial security. Maybe you want to get better organized for taxes. Maybe it's finally time to figure out where all that money is going. Perhaps you need to retrieve more information about a particular mutual fund to see if it fits your investment objective. When you start to give yourself a financial checkup and want to learn how to manage your money, consider consulting one of the following software packages.

➤ Kiplinger's CA-Simply Money (800/225-5224) is available for both DOS and Windows and is very user-friendly and visually non-intimidating. There is an icon that represents every transaction that you would ever need to perform. It shows you in three simple steps how to balance your checkbook and your credit card statements. It can forecast annual budget expenses and even update prices on your investments if you have a modem. You can also print checks and create and monitor your investment portfolio. If you have a home-based business, it allows you to create all necessary financial accounts.

➤ Quicken, available from Intuit (520/295-3220) as of March 1995, is probably the most well-known financial software package available. The package provides you with features to pay your bills, reconcile many types of financial accounts, and create financial records and a custom-tailored investment portfolio. This program updates security prices for you on all of your investments listed in your portfolio.

Since there are so many software programs that help you choose stocks, the best resource to initially contact is the *Individual Investor's Guide to Computerized Investing*, which is available through the American Association of Individual Investors (312/280-0170).

➤ StreetSmart (800/334-4455) is offered through Charles Schwab & Company and is mostly used for creating and monitoring your investment portfolio. In fact, if you have an account at Schwab, you can retrieve all of your information and analyze your account portfolios. Plus, you have the ability to keep up with current financial news and obtain research reports from investment analysts.

Want to buy a home? The following computer software packages make it a bit easier for you.

➤ Mortgage Analyzer (801/295-1890) helps you determine whether or not you can qualify for a mortgage, whether it is worth refinancing your mortgage, and the different types of mortgages available and how they affect your taxes.

➤ Buy or Rent (800/289-6773) helps you analyze your situation—can you buy a home and *should* you buy a home? Or would it be better to rent based on your tax rate and housing costs?

If you want help with your insurance needs, check out PC Life Services (212/408-0529). It explains the different types of insurance products available, such as disability insurance and all types of life insurance.

The second largest expense in your life is paying for your children's college education—or even yours! So here's a few software packages designed to help you prepare for tuition day:

➤ Scudder Tuition Builder Kit (800/225-2470) estimates how much college costs will be in the year you send your child to school and tailors an investment program to meet those costs. It also projects future inflation rates and the potential rate of return on your investments.

➤ College Cost Explorer (800/323-7155) will also help you calculate your expected family contribution to college costs. This financial software program allows you to access a database of thousands of private sources of scholarships, financial aid packages, and loans.

Want a painless way to do your taxes? Check out some of these tax planning software packages:

➤ TurboTax (800/964-1040) will print out your completed federal and state tax returns after you complete a number of tax preparation exercises. TurboTax also lets you file your return electronically, too.

➤ Kiplinger TaxCut (800/365-1546) is easy-to-use software that not only lets you fill out your federal and state returns but also project the tax consequences of your actions before you take them.

Retirement planning can be easy if you use one of the following computer software packages:

➤ T. Rowe Price Retirement Planning Kit (800/638-5660) allows you to estimate your retirement expenses and figure out how much you're going to need to save so you can live comfortably in your golden years.

➤ Harvest-Time (800/397-1456), in its easy-to-understand format, helps you calculate how much you'll need to save toward retirement. It also tracks different types of retirement-oriented investment products, such as municipal bonds, IRAs, and annuities.

If you want help with estate planning, here are a few financial software packages that can help you:

➤ Home Lawyer (800/288-MECA) is a user-friendly software package that allows you to write your own will, a residential lease, an employment agreement, and other frequently used legal documents.

➤ Willmaker (800/992-NOLO) takes you through a step-by-step process of writing a will. You can also create different types of trusts as you are working on your estate plan.

➤ It's Legal (800/223-6925) provides power of attorney forms, estate-planning worksheets, different types of wills, and a living trust.

The Least You Need to Know

➤ Online services can be a good way to get financial information. The three largest ones are CompuServe, America Online, and PRODIGY.

➤ Online banking is becoming increasingly popular. Contact your financial institution to see what kind of online opportunities they offer and what fees are involved.

➤ There are many software packages out there that are designed to help you with financial issues. You can find packages that help you manage a budget, run a home-based business, save for college costs, and even plan for retirement.

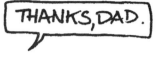

THANKS, DAD.

Chapter 26

Getting the Kids Through School

In This Chapter

➤ How to teach your children about money—even at an early age

➤ Getting a ballpark figure of how much Junior's college is going to cost

➤ How you can afford to send your kids to school

➤ Programs that offer parents a break

A college education is one of the best investments you can make. Studies show that the earning power of a college-educated individual is one-half million dollars more than that of a person who has a high school degree. However, a college education is also one of the largest investments you will ever make. As of December 1994, the average cost of one year of education at a state university is $7,274—and that's just for tuition, fees, and room and board!

That's why you need to arm yourself with enough information as soon as possible. Why? Two reasons: One, the rate of inflation of college costs is averaging 6.7 percent annually and two, the more time you have on your side, the better off you'll be—the younger the child, the less you need to save each month. This chapter shows you how to teach your children important lessons in financial planning and help you plan specific financial strategies for getting your kids through school.

Children and Money—They Go Hand in Hand

Before you tackle the problem of learning different money strategies to finance your child's college education, it's time for a little homework for your kids: Money 101.

Start talking to your children about money: how to save it and how to invest it. The earlier you begin, the better off your children will be in the future. People who don't learn about handling money at a young age often don't know how to handle it as an adult. The following are some strategies for teaching your child about this important topic:

➤ **Tailor your lessons according to your children's age.** For example, if you have a four-year-old and a ten-year-old, speak with them separately. Why? Because the ten-year-old already knows how to add, subtract, multiply and divide (if our fifth-grade education serves us correctly!) and your youngest does not. However, your four-year-old can understand the importance of "how much." Older children can handle more financial responsibility and grasp more difficult financial subjects, such as comparison-shopping and the value of a dollar.

You can teach your kids at any age about saving by using the "penny jar" concept. Keep a large, clear jar in their room and whenever they get any change, have them put it in a container. It's financial planning at its easiest; they get to see what happens when the money grows.

➤ **Teach your children that they can't have everything they want.** (Some adults need this lesson, too; remember the '80s when the motto was "Greed Is Good?") A good way to start is to let them know that the next time they're wailing for the latest toy fads, they should make a decision to have one or the other but not both. An example: If you're shopping and your five-year-old wants a Power Rangers megablaster survival kit or a Barney and Baby Bop sleeping bag, have your child make a decision between the two. Child psychologists advocate that this is the first—and most crucial—concept to convey to kids in basic financial planning: decision-making.

➤ **Teach your younger children about the differences between coins.** Explain that all coins are different in value: Show them how a quarter is worth more than a dime, a dime is worth more than a nickel, and so on. Studies show that the earlier you begin, the better. Plus, it gives your child the opportunity to recognize different types of coins and to become comfortable with numbers. Children between the ages of five and seven often handle this concept well.

➤ **Explain how you get money.** Many youngsters think ATM machines are magical—press a few numbers and *poof!* Instant cash. We grownups wish it were that easy. If your children frequently visit the ATM machine with you, make sure they understand that in order to take money *out* of the machine, you have to put money in. Explain that you get your money from your job. If you have the opportunity, take your children to work with you to help them learn why mom or dad is gone all day. It will teach them that people have to work to pay bills, such as for the house, food, and clothing. Explain that you receive a paycheck you deposit into your bank account and that's why you can take money out of the ATM machine.

➤ **Give them an allowance.** Children who receive an allowance tend to adapt better money-management skills and will feel more in control of their own finances later on in life. It is up to you whether you tie the allowance to household chores, but if your children do more than their fair share of household chores, you can reward them—like a "bonus."

Child psychologists indicate that six- to seven-year-old children are capable of handling an allowance. The rule of thumb is to give your child a specified amount of money at regular intervals, typically on a weekly basis if possible. Never skip a payment either! (You wouldn't want your boss to accidentally forget to pay you, would you?) Tell them it's their "paycheck," just like mom and dad receive a weekly/monthly paycheck from their employers.

If you do give your children an allowance, make sure you give them more than just the right amount to cover school lunches or transportation. The extra money you give them should allow them to learn about saving and investing.

Make sure you increase the amount, too, such as every six months or on their birthdays.

Teach them how to plan and save with the allowance. How should allowance money be spent? It is really up to the child. If Junior wants to spend all five bucks on candy as soon as he receives his allowance, let him. But let him know that once all the money is spent, he has to wait until next week for his next allowance payment. Missing out on other opportunities later in the week will give Junior a good indication of why he should save his money.

➤ **Have your child keep a money diary.** Every time he or she receives an allowance or even a gift, have your child write the date, the amount, and the total received. Usually, by the time children turn seven, this is a good habit for them to practice. If your child takes out any money, it should be recorded, too. It's a great way to have your children learn the answer to that perennial question: "Where does all the money go?"

➤ **Open savings accounts for your children.** One of the best ways to teach your children about the interest that they can earn from a savings account is to take them to the bank with you when you

Make sure you open up a no-fee account for your child. Why? Because the amount of money that will be deposited probably won't meet typical minimum-balance requirements—no need to have Junior get nicked by fees and charges at a tender young age.

open up their account. Tell your child that in exchange for letting the bank "hold onto" his money, the bank will give him a bonus by paying interest on that money. (You don't need to explain to them the mathematical equations on whether the account should have its interest compounded annually or quarterly! But *you* should know the difference!) The policies for opening an account for a minor—those under the age of 18 or 21, depending on the state— are not the same in each state. Industry standards stipulate that one parent has to co-sign on the account and on any subsequent deposits and withdrawals.

358

➤ **Make sure they understand the basic elements of borrowing.** Not that your child is going to be applying for a mortgage loan, but he or she should understand the concept of what it means to borrow money. If your child knows the basics about earning interest on a savings account, then he or she can understand this lesson: If they come to you to borrow a few dollars, tell them that you are going to charge them interest. And then duck. Really, folks, children need to understand that they have to pay the money back—and at a price. You don't have to charge them 10 percent—one percent will do. And then have them figure out the amount.

Make sure you know what your child's bank policy is about service fees and charges. Explain to the bank representative that this is a child's account to see if there can be a reduction in fees and charges or if they could waive the service charges that could wipe out all of the interest on Junior's account. You'll see in Chapter 8 where to find the best deals on savings accounts.

A great way kids can learn about the stock market is through a 10-week Stock Market Game for students nationwide by the Securities Industry Association (212/608-1500). Children from fourth through twelfth grade participate in different types of divisions; they are given a fictional $100,000 portfolio to make buy-and-sell decisions on their investment portfolio. The results are recorded and posted in a centralized computer program. Plus, your children are encouraged to keep up with the stock tables in the financial section of your newspaper and keep tabs on current market news from financial TV programs. Who knows? Your child may make it to the *Forbes* list of the richest by age 16.

These lessons in financial planning are imperative for you and your children. Once you have these tasks accomplished, you can involve your children in planning for their financial future.

Figuring Out How Much Junior's College Is Going to Cost

Many parents fret over future college costs—whether it's one year or 18 years away—and often find that they're defending themselves against staggering tuition bills. For students entering college in 1995, the four-year cost, including tuition, room and board, books, and other expenses, will average $94,818 at a private school and $44,138 at a public university. The projection for college costs in the year 2010 is $121,779 for a four-year public college and $261,605 for a four-year private university. Ouch!

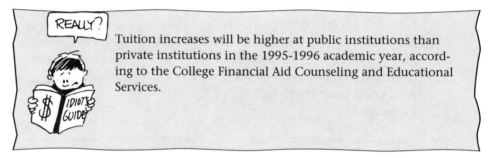

REALLY?

Tuition increases will be higher at public institutions than private institutions in the 1995-1996 academic year, according to the College Financial Aid Counseling and Educational Services.

Why is it going to cost so much? Because of the increase in college costs. On average, the costs at public colleges have risen 6.8 percent a year for the past 20 years, which happens to be faster than the overall rate of inflation. For future students who plan on attending a private school, you may need to adjust this figure.

If you haven't started planning for your child's education, it's time to swallow a bitter pill. In order to meet the rising costs of a college education, you need to have a plan. To formulate your plan, follow these steps:

1. Consider all of your options and gather as much research as possible.

   There are a number of choices available to get you and your kids on the right track, including mutual funds designed specifically for kids, certificates of deposit for college-bound children, various types of bond investments, scholarships, Pell grants, financial aid, and student loans. You can even borrow against your house or retirement plan from work. You will learn more about how each of these types of choices work and whether or not they're for you later in this chapter.

2. Figure out how long it is going to be before your child or children begin college.

   Easy enough. If little Suzie is six years old and she starts college right after high school, with the typical age a student enters college being 18, you have 12 years to work your plan. Write down what year your child will start college and remember it— you're going to need it later on.

3. Determine your child's total college cost.

   Oy! This is the figure that always stumps parents. First, figure out if your child will be attending a private university or a public university. If you don't know, you can hypothesize.

   Then find the year your child will enter school (which you figured out in step 2) in column A in Table 26.1. This table gives you a good indication of how much college costs are going to be, based on the average cost increase of public college at a 6.8 to seven percent annual rate, for four years of both a private and public education.

Table 26.1 College Cost Projections

Year the Student Enters	Cost of Private College	Cost of Public College
1995	$87,025	$34,810
1996	$93,378	$37,350
1997	$100,194	$40,078
1998	$107,508	$43,003
1999	$115,356	$46,143
2000	$123,777	$49,511
2001	$132,813	$53,125
2002	$142,509	$57,003

continues

Table 26.1   Continued

Year the Student Enters	Cost of Private College	Cost of Public College
2003	$152,912	$61,165
2004	$164,074	$65,630
2005	$176,052	$70,421
2006	$188,903	$75,561
2007	$202,693	$81,077
2008	$217,490	$86,996
2009	$233,367	$93,347
2010	$250,403	$100,161
2011	$268,862	$107,473
2012	$288,296	$115,318
2013	$309,341	$123,737

Sources: Annual increases are estimated, and taken from College Savings Bank. Actual college costs may vary. Source for 1994-1995 private college costs: the College Board's *Independent College 500 Index*. Source for 1994-1995 public college costs: U.S. Department of Education.

4. Determine how much money you will need to save.

   Get your pencils ready, folks. Now that you know what your tuition cost estimate is going to be for your child, it's time to do a little math. The following worksheet will help you figure out where you are financially, how much your current investments will grow, and the additional amount of money you're going to need (not counting financial aid and loans).

How Much Do You Need to Save?

If you save $100 a month for your children's college expenses, here's an idea of how much you'd have—based on a return of five, eight, or

10 percent, and a time frame of five, 10, 15, or 20 years. (We're assuming that *all* dividends and capital gains are reinvested.)

Table 26.2   Saving $100 a Month for College

Return %	5 Years	10 Years	15 Years	20 Years
5 percent	$6,829	$15,592	$26,840	$41,275
8 percent	$7,397	$18,418	$34,835	$59,294
10 percent	$7,808	$20,655	$41,799	$76,570

Because figuring out how much you need to save for college expenses is tricky—and often overwhelming when you add up all the expenses—we've included a college cost worksheet to help you. The calculations in the worksheet are based on the figures in Table 26.3, the CollegeSure Savings Table.

Table 26.3   The CollegeSure Savings Table

Years Until Freshman Year	CollegeSure Growth Multiplier	Monthly Savings Divisor
1	1.154	13.429
2	1.221	27.637
3	1.291	42.670
4	1.366	58.574
5	1.446	75.400
6	1.529	93.203
7	1.618	112.038
8	1.712	131.965
9	1.811	153.048
10	1.916	175.354
11	2.027	198.954

continues

Table 26.3 Continued

Years Until Freshman Year	CollegeSure Growth Multiplier	Monthly Savings Divisor
12	2.145	223.923
13	2.269	250.340
14	2.401	278.289
15	2.540	307.859
16	2.688	339.144
17	2.843	372.243
18	3.008	407.263
19	3.183	444.313

Note that these figures make some important assumptions. They assume a constant amount put aside every month—as well as the reinvestment of all earnings, *and* an average annual rate of increase in college costs of 7.3 percent.

The College Cost Worksheet first helps you determine how much you should save each month to fully fund four years of college tuition, fees, room, and board. If this amount is more than your budget allows, it can also help you create a plan based on your own financial situation.

College Cost Worksheet

1. What year does your child begin college?

   _____

2. What is the estimated total college cost (refer to Table 26.1)?

   _____

3. How much do you currently have socked away for your child's education? _____

4. How many years until your child's freshman year of college (subtract the current year from your answer in Question 1)?

   _____

5. What is the rate at which your *current* savings are expected to grow? (This rate is the *growth rate*, technically known as a *multiplier*; to find this, look at the CollegeSure Savings Table, match the number of years your child has until freshman year, and look across for the growth multiplier figure—that's your answer to this question.) _____

6. Multiply the number you gave in Question 3 by your answer to Question 5. This answer is an estimate of how much your current savings will have grown at the time your child will be attending college.

   _____

7. Subtract your answer to Question 6 from your answer to Question 2. This answer is the remaining amount you will need in order to fully fund your child's education.

   _____

8. Now that you know how much you need to fund your child's education, calculate how much you need to save each month to reach that figure you got in Question 7. How do you start? Look at your answer to Question 4 (how many years until your child's freshman year of college). Find the CollegeSure Savings Table and then look across to the right column for the monthly savings divisor. What is the number listed?

   _____

9. Divide the number from your answer to Question 7 by the number that answers Question 8. This will tell the remaining amount of money you need to pay for college, divided by the monthly savings divisor. The resulting number is how much money you need to deposit each month to meet all of your child's educational costs.

   _____

Source: CollegeSure Savings Worksheet, College Savings Board

Let's plug in some numbers to see how this might work.

Sample Worksheet

1. What year does your child start college? **2003**

2. What is your estimated total college cost for a public university (refer to the College Cost Projection Table)? **$61,165**

3. How much have you already saved for your kid's education? **$2,500**

4. How many years until your child begins college? **8 years**

5. What is the CollegeSure growth rate in the CollegeSure Savings Table that corresponds with the year your child starts college? **1.172**

If the number in your answer to Question 9 is more than your budget will permit, don't worry! You'll learn more about additional means of paying for a child's college education in this chapter.

6. Multiply your answers from Questions 3 and 5. Answer: **$2,500 × 1.172 = $4,280**

7. Subtract your answer in Question 6 from that in Question 2. What is the remaining amount? **$61,165 – $4,280 = $56,885**

8. What is the monthly savings divisor in the CollegeSure Savings Table? **131.965**

9. Divide your answer in question 6 by your answer from Question 7. The result: **$56,885 ÷ 131.965 = $431.06/month**

According to this sample worksheet, you have to save $431.06 a month until your child starts college. The next section explains how to figure out where to put that savings so that you'll have enough for T-Day (tuition day).

FYI on Your Kids

When you are saving money for your children's education, it pays to know how to set up the account. You should open the account as a custodial account—known as a "uniform gift to minors"—with you as custodian and the child's name on the account. Know that, depending on what state you live in, at age 21 the money is *theirs*.

In addition, keep the following information in mind before you open an account. The first $650 that a child under the age of 14 earns in interest or dividend income (like dividends from stocks) is completely tax-free. The second $650 of income is taxed at the child rate, which is currently 15 percent. Any interest or dividend income beyond that is taxed at the parents' rate until the child is 14. Once the child reaches age 14, the income is taxed at the child's rate.

Make sure you keep your children involved in the money that you invest for their college education. The more informed they are at a younger age, the better equipped they will be to handle financial responsibilities in the future.

Paying for Megabuck University

Figuring out what you are going to do with your monthly college savings is the next step. You have many options available to you and your children—growth stock mutual funds, zero-coupon bonds, and savings bonds. The best way to make heads or tails of all of these choices is to start from square one. What are they? Let's break them down.

Investment Tailoring for Tots

Mutual funds represent a pool of money managed by professional money managers and invested in a group of securities, like different types of stocks and bonds. They offer a great way to *diversify* your investment portfolio because you spread your risk among the different types of securities.

There is a mutual fund for everybody—even the kids. For example, Stein, Roe & Farnham has created a mutual fund dubbed the "SteinRoe Young Investor Fund," created specifically for families with young children and teenagers trying to meet future college costs. It is an *equity mutual fund* that tries to increase your earnings by investing in companies that

WHAT?

When you **diversify** your investment portfolio, you practice the art of not putting all of your eggs in one basket. By doing this, you spread the risk around and therefore, if one of your securities takes a tumble, all of the others are still in tact.

affect the lives of children, such as toy companies (of course!), entertainment companies, restaurant franchises, and computer manufacturers. One example of a company would be Procter & Gamble, whose products include Pampers diapers, Crest toothpaste, and Hawaiian Punch fruit punch. Another benefit for the kids: There is a quarterly newsletter, called *Dollar Digest*, written for kids only. This fund is also a *no-load fund*, so there are no sales charges or commissions. Since inception (April 1994), the fund posts an average return of 11 percent to February 1995.

When you invest in an **equity mutual fund**, your money is invested in a mutual fund that invests solely in equities, which is a synonymous term for stocks.

When you invest in a **no-load** mutual fund, you don't pay any sales charges or commissions. However, keep in mind that there are fund expenses, such as management fees and administrative costs.

With the SteinRoe Young Investor Fund, you have a choice of how much you can initially invest ($1,000 minimum to open a custodial account), or you can practice the strategy of dollar-cost averaging with this fund by enrolling in their automatic investment plan. It takes $500 to begin, and thereafter subsequent investments ($50 minimum) are debited automatically from your bank account into the fund. For further information, contact Stein, Roe & Farnham directly at (800) 338-2550.

Another mutual fund company that provides parents a "stress-free" investment program is the Twentieth Century College Investment Program. Here's how it works: Initially, your money is invested (and continuously, as you make monthly investments) in Twentieth Century Select, one of their top growth-stock funds. Tracking its past five-year performance, the fund posts an average annual return of 7.34 percent. Then, as the day you send Junior off to college gets closer, your money is moved automatically to a money-market fund over a period of four, five, or six years. It's up to you. To find out more about this program, contact Twentieth Century at (800) 345-2021.

The biggest piece of advice to keep in mind? Start early and don't be too conservative. You can choose other types of mutual funds—especially those that invest in growth stocks, which will outperform all other financial securities over the long haul. The proof is in the pudding: The NASDAQ Index (considered the bellwether for growth stocks) has an average annual return of 11.76 percent over the past 10 years, compared with 9.96 percent if you kept your money in the bond market—according to the Lehman Aggregate Bond Index—or even compared with the Dow Jones Industrial Average, which posts 16.11 percent for the same time period (December 1984 to December 1994).

Keep the following tips in mind when searching for the right mutual fund to stash your cash in. (You can find mutual funds that will fit your investment objective from some of the newsletters listed here.)

➤ Find a mutual fund company that will waive the minimum investment requirement, which is typically $1,000 to $2,500 as long as you participate in their automatic investment plan.

➤ Subscribe to a mutual fund newsletter that will allow you to track ongoing performance information on how your mutual fund(s) are doing. Some of the most popular include these:

Morningstar No-Load Mutual Funds at $145/year, (800) 876-5005

Standard & Poor's/Lipper Mutual Fund Profiles at $132/year, (212) 208-8000

CDA Wiesenberger's *Mutual Fund Report* and *Mutual Fund Update*, with three-month trial subscriptions at $75, (800) 232-2285

Sheldon Jacobs' *No-Load Fund Investor* packs a lot of information into its monthly newsletter. For information on its monthly $119/year subscription, call (800) 252-2042.

➤ Make sure your mutual fund "family" offers you telephone switching privileges. Why? Because as you get closer to sending your children off to college, you are going to have to alter your investment strategies.

For parents of young children, the earlier you begin, the better off you'll be. Use the following guidelines as rules of thumb when you start charting your course:

From Ages 1 to 10: Pick a no-load mutual fund with a good, solid track record. Although past performance is not an indicator of future performance, it will give you an idea of how a fund performed during different phases of the economic cycle and financial market changes. The idea is to focus on stock funds that traditionally deliver a better return over the long haul, and that meet your investment objective of long-term growth. Plus, because you have more time on your side until the kids start college, you don't have to be as conservative in your investment strategy.

From Age 11 to the First Day of College: Because you are working within a smaller timeframe—a maximum of seven years— you'll need lower volatility. Time to start shifting a portion of your investment out of stocks and into fixed-income investments, such as conservative bond funds or money market funds. The closer the first day of college, the more you allocate to the money market fund. Why? Because of the safety of principal. So, by the time your children reach 15 or 16, you should begin shifting out of stocks entirely.

From the First Day of College and Beyond: Most folks make the mistake of working so hard to meet those educational expenses on the first day, and then quitting. Wrong! You need to work constantly at your investment strategy throughout Junior's college years. The bottom line is to maintain safety of your principal, so a money market fund with check-writing features fits the bill here.

Savings Bonds

The guaranteed rate on Series EE savings bonds, if purchased after March 1, 1993, is 4 percent. In fact, a 4 percent floor applies if the bonds are held five years or longer. However, the major advantage to investing in savings bonds to pay for your child's education is this: all the interest you earn on those savings bonds will be tax-free—as long as you meet the following conditions.

➤ You must buy Series EE savings bonds.

➤ You must have purchased the bonds in 1990 or thereafter, in both the parents' names (NOT in the child's name).

➤ You and your spouse must be at least 24 years old when you purchase the bonds.

➤ You must cash in the bonds in the same year that you are going to use them to pay for tuition (*not* room and board).

➤ You must meet the following income limitations: For 1995, the Series EE bond interest is tax-free for married couples with adjusted gross incomes below $63,450, and singles with incomes below $42,300. If you are above either of those two levels, the tax benefit is gradually phased out until you get no tax break. The levels at which you no longer get any tax break are currently $93,450 for married couples and $57,300 for singles. Because the income limitations are indexed to inflation, they should rise every year.

> To find the most recent rate on your savings bonds, call (800) US-BONDS.

College Bonds for the College-Bound

If you don't get the tax break on savings bonds, zero-coupon bonds can be just your ticket to help with Junior's college costs—as long as you either hold onto them until maturity, or buy them low and sell them high.

Here's how they work. You purchase them at a discount from their face value, and the interest you earn each year allows the bond to increase in value. You collect the principal plus the accrued interest at maturity. (Although you don't receive an interest check, you are required by the IRS to report the interest as income, which is known as the *phantom tax*.) Once the bond reaches maturity, the bond is worth its full face value. The longer the maturity of the bond, the lower the price you'll initially pay. Why? Because there's more time for the interest to build up the value of the bond. That's why they're so popular for long-term investors: they allow you to match up future liabilities, such as your children's hefty tuition bill.

> If you are close to the income limits, and you stand to gain a profit from the bonds when you cash them in, only cash in a small amount of the bonds for each tuition year.

When you buy a zero-coupon bond, make sure you pay no more than the bond's *accrued value*, which is the purchase price plus the interest that's built up so far. It should be stated on the confirmation trade notice you receive from your broker or discount broker.

All bonds react intensely to the direction of interest rates. So if you bought a ten-year zero-coupon bond at a discount, and plan on selling it within the next 6 years instead of waiting until maturity, you have no idea what interest rates and bond prices will be. You may get lucky and the value of the bond will rise, so you can sell it and get a profit. If bond prices fall, however, you're better off waiting until maturity to get the full face value of the bond. You can purchase zero-coupon bonds in maturities from six months to 30 years with as little as $1,000.

If you are concerned about the tax ramifications of a zero-coupon bond, you can purchase municipal zero-coupon bonds. The interest you earn on these is exempt from federal taxes. You can also escape state taxes if you buy a municipal zero-coupon bond issued in your state. And if you're in the 28 percent tax bracket, a 7 percent tax-free yield on a zero-coupon bond is as good as a 9.72 percent taxable yield (see Chapter 24 on taxable versus tax-free). Plus, the zero-coupon bond still allows you to purchase the bond at a discount and realize its full face value at maturity—just about the time the bill from State U arrives!

Make sure you have *call protection* if you invest in zero-coupon municipal bonds. If an issuer "calls your bond back" before maturity, the price of your bond drops in value. To avoid this, buy a non-callable, triple-A-rated, insured zero-coupon bond.

Zero-coupon bonds sound like an intimidating investment, but slap the title "college savings bonds" on them, and parents think they're the next best thing since sliced bread. And they're hot: Illinois college bonds are so popular brokers cannot fill all the orders. Connecticut started its college savings bond program in 1988 to the tune of $110 million—twice what was expected. About 22 states offer them today. If you need additional information, contact a brokerage firm; these bonds are sold through such firms, and not through the state. Keep in mind that you *have* to pay taxes on the accrued interest!

I'm So Sure, It's CollegeSure

Offered through the College Savings Bank at (800) 888-2723, the CollegeSure CD aims to meet the rising cost of college by linking its interest rate on its variable-rate certificate of deposit to the rising cost of a college education, which is measured by the College Board Independent 500 Index. Although the rate changes annually, it has a 4 percent floor.

Here's what you need to know:

➤ The CDs are sold in maturities of from one to 25 years, with all of them maturing on July 31 of each year.

➤ The CDS are sold in units and/or fractional units. For example, one full unit at maturity on July 31 each year is equal to one full year's average cost for tuition, fees, room and board at a four-year private college.

You do not have to purchase a full unit, but keep in mind how a unit measures college costs. According to the College Savings Bank, one unit prepays approximately one year at the average private college; 0.40 units prepays approximately one year at the average public college (in-state), and 1.43 units prepays approximately one year at the average Ivy League college. It's up to you to calculate how many units you'll need.

➤ When you buy a unit CD, it is priced above the current index value (according to the College Board Independent 500 Index) for one year of college today, but at a deep discount to the possible cost of one year of college at maturity. That's why it pays off to start this program early.

➤ Each unit pays one full year of average college costs—even if they hit the roof!—assuming interest and principal remain on deposit until maturity.

You'll get penalized if you take out any of your principal BEFORE the date of maturity: 10 percent of the principal within the first three years, 5 percent thereafter until the final year, which only charges you 1 percent. You may withdraw interest without penalty, provided that you notify the bank in writing between June 1 and July 15 preceding the interest payment date.

➤ The minimum first investment in a CollegeSure CD is $1,000, which buys you a certain number of units. Subsequent investments must be at least $250. If you automatically enroll in their payroll-savings program, you can invest $50 per paycheck. For the CollegeSure Plus CD, the minimum investment is $10,000.

➤ The CollegeSure CD has a four percent floor—it will never pay less than that in any year, regardless of the college inflation rate. So, if the indexed increase is less than four percent annually, your investment will earn no less than four percent annually.

➤ If your child decides not to go to college when the CD matures, you can get your investment back—plus the same amount of interest as if your child were to attend college. No ifs, ands, or buts.

➤ Keep in mind that the interest credited to a CollegeSure CD is subject to current taxation, even if the interest is not withdrawn until maturity.

If you don't qualify for the tax exemption from investing in savings bonds, you'll end up with a better return as long as you keep the money in a custodial account invested in the CollegeSure CD. Here's why, according to the College Savings Bank, assuming that $10,000 was invested in June 1993, the investment matures in July 2000, the child is five years old, and the parents are married, filing a joint tax return.

	CollegeSure CD (custodial account)	**Series EE Bond (above income restrictions)**
Pre-tax Rate of Return	5%	5%
After-tax Rate of Return	5%	3.87%
Total Return	**$18,933.32**	**$16,431.99**

Contact the College Savings Bank at (800) 888-2723 to receive its selected college cost list, which includes unit values. If you tell them where you're sending your kids, the College Savings Bank will also calculate approximately how many units you'll need for each year of college, and how much money you'll need to save every month

Finding Financial Aid

What if you fall a few dollars shy of your goal? Don't rule out financial aid—even if your income puts the Rockefeller family fortune to shame. Remember the worksheet you filled out in the beginning of this chapter? Refer to it to determine what your expected contribution is going to be. The difference between what you contribute and the total cost of attending college is the amount of aid for which your child is eligible.

The best time to begin looking for financial aid is one year prior to when you will actually need the funds.

There are two types of financial aid forms. The FAF form is typically used by private colleges; the FAFSA (Free Application for Federal Student Aid) is used by all universities.

What can increase the potential to receive financial aid? Having more than one child in college, some experts say. Here are a few other tips for you to adjust your financial picture to qualify for financial aid:

➤ Spend the student's savings first, because they're typically considered the first source of a contribution to college costs.

➤ Good news—money built up in retirement plans—such as 401(k) plans, IRAs, annuities, and Keoghs—does NOT count against you in the "assets" category on the FAF form.

➤ Don't take any big lump-sum distributions or big tax refunds in the year you are being approved for financial aid, because this will only increase your level of income.

➤ Don't sell any investment securities for a profit in the year before applying for financial aid. Why? Because the profit you realize is considered income.

➤ Reducing your income—for example, when you start a business and need to deduct business losses and expenses—helps. Any way you can defer income to keep that income out of the financial aid picture can help.

Whatever your strategy, make sure your child completes the Free Application for Federal Student Aid (FAFSA), which is available in the guidance counselor's office at your child's high school, or at the college's financial aid office. Don't be surprised by what they ask for— it's almost as daunting as filling out your tax forms. In fact, some colleges require that you enclose copies of your tax returns.

Once the application is complete, it is sent to a *needs analysis* department, which assesses your income, your assets, and your potential contribution. There's no guarantee that you'll receive financial aid, but don't overlook it. Remember: If you want your child to receive financial aid, you must go through this process *every year*, filling out the new aid forms and sending them in by the deadline dates until your child is finished with school. For more information, call the Financial Aid Hotline at (800) 4-FED-AID.

So You're Looking for Some CASHE

CASHE stands for College Aid Sources for Higher Education; it's an automated computer program sponsored by the National College Services, Ltd. in Maryland. This database provides information on various types of financial aid: over 150,000 awards and 14,000 other resources to help pay for school. Examples include scholarships, loans, grants, and work-at-school programs.

All your child needs to do is complete the application, which requires information such as work experience, class rank, student activities, and intended colleges. The more the information they have, the easier it will be to match up your child's application to an appropriate source from the database. The deadline dates for private-aid applications typically range between October and March of the year that precedes the academic year your child is planning to attend college. The cost of the service? There is a $30 processing fee, and you will get results within ten working days. For more information, call (301) 258-0717.

And the Scholarship Goes to...

All high school sophomores, juniors, and seniors—even college students—are encouraged to apply to the National Scholarship Research Service. For $75, the NSRS will provide you with a list of funding sources that match your personal background and educational goals. The funding comes from the private sector, such as corporations, memorials, trusts, foundations, and other philanthropic organizations. In fact, private-sector funding is on the rise—it has grown an average of 13.4 percent every year for the last 10 years.

If you apply, you will receive a computer printout containing a list of scholarships, fellowships, grants, and loans that match your application. Plus, there are tips on applying for awards, a list of general publications containing further post-secondary and financial-aid information, and a scholarship calendar for keeping track of application deadlines. For further information, call (707) 546-6777.

Gifts from the Government

Here's a list of grants that are available for government assistance with financial aid. For further information about federal grant programs, call the Federal Student Aid Information Center at (800) 433-3243.

➤ **Pell Grants**   These are from the U.S. government and are for low-income undergraduate students. Typically, between $200 to $2,300 is awarded per year. No need to fill out any additional forms: you automatically apply when you fill out the FAFSA.

➤ **State Grants**   Although the amount of money awarded varies state by state, don't overlook this source of financial-aid assistance. These grants are for resident students attending state schools. Application is automatic with FAFSA forms.

➤ **Supplemental Educational Opportunity Grants**   Also known as SEOG, low-income undergraduate students are awarded these grants from the U.S. government and some colleges. Award amounts fall anywhere from $200 to $4,000 per year.

Shopping Student Loans

Not to be missed—student loans. But remember: You must pay them back! Most recent figures show that the Federal Family Education Loan Program (FFELP) in 1993 provided almost 5.8 million loans, amounting to $18 billion.

There are two different types of loans: subsidized and unsubsidized. If you meet certain financial-need criteria, you may qualify for a subsidized loan. The federal government pays the interest while you are in school. If you don't meet the financial criteria, you may apply for an unsubsidized loan; you must, however, repay the interest that accumulates while you are in school. If not, the interest will be added to your principal balance.

Various loan programs exist. The Stafford Student Loan Program offers up to $23,000 total for undergraduate years; the Perkins Loan Program offers a maximum of $9,000 for four years; under the PLUS Loan program, the parents take out the loan on behalf of the student, and they apply directly to banks, savings and loans, and credit unions. Note: The PLUS Loan program is not based on need, but rather on the parents' good, solid credit report. This means that if you are a student, your parents are legally responsible to pay back the loan. (To learn how to obtain a good credit report, read Chapter 16.)

The industry standard indicates that the interest rate charged on a student loan is usually tied to the 90-day Treasury bill rate plus 3.1 percent. Most often a cap is given—around 9 to 10 percent. If you'd like more information about loan programs, call United Student Aid Funds at (800) 562-6872.

The Least You Need to Know

> ➤ Teaching your kids about money while they're young will help them handle it better when they're older. An allowance can be a useful tool in helping them understand basic financial planning.

> ➤ To figure out how much you're going to need to save and invest for college, complete the worksheet listed in this chapter—which includes figuring out how long it's going to be before Junior starts school, projecting your

children's future college costs (believe us, they're a doozy!), and determining how much the current savings you're allocating to college costs will grow.

➤ Start saving and investing early. Don't worry about being too aggressive in your approach in the beginning; for example, investing in growth stock mutual funds could be an option. As time passes, however, you'll want to switch your assets into more conservative investments, such as a money market fund.

➤ Some investments worth looking into include mutual fund programs geared towards saving for college, such as the SteinRoe Young Investor Fund and the Twentieth Century College Investment Program, Series EE savings bonds, zero-coupon college bonds, and the CollegeSure CD program.

➤ Available financial aid includes government grants, scholarships, and student loans. Make sure your child completes the FAFSA form; start looking for aid resources about a year in advance of your child's anticipated enrollment.

You're Never Too Young to Think About Retiring

In This Chapter

➤ The top five "must-dos" for retiring comfortably

➤ Common mistakes you should avoid

➤ Different types of retirement accounts—in simple English!

➤ You're in your golden years—now what?

How many of you had a piggy bank during your childhood? That big, plump porcelain pig that held all your loose change was the only method of saving you knew about. You knew you were supposed to save for a rainy day, but not many people understood *why* they were supposed to do it.

That rainy day is closer than you think. So why save for it now? The earlier you start saving for retirement, the less you'll need to save to have enough money to live well. Many people live an average 15 to 20 years in retirement, yet only save enough money for about half of that.

If you're counting on Social Security, forget it. Given the funding problems in the Social Security system, benefits are projected to provide only 21 percent of your current income. If you earn $26,000 a year, expect to receive an average estimated monthly benefit check of $455.

You may think you're young enough or ambitious enough to avoid thoughts of retirement. Perhaps you're counting on Uncle Gilbert to leave you a fortune in his will. But that's not always the case. Planning for your future does *not* mean you're expecting something terrible to happen. Buying a life insurance policy doesn't mean you're going to die right away, does it? This chapter explains what you can do for retirement starting today, some common mistakes you should avoid, and the different types of investment products that will get you from here to there.

Why Can't We Think About Tomorrow?

The statistics on how we relate to saving money are not encouraging. A Merrill Lynch study concludes that if Americans continue to save at the rate they do now, they may end up with only 36 percent of the money they'll need to maintain their current standard of living. Why have we developed such a nonchalant attitude toward the future, anyway?

Saving money for the future is B-O-R-I-N-G, many folks tell us. Put an extra $100 bucks in a savings account to earn a few pennies? Big deal. Credit cards have cured this boredom by enticing consumers to charge now and pay later. This bad habit hurts you in the long run because you'll be so busy climbing out of debt that you won't have any money to sock away for the future, let alone even think about it. Get rid of the credit cards. Make the transition from "see-it-buy-it" to "save-it-for-tomorrow." You're not a millionaire just because you have a $25,000 line of credit that makes you *think* you are.

Many consumers think they can count on a company pension. After all, their parents had one. But you can't always count on a pension. Alarmingly, only 45 percent of all men receive a pension. Women? Just 23 percent—and those who do only get about two-thirds as much as men. Companies are doing away with traditional pension plans, either by reducing the amount of benefit payments or eliminating the plans altogether. Instead, many companies offer other types of retirement savings programs (you learned about a few in Chapter 22) that shift the burden of saving onto you, the employee. There are, however, alternative or additional means of saving for retirement that work just as well—and sometimes even better! You'll learn more about them in this chapter.

Finally, people think that retirement is far, far away. A 25-year-old person working hard to make ends meet never ponders what life will be like at 65. But tomorrow always comes, you know. Know that if you delay any longer, you're going to have to come up with more money down the road for the same end result. Keep reading to learn how you can start saving today.

The Power of Saving

Read these motivating facts:

➤ A 25-year-old woman who saves $100 a month until she retires will have six times more money when she retires than if she were to begin saving $100 a month at age 45.

➤ A 50-year-old woman who contributes $500 a month to a retirement plan will never catch up with the 30-year-old woman who has been socking away $100 a month.

➤ If you save $2,000 a year at 6 percent for 30 years in a regular savings account, you'll have close to $120,900 after paying taxes. However, if you shelter your $2,000 each year in your IRA at six percent, your savings increases to almost $168,000 because of the tax-deferred feature.

Let's get started.

Excuses, Excuses, Excuses

Each person's situation is unique. Perhaps you don't have access to a company-sponsored program. Or you're saving your wad of dough for your children's college education. No matter what the excuse (because that's what they really are), you can still save for retirement.

Don't think that you don't have enough money to save. If you don't take advantage of saving your money from taxes, then you *really* don't have money to save! Sure, you may be saving for a child's college

Most people live longer than their parents, and most women live longer than their husbands. You may wish to increase your projected estimates of how much you'll need to have on hand in personal savings if this is the case. For example, if you retire at 65 and live to 86, you'll need—based on current projections of the lifespan of a 40-year-old, non-smoking woman—more than *20 years' worth of income* to live on. You may not have an idea exactly how much you'll need at retirement, but that's not an excuse to buck your duty of making a savings plan.

education or saving your money to buy a home—but that money is typically in taxable accounts. So, you're paying "extra" taxes by keeping your money in those accounts. Of course, you must continue to save for those financial goals, but *your financial goal of retirement is important, too*. Scholarships, Pell grants, and student loans are available for your children (remember Chapter 26?)—but Social Security won't provide for you the way a scholarship can provide for your child. You can save for retirement if you reduce some of your current living expenses.

Just because you contribute to a retirement plan doesn't mean that you'll never have access to your money until you're older, either. Although the IRS will hit you with a penalty if you withdraw your money before age 59 1/2, you can access your money, depending on the circumstances. For example, if you contribute to a 401(k), some companies will allow you to borrow against your cash balance—but that's up to the company. There are also hardship withdrawals you can take—not for a whirlwind vacation, but for when you're in a financial pinch (as a result of a medical emergency, for example).

Finally, don't count on your cash value life insurance policy to take advantage of tax-deferred growth. True, cash value life insurance policies provide tax-deferred growth, but there's no tax deduction. And you don't "benefit"—your heirs do. You can borrow against your life insurance policy, but if you die with the loan outstanding, your intended heirs will receive less than you planned.

Turn These Must-Do's into Can-Do's!

Part of your everyday money management should include planning for retirement. You don't need to go overboard and deny yourself day-to-day necessities (like food) because you fear you'll wind up impoverished if you eat today. That's not the point. But if you have the benefit of time when it comes to evaluating your retirement plan, take advantage of it.

The earlier you begin to plan for your golden years, the less money you'll have to save to live well in the future. Why is this? Because the sooner you begin, the more your money has time to compound. If you invested $1,000 in the stocks of the S&P 500 back in 1940, you would have close to $390,000 today, counting dividends being reinvested and before any taxes on capital gains were paid.

If you have more than a 10-year time frame, invest your retirement money for the long term. Younger people can take advantage of the potential growth that some investments offer, especially equities. Obviously, you don't want to gamble your retirement savings the closer you get to retirement, but if you have time on your side, take advantage of more aggressive investments that offer higher degrees of potential growth.

Don't be *too* conservative in your retirement savings. This tip is aimed especially at the younger generation saving for retirement. Too often, younger people make the mistake of being conservative in their retirement-savings strategies. The biggest mistake is when they invest their 401(k) money in a Money Market fund as their long-term retirement choice. Bad move, especially when the Money Market rates can barely keep up with inflation. Even if you are closer to retirement, don't forget that you will probably live for a long time as a retiree, so your funds will still need to grow.

Take advantage of *every* opportunity to shelter your retirement money from current income taxes. These opportunities, which will be discussed in detail later on in this chapter, are different types of investment products that offer a tax-deferred feature. You can shelter your money from current income taxes through an individual retirement account, a company-sponsored retirement plan, or an annuity.

Even if you have a retirement program at work, open and contribute to an IRA to take advantage of tax-deferred growth. Depending on your income level, if you are covered by a company-sponsored plan, you may not receive a tax deduction on your IRA contributions. Are you still going to *not* open an IRA because you don't receive a tax deduction? You still get the tax-deferred growth, just not the perk from

Uncle Sam. Look at Table 27.1 to see whether or not you get the deduction based on your adjusted gross income. Even if you can't deduct your IRA contribution, the tax-deferred compounding makes it a worthwhile forced savings plan.

Table 27.1 IRA Tax Deduction: Yes or No?

Deduction	Single AGI*	Married Filing Jointly AGI	Married Filing Separately AGI
Full deduction	$25,000 or less	$40,000 or less	$10,000 or less
Partial deduction	$25,000 to $35,000	$40,000 to $50, 000	$10,000 or less
No deduction	$35,000 and up	$50,000 and up	$10,000 and up

*AGI = Adjusted Gross Income

Retirement Accounts Explained in Simple English

The most common type of retirement account is an *Individual Retirement Account.* An IRA is available for you to make an annual contribution of $2,000 or 100 percent of earned income that year, whichever is less, up until the year you reach age 70 1/2. In other words, your contributions must come from a salary, wages, or self-employment income. Even alimony counts.

What if you're a non-working spouse? If you are part of a couple with one spouse working and the other not working, the working spouse may contribute an extra $250 (for a total of $2,250). The contributions must go into separate accounts, however—one bearing the name of the working spouse, and one bearing the name of the non-working spouse. The account held by the non-working spouse is called a *spousal IRA.* Spouses who work part-time and have no company benefits can open up their own IRAs. The same rules apply.

Ironically, an IRA causes a lot of confusion. Many people will ask, "Should I invest my money in a mutual fund *or* in an IRA?" The truth is that you should invest your money in a mutual fund *inside* an IRA. An IRA is an account that shelters your contributions from current income taxes. The contribution you make should be made by your tax-filing due date.

The earlier in the year you make your contribution, the longer your money has to grow tax-deferred.

They're for Your Benefit

The range of retirement plan alternatives is broad, but most plans fall into one of two major categories:

Defined contribution plans provide an individual account for each participant (that's you), and for benefits based solely upon the amount contributed to the participant's account. These include—but are not limited to—money-purchase plans, profit-sharing plans, and 401(k) plans.

Defined benefit plans are retirement plans other than an individual account plan (like a defined contribution plan). Retirement benefits must be definitely set. For example, a plan that entitles you to a monthly pension for life equal to 25 percent of monthly compensation is a defined benefit plan.

401(k) Is the Way to Play

In Chapter 22, you learned the basics of a 401(k) plan. They allow you to deduct a portion of your earnings—before taxes—and put the money into various investment options. The beauty of the 401(k) is that the money comes out of your paycheck in *pretax* dollars and it grows tax-deferred until you take it out at retirement.

Typically, you have a choice between a money market fund, a fixed-income option, a growth or equity stock fund, and perhaps an option to invest in company stock. Typically, you can make changes every quarter—some companies offer the chance to do so every month.

Rules, Rules, Rules

You must leave your contributions in the plan (or roll it over into an IRA if you leave the company, or take it with you to a new employer's plan) until age 59 1/2. There are hardship cases when you can withdraw money, such as purchasing a home, emergency medical expenses, or college tuition.

What constitutes a hardship? The withdrawal must be made on account of the participant's (that's you) immediate and heavy financial need—and the withdrawal must be necessary to satisfy such need. Check with your employer to find out exactly what your company's plan will allow.

What happens if you leave your job and you want to take your money with you? You *must* have the transfer made directly from your old plan to your new plan, or roll it over into an IRA account. If you take possession of the money yourself—even if you plan on "rolling it over" into a new plan (whether it's at your new employer or in an IRA)—you will get hit with a 20 percent federal income tax penalty. Wait—there's more. Unless you replace the 20 percent penalty with new funds put into the new plan, it will be treated as a withdrawal and WHAMMO! You'll owe ordinary income taxes on it.

If You're Self-Employed...

You can create your own retirement savings program! Plus, you can contribute much more than the $2,000 IRA maximum. There are *Keogh plans*, which fall under two types: *defined benefit* and *defined contribution* plans. The choice is yours, but make sure you review the paperwork about requirements, especially if you have employees—then you *must* include contributions for them as well.

There's a lot of legal mumbo-jumbo to the paperwork when you set up a Keogh plan, but most mutual fund companies and brokerage firms (full-service, discount, and deep-discount) just need you to fill out the basic paperwork to set one up. A Keogh plan must be set up by the end of the year, and contributions must be made by the tax-filing due date.

As a self-employed individual, you also have access to opening up a SEP-IRA, which is a Simplified Employee Pension IRA. A SEP is easier to understand and administer successfully than a Keogh. Sometimes dubbed an "easy-to-manage retirement plan for individuals," a SEP-IRA can be opened and contributions can be made up until the last day of your tax filing deadline, including extensions. You can contribute up to 15 percent of your compensation or $22,500, whichever is less.

Another Way to Save for Retirement

Socking away $2,000 a year into a retirement program is great. But for those of you who have more money to invest and want to take advantage of tax-deferred growth, you may want to think about an annuity.

What exactly is an annuity? You already know what CDs and no-load mutual funds are, right? Well, an annuity is an insurance company product with fixed-rate CDs and no-load mutual funds in it.

It's like creating an IRA that you can contribute an unlimited amount of money to. Plus, you are not obligated to take out the money by age 70 1/2, as you are required to do with an IRA. However, unlike an IRA, you cannot deduct your contribution on your income tax returns, but you can still take advantage of their tax-deferred feature. The money you invest in an annuity is made with *after-tax* dollars.

Once you put your money in, you must leave it there until you turn 59 1/2. If you dip into the money, watch out! You'll get nicked with a 10 percent federal tax penalty on any interest earnings to date—but not your principal. Plus, the insurance company hits you with *surrender charges*—sometimes as high as seven percent in the first year, although they do gradually decline one percent each year until they vanish.

So how can you get there from here? If you are a 25-year-old single person earning $30,000, you should try to save almost 11.5 percent of your net income if covered by a company pension plan. If you don't have access to a company plan, boost your savings to 15.4 percent of your net income.

Because annuities are insurance products, make sure you look into the financial health of the insurance company. Sources such as Weiss Research and A.M. Best, which are listed in detail in Chapter 23, will provide this information.

They come in two different types: an immediate annuity or a tax-deferred annuity. With an immediate annuity, you give a lump sum of money to the insurance company. Based on your age, life expectancy, and current interest rates, the insurance company calculates how much they'll send you each month—no matter how long you live—and invest it accordingly to provide for these specific dollar amounts.

To set up a tax-deferred annuity, typically you give the insurance company a lump sum of money to invest, and it grows on a tax-deferred basis over a number of years. They beauty of a tax-deferred annuity is that you don't pay any taxes on the earning or profits that are built up in the annuity until you take the money out. If you want, you can add money to your tax-deferred annuity in various amounts over time; this is known as a *flexible-premium deferred annuity*.

Within a tax-deferred annuity, you have two options: a *guaranteed-rate* or a *variable* annuity. Guaranteed rate is just like it sounds—it pays a fixed interest rate that is guaranteed for a period of one to ten years (it's up to you). A variable annuity, though, allows you to choose among a wide range of mutual funds—such as stock, bond, or money market funds. Obviously, because these types of investment products don't guarantee a rate of return, your return in a variable annuity can fluctuate.

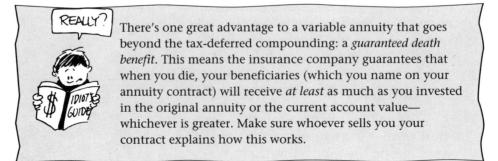

There's one great advantage to a variable annuity that goes beyond the tax-deferred compounding: a *guaranteed death benefit*. This means the insurance company guarantees that when you die, your beneficiaries (which you name on your annuity contract) will receive *at least* as much as you invested in the original annuity or the current account value—whichever is greater. Make sure whoever sells you your contract explains how this works.

Most often, if you have more than a 10-year time horizon and want to take advantage of tax-deferred growth, a variable annuity is a great place to begin. But there are some questions you should ask the insurance agent before you invest your cash.

➤ **Find out what the total expense, including all fees, would be for maintaining this account.** Even though there are no up-front sales commissions or loads that are charged (remember, these are no-load funds), there are still expenses involved. Find out what the surrender charges are, management fees (no-load funds have them, although they vary), and mortality fees, which take into account your projected life span.

➤ **Have the agent explain what funds are available within the annuity.** Just as you do when you are mutual fund shopping, check out what types of funds are available and the performance history of each. Within each variable annuity is a pool of mutual funds. Make sure they're well-established funds that you have heard of from your research—you can even get performance information from some of the sources listed in Chapter 19.

➤ **Determine upfront if you can add more money to the annuity.** If it's possible, find out how much the minimum amounts are and if the additional money you invest will also extend the period of surrender charges. You don't want that to happen. Additionally, find out if the annuity will allow an automatic investment program—similar to an automatic investment plan set up by a fund company. This way, you can have your monthly investment electronically transferred from your bank account to your annuity. Discipline, discipline, discipline!

If you need help annuity shopping, call Independent Advantage Financial Services at (800) 829-2887 for more information. Depending on your objective, they can research and find an annuity that best suits your financial goals and retirement needs.

If you want to save on expenses, buy a variable annuity directly from mutual fund companies, if they offer them. You are limited to that particular family of funds, but the overall expense (such as management fees) tends to be lower, and many times there isn't a surrender charge. Vanguard (800/522-5555), one of the lowest-cost fund companies around, offers variable annuities with no surrender charges.

You're Retired—Now What?

For the past thirty-some-odd years, you've spent a lot of time doing your homework—and contributing as much as possible to retirement accounts. After all, you want your retirement lifestyle to be comfortable, right? Right! But there are some rules you still have to follow *during* your retirement to keep the money growing so it can keep on flowing.

➤ Continue to have your money grow and compound tax-deferred as long as possible.

➤ Be flexible with your funds so you can cushion yourself against any changing market conditions.

➤ Monitor the changing tax laws and how they affect your distributions.

➤ Keep a small portion of your retirement assets in growth investments (depending on your risk tolerance).

Your retirement income is probably based on how much you decide to receive in *distributions* (the money you eventually take out from your retirement plan)—and when. You must begin taking distributions from your IRA by April 1 of the year *after* you reach age 70 1/2. It's okay if you start taking distributions before you reach 70 1/2—but not before 59 1/2, if you want to avoid the penalties imposed by the IRS—and there are no limitations on how much or how little you can take out.

Once you turn 70 1/2, it's a whole new ballgame. IRS rules indicate that you must take out enough money in distributions each year to use up your IRA account over your life expectancy. So how does the IRS know how long you're going to live? It's based on IRS mortality tables; your IRA *custodian* (the firm or company where your IRA is held) can help you calculate the amount.

You should have other retirement savings that you have put aside if you outlive your IRA and the IRS' mortality table. If you want to make your money last longer, have your annual distributions based on the joint life expectancy of *both* you and your spouse. If your spouse is much younger than you are, that would extend the payments over a longer period of time. If you are not married at the time, your calculation can be based on the life expectancy of you and your beneficiary (although there is a 10-year maximum age difference allowed).

A Final Word

Geez, all these calculations and numbers in the retirement world? It doesn't have to be intimidating. No matter if you're single, married, divorced, or widowed, you should do something to prepare for retirement. Much of your fear will quickly disappear once you realize how easy it is to make your savings grow for retirement. The name of the game is to take one buck and turn it into two (then four, then sixteen…) for a financially healthy tomorrow.

The Least You Need to Know

➤ Company pensions and Social Security won't cover all your financial needs for retirement. In order to be fully prepared, you need to start a retirement savings plan now.

➤ Take advantage of company retirement plans such as the 401(k).

➤ If you don't have a company retirement plan or you would like have additional retirement savings, open an IRA. If you're self-employed, your options include a Keogh plan or a SEP-IRA.

Chapter 28

Estate Planning

In This Chapter

➤ Learning how you can pass it on without passing out

➤ How to set up a living trust

➤ Creative financial strategies to cut estate taxes

➤ Saving money in the long run by giving it away now

It's never too early to start thinking about estate planning, even if you only have a few possessions. Why? Because taxes are the only certainties in life other than death. Effective estate planning now can help prepare you for both eventualities later on. You can't avoid Uncle Sam when it comes to estate planning, but you can be prepared and save a few bucks if you've done your homework.

This chapter won't replace the type of professional estate planning advice you should get from an attorney, but it will get you started. In this chapter you'll find a few smart—and creative—money strategies that will help you save the maximum dollar amount possible on estate taxes by using the existing laws.

It's Never Too Soon to Get Started

You're 29 years old, drive an '89 Buick, and rent an apartment. You don't have many assets, so you think you don't need an estate plan. Right? Wrong!

No matter how old you are or how much you're worth, you still need to think carefully about how you want your possessions distributed when you die. Estate planning is not just for the wealthy. As you know, the more you have, the more complicated it can get, especially when Uncle Sam steps up to the plate to take out a big bite in the form of estate taxes.

If you decide not to give any legal instruction for how your possessions should be handled when you die, guess what? The state where you live makes all the decisions. Even if you become incapacitated, you need special instructions—and a person—to help you. So if you do nothing, you run the risk of having Uncle Willie's antique pocketwatch wind up in your punk-rocker cousin Elmo's hands. And, depending on your state's laws, if you die without a will (a condition known as *intestate*), the state will give the largest portion of your estate to your surviving legal spouse. Next in line are your children, your parents, and then close blood-relatives.

Suppose you are married, have no children and no will, either. You and your spouse are in a severe car accident, and you die from the wreck and then your spouse dies a few weeks later. Since you died first, all of your assets go to your spouse. However, when your spouse dies— because you didn't have any children—your in-laws wind up with both your assets *and* your spouse's *because there is no will*. Now can you see why estate planning is so important?

Another situation to consider is if you are incapacitated and need someone to care for all of your financial obligations. You need a special kind of document to help you: a durable power of attorney, which is a legal document that gives a family member or trusted friend 100 percent legal authority to act on your behalf.

"I don't want to think about it," many people say, because estate planning is a concept that makes people realize their own mortality. It's a common phobia, but it doesn't mean you should overlook this important element in your financial planning—especially if you have children.

What if you don't do anything? Just take a peek at the following situations that could arise if you *don't* do any estate planning.

➤ The court will appoint a guardian for your minor children. It will be up to the probate court to name a guardian for your minor children if you have not made any legal provisions for someone to care for your children and manage their inheritances. Sure, it could be a family relative, but maybe you wanted your Cousin Frankie raising your three sons and not Aunt Matilda.

➤ Your state laws determine who the beneficiaries of your estate will be. Typically, each state sets up the distribution of your assets and property to your spouse and relatives in an established order. Many times, the distribution of your assets may *not* be according to what you would have wanted—and quite often, the process can be delayed, up to two years at times. Your estate will be subject to probate, which is the legal process used to value your estate. The probate process also pays any estate taxes, settles any outstanding debts, and supervises the distribution of your assets to beneficiaries.

➤ The government gets a huge chunk in the form of estate taxes. Any amount you leave over $600,000 in assets is subject to federal estate tax (even insurance proceeds and retirement plan assets). Just how much federal estate tax? It depends on current tax law, although amounts over $600,000 may be subject to a maximum tax rate of 55 percent.

Before you learn about simple estate planning strategies, you must do the following:

Set up an "Asset and Liability Inventory Worksheet." This won't be difficult—you should have filled this out in Chapter 2 in the worksheets provided.

Make sure your objectives sheet lists your instructions in detail so that in the event you become disabled or die, your instructions are carried out the way you intended. Also, once you review your plan with an attorney, make sure you implement strategies that will shelter as much from taxation.

Determine what your objectives are by reviewing your current situation. Are you married? Divorced? Do you have children? How many? Who do you want to provide for if you become incapacitated or if you die? Your objectives sheet will list the needs of your beneficiaries and how you will provide for them in the manner you intend.

Seek professional legal help. This is one area of your financial life that you don't want to skimp on. You can contact some of the professional organizations listed in this chapter for help. No matter what, make sure you have done steps 1 and 2 before you do so; it will save your estate planning attorney some time and save you some money!

Making a will is *not* a "do-it-on-your-own" financial planning strategy. Handwritten wills are illegal in many states unless proper procedures are followed. Videotape wills don't really count, either, unless they're used to "back up" your state of mind when creating the will. That's why you need to make sure you get yourself a qualified lawyer who specializes in estate planning.

By now you know that we advocate doing your homework as much as possible, and taking charge of your financial picture—especially if it means you can save money along the way. When it comes to estate planning, however, you need good, solid advice. It may cost you a bit extra, but it's better to ward off any mistakes now so your heirs don't have to suffer. The bottom line is that you need to protect your assets. The two most common ways of providing for the distribution of your assets are creating a will or creating a trust. You will need a professional to help you do either, but it's important to understand the basics before you hire an estate planning pro. So let's get started.

Will You or Won't You: Creating a Simple Will

An *estate plan* is just a glorified phrase that represents a legal, written document that explains who gets what and how you want things distributed. An estate plan also can help you save on taxes, too, if you're smart.

If you're young and single, consider having a simple will. Even if you have named a beneficiary to your bank account in the event you die, that's just one part of the process. You probably have furniture, a car, or some other personal items that need to be addressed. So unless you live alone and have no personal possessions, you need to do something—and a simple will is a good way to get started.

A simple will can be drawn up by most attorneys who handle basic estate planning situations. The legal costs for you to draw up a will range from $100 to $2,000, depending on where you live and how much work needs to be done—and your attorney's hourly billing rate! A simple will accomplishes the following:

➤ **It provides instructions for who should get what.** These people are known as *beneficiaries*. This is typically the first part of the will. You decide to whom you want to bequeath your assets, and in what amounts. When you designate your beneficiary, make sure you clearly name who the recipients are, such as "To my sister, Robyn-Jo," etc. As for any property or valuables, clearly describe them in detail.

For those of you who are still young, you don't have to decide how much you are going to leave your beneficiaries now, because you don't know what the value of your future estate will be. Instead, designate a percentage of your assets. And for those of you who designate financial assets, such as shares of stock or bond certificates, if you sell them before you die—but forget to remove them from your will—your estate will have to go out and re-purchase them to give to your heirs. Be careful!

REALLY? You cannot disinherit your spouse, according to some state laws. You must provide for your spouse if you are still married; he or she is entitled to at least one-third of your estate. The only way to eliminate this exception is through a pre-nuptial agreement. Check with your estate planning attorney for details.

➤ **It designates who handles the distribution of your assets.** This person is known as your *executor*, although there are also *trustees* and *guardians*. Typically, an executor is someone who you trust to handle the distribution of all of your financial affairs. An executor's responsibility is twofold: (1) follow through with the

In your will, give your beneficiary the right to change trustees on the basis of certain circumstances, so your will is not locked into a bank trust department that it can never get out of.

distribution of your assets and (2) comply with all tax rules and tax laws that apply to your estate. You need to find someone who is competent in handling this information.

A trustee can be a person, a financial institution (usually a bank, their "trust" department), or an investment professional. You can choose more than one trustee, although you should make sure you designate who gets the last word on important legal and tax matters relating to your estate.

➤ **It designates guardians when you have children and in the event you and your spouse die.** When divorce is involved, matters can get tricky, so make sure you review this material with your estate attorney.

➤ **It limits your estate tax liability as much as possible.** The amount of taxes owed is based on the size of the estate—and boy, at times, these owed taxes can be doozies! Current estate and federal tax laws say that taxes are due in cash nine months after the date of death. The amount of taxes you owe is based on the *Unified Tax Credit* rule that exempts the first $600,000 of an estate from federal taxes.

Here's how it limits your estate tax liability. For example, you can transfer any amount directly to your spouse (or a qualified trust—you'll learn more about this later on) *free of estate tax*. This is known as an *unlimited marital deduction*.

Let's plug in some numbers. If your estate is valued at $1 million, based on the unified tax credit (where $600,000 is exempt from estate taxes) you could use the unlimited marital deduction as follows:

Value of your estate:	$1,000,000
Unified tax credit:	600,000
Amount subject to estate taxes:	$400,000

But...

If you transfer or "bequeath" this amount to your spouse, making use of the *unlimited marital deduction*, watch what happens.

Remaining value of your estate, which is the amount subject to estate taxes:	$400,000
Transfer this amount to your spouse using the *unlimited marital deduction*:	$400,000
Amount subject to federal estate tax:	-0-

What happens when your spouse dies? Your heirs must pay estate taxes on anything that your spouse leaves to them, unless you implement a tax-saving plan that has been set up in your will. Make sure you review this information with your attorney, since each person's estate plan varies.

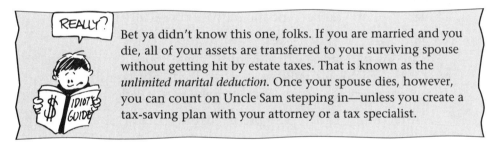

REALLY? Bet ya didn't know this one, folks. If you are married and you die, all of your assets are transferred to your surviving spouse without getting hit by estate taxes. That is known as the *unlimited marital deduction*. Once your spouse dies, however, you can count on Uncle Sam stepping in—unless you create a tax-saving plan with your attorney or a tax specialist.

If you have a will and you die, your will must be probated (remember that legal process?). During the *probate period*, the executor of your will notifies your beneficiaries and they get a copy of your will. Creditors are also notified of your death—usually a copy of the death notice published in the newspaper is sent to them—so they can present any outstanding debts to the executor. Your executor must also file your personal tax return *and* a separate tax return for your estate. Papers are filed in court while your executor evaluates your estate by:

➤ Taking inventory of your assets

➤ Having your assets valued

➤ Paying any outstanding debts

➤ Filing any necessary income tax returns

Once this process is complete, your executor will obtain an *Order of Distribution* (who gets what) from the court. Distributions are made, and then your estate is officially closed.

Keep in mind that even if you do have a will, your will *does not* protect your financial assets and should you become incapacitated while you are alive. But a durable power of attorney *does*. If you cannot handle your own financial affairs—paying bills, writing checks, making decisions about distribution of your financial assets—your heirs are going to have to petition to have a guardian or *conservator* named to run the show. Trust us, it's a pain in the keester. To avoid this hassle, consider setting up a durable power of attorney, since a will is effective only at your death. If you can't manage your own financial affairs, a durable power of attorney can help. It is a legal document that is also part of your estate plan. Most people with wills have this drawn up.

A *living will* must be enforced while you are alive, and it is different from a simple will. A living will states that you do not wish to be kept alive by life-support and special care by doctors. A living will is activated when you become mentally *or* physically incapacitated and recognizes your regret to die.

A copy of a living will should be given to your executor of your estate. These wills are valid (unless revoked), but you should review the document every five years or so to make sure it reflects your wishes.

After your will is legally prepared, all you do is sign it. Your attorney should keep a copy, but most importantly, make sure you make a copy and keep it in a safe place. Be careful—if you keep it in a safe deposit box and the bank closes, your executor or heirs will not be able to get to it!

Here are some problems with probate you should be aware of:

➤ The process of probate at times can take less than a year to finish, although it can take as long as *two years* to go through the entire process.

➤ With or without a will, your heirs will go through the process of probate. And guess what, folks? Probate costs are in addition to any federal or state taxes that your estate is responsible for. Many states' probate fees are based on the percentage gross of the estate's value. Legal fees have run as much as 10 percent of your estate's gross value, although you can shop around for an attorney. One guy we know found an attorney who charged only $100 to have his father's will probated—and it only took a month!

➤ When you go through probate, all your financial records and intimate financial details are public knowledge—no stone gets left unturned. All your financial affairs are public information and can be found in public records so anyone can see them.

If you need to make changes to your will, you can revoke the earlier will and replace it with a new one or add a *codicil*, which is an amendment, to the earlier will. A codicil can work in situations like when you have a child or get a divorce. If you sell a major asset that's listed in the will, you'll need a codicil, too, if you don't create a whole new will. Make sure you make additional copies of your new will or codicil and date the copies.

So how can you avoid probate? You can hold assets in *joint tenancy with rights of survivorship*. This means that everything you own automatically transfers to the survivor (usually a spouse, although it can be another person you designate) *without* going through probate court. But be careful: if you both die at the same time, chances are the estate will have to pay an enormous amount in estate taxes. Make sure you review this with your attorney because this may not be a good option for you, depending upon the value of your assets.

You can also give your assets away as gifts while you are still alive. Under current IRS law, you can give $10,000 a year (in cash or property) to each of any number of people without incurring a gift tax. But be careful; you don't know how long you will live, so you don't want to impoverish yourself.

Finally, if you want to avoid the hassles of probate you can set up a trust.

Setting Up a Trust

A trust does not save on estate taxes, but it does keep your private financial affairs just that—private. Plus, the whole mess of probate—its costs, its process, and the headaches—are avoided.

Who should have a trust? People who want their assets held separately for their young children often establish a trust. Trusts are also established for someone who is mentally or physically incapacitated.

403

A trust can either be *revocable* or *irrevocable.* A revocable trust allows you to change it or even cancel it any time after it is established. An irrevocable trust cannot be altered or cancelled at all. Why even set up an irrevocable trust? Because once you transfer your assets into this trust (and it doesn't have to be all of your assets) the trust becomes a separate taxable entity that pays taxes on the profits and income it generates. Therefore, when you die, the appreciation of those assets is not considered part of your estate and avoids estate taxes!

To determine whether you need a will or a trust, review your "Asset and Liability Worksheet" and your objectives with your attorney, since every person has a different set of circumstances. Typically, if your estate is substantial, the cost of settling a trust agreement will be lower than probating a will.

There are two types of trusts: *testamentary trust* and *living trust.* A testamentary trust is created within a will and it only goes into effect when you die. A living trust is just like it sounds—it operates while you are alive and is enforced once the trust is funded. The living trust can be revocable or irrevocable.

Your trust should specify the management and distribution of assets to your beneficiaries and make provisions for a trustee (who will be known as a *successor trustee* when you die) to manage your assets for the benefit of your heirs (unless you are the trustee in the living trust).

Where can you find estate planning attorneys? Contact the National Network of Estate Planning Attorneys, 410 17th Street, Suite 1260, Denver, Colorado 80202. Their phone number is (303) 446-6100. Also available are the Estate Planning Specialists at (800) 223-9610. Don't forget your local Bar Association when looking for an estate planning attorney in your area.

If you set up a living trust, you will change the title of all property you're placing in the trust from your name to the name of your trust. When you open up a trust, your account will be named similar to the following: "Joe Schmoe revocable trust dated __/__/__, Joe Schmoe trustee (or TTEE)." You can even have a checkbook and checks associated with your trust account. Just make sure you put "trustee" after your signature when you sign your name on those checks. Your trust can also be a joint trust, with you and your spouse listed as trustees.

To set up a revocable or irrevocable living trust, you need to contact an estate planning attorney. An example of how assets need to be changed—depending on which assets you are placing in the trust—is as follows:

➤ The title to your house, unless you have a mortgage, in which case you need to notify your lender. If a new deed to the house is required, the typical cost is about $30.

➤ Your investment accounts. You have to rename your brokerage accounts, your mutual fund accounts, even your bank CDs and your other major financial assets. To rename these accounts, write to your bank, broker-age firm, or mutual fund company, and enclose a certified copy of your entire trust document (the front and back pages *won't* work). Make sure you send everything by registered mail. It may be time-consuming, but it is worth is in the long run, especially since you don't have to go through probate.

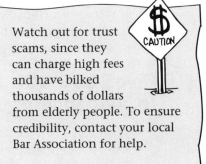

Watch out for trust scams, since they can charge high fees and have bilked thousands of dollars from elderly people. To ensure credibility, contact your local Bar Association for help.

➤ Your car, if it's an expensive one. But for those of you who aren't driving a Rolls, you don't have to transfer the title of your car to your trust. It's up to you.

For those assets that you keep outside of the trust, you will need a *pourover will*. This part of your estate will go through probate. Typically, these assets include your checking account, used cars, etc.

Creative Financial Strategies That Will Help You Now... and Then

To save some money on estate taxes, you might want to consider one of the following financial plans. No matter what creative strategy you use, you must consult with your tax advisor and your attorney to find out which plan will work best in your situation.

Give All Your Money to Your Spouse

A creative estate planning strategy—and probably the simplest to do—is to title most of your assets in *joint tenancy with rights of survivorship*.

This means that everything you own automatically transfers to the survivor (usually a spouse, although it can be another person you designate). You don't have to go through probate, and you can take advantage of the unlimited marital deduction. However, if you both die at the same time, chances are the estate will have to pay an enormous amount in estate taxes. Make sure you review this with your attorney because this may not be a good option for you, depending upon the value of your assets.

Give $600,000 to Your Kids and the Rest to Your Spouse

You can still take advantage of the unlimited marital deduction using this strategy and reduce your taxable estate when your spouse dies. Here's how it works: if your estate is worth $1 million and you give $600,000 to your kids, that $600,000 is not subject to estate taxes. The remaining $400,000 goes to your spouse, which is also exempt from estate taxes because of the unlimited marital deduction. But, its $600,000 *less* that would be subject to estate tax when he or she dies.

The A-B Trust

An A-B trust allows married couples and their families to save up to $1.2 million on estate taxes. First, every person gets a $600,000 exemption from estate taxes, which is the Unified Tax Credit. When you die, your estate is exempt from taxes of up to $600,000. If you're married, there's an additional perk: the unlimited marital deduction. There is no taxation on the estate upon the death of the first spouse; when the second spouse dies, everything over $600,000 is subject to estate taxes.

Make sure you address the situation of "simultaneous death" because of the tax consequences involved. Have your estate planning attorney include this information in your living trust documents.

With the A-B Trust, the "A" part of the trust (sometimes called the *marital trust*) goes to the surviving spouse, to be managed and used however he or she wants. You don't really save on taxes, you just get the unlimited marital deduction as the surviving spouse—and all the assets, too. The second part of the trust, the "B" part, is where the benefits kick in. When the surviving spouse dies, the first

$600,000 of assets are exempt from federal estate taxes. Those assets can grow above $600,000 within the trust, and even the growth of the assets is not subject to estate tax. Upon the death of the surviving spouse, the entire "B" trust will pass tax-free to the children or grandchildren for whom it was intended.

Here's a simple way to remember how this works. The "A" trust stands for "alive"—money that goes directly to the surviving spouse. The "B" trust stands for "buried"—money buried in a trust at the death of the first spouse, held in the trust until the second spouse dies, and then dispersed to children and grandchildren.

An Irrevocable Trust

Concerned about giving money to children or grandchildren who might spend it foolishly, but still fretting over your estate tax problems? Set up an *irrevocable trust*. In fact, you can set up as many of these as you want, depending on the number of beneficiaries you name. Each year you make your $10,000 gift to each trust. The trust will dictate when your heirs can receive the income or assets from the trust.

The Family Limited Partnership

Considered as a thorn in the government's side, this *family limited partnership* is still making its way through the legal system. It's a simple idea where a legal family limited partnership holds assets outside the taxable estate. One of the spouses, acting as general partner, holds 10 percent of the assets of the partnership. The remaining 90 percent of the assets are divided among the limited partners, who initially are husband and wife.

After the partnership has been set up, each year the parents give a small partnership interest to their kids, subject to the $10,000-per-year-per-person gift tax exclusion. Over a period of years, the children will own 90 percent limited-partner shares in the entire family limited partnership. The advantage is that the remaining 10 percent controls the 90 percent owned by the limited partners—the children. This controlling interest decides how the money is to be managed. Once this spouse dies, the surviving spouse receives controlling interest. The good part? Ninety percent of the assets are not subject to estate taxes once either spouse dies.

An Irrevocable Life Insurance Trust

It's a wee bit complicated, but here goes. By using the $10,000 annual gift exemption you're allowed, you use the gift money to pay the premiums on an insurance policy every year. (For a review of insurance strategies and how to find a strong insurance company, re-read Chapter 27.) Because the death benefits from a life insurance policy are considered part of the estate of the deceased, estate taxes will be owed.

Believe it or not, there's a special no-load mutual fund that allows you to set up an irrevocable trust account for your children or grandchildren. It is available from the Twentieth Century Giftrust Investors (800/345-2021). The catch? The money you gift to the children (or grandchildren) must stay in the fund for 10 years or until the child reaches the age of 18 or 21 (or whatever the majority age is for your state). Plus, any contributions you make to the fund must be reported on your tax return and taken against your $600,000 exemption. Fidelity has a fund similar to Twentieth Century's, too. Call (800) 544-8888 for information.

This is not the case if you set up an irrevocable life insurance trust. You can purchase the maximum amount of term or cash value life insurance on the life of a single person. In this case, the trust is the owner and beneficiary of the life insurance policy.

This is a popular method to saving on estate taxes because the insurance proceeds can be removed from your taxable estate (depending on the requirements, which you should review with your attorney). Plus, the insurance proceeds can be used to pay for death-related expenses, such as funeral costs or as wealth replacement for your heirs once you pay estate taxes. Or proceeds can pay estate taxes!

If you are the creator of the trust, you cannot be the trustee; you must appoint someone else who is independent of the trust. There is a checking account "attached" to the trust, which is used to pay the insurance premiums. Above all, make sure you review your options with your estate planning attorney before you do this, because it's a bit more involved.

Don't Give It Away, GIFT It Away

You can give up to $10,000 per year to any number of people, free from the unified estate and gift tax. So if you and your spouse want to give away $20,000 a year (while you're alive), that's $10,000 × 2 individuals = $20,000—happy giving! The rule of thumb is $10,000-per-parent-per-year-per-person if it's Mom and Dad. Why do this? Because you lower the value of your estate for tax purposes and the money is going to people who you probably would have named anyway as beneficiaries in your will when you die.

For example, you can make a gift to your favorite charity and deduct it on your income tax return. Current tax laws say you are entitled to an itemized deduction for cash contributions in an amount up to 50 percent of your adjusted gross income. This is only reflective in the year you make the contribution. Other tips on giving are in the following sections.

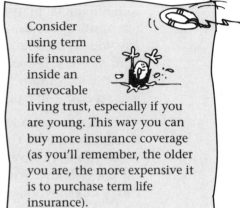

Consider using term life insurance inside an irrevocable living trust, especially if you are young. This way you can buy more insurance coverage (as you'll remember, the older you are, the more expensive it is to purchase term life insurance).

Educational Gifts to Grandchildren

In addition to the $10,000 gift provision per person per year that you are allowed and the $600,000 exemption, grandparents may make unlimited gifts of money for the education of their grandchildren—from kindergarten all the way to college—without incurring any gift taxes. All tuition payments must go directly to the institution and bypass the children.

But be careful; sometimes the IRS frowns upon this because of the income tax ramifications it puts on the parents of the grandchildren. The IRS has been known to consider the amount of the tuition payment as taxable to the parents because it relieved the parent of the legal obligation for support and education.

When giving monetary gifts to your grandchildren, be careful about the Generation-Skipping Transfer Tax. This tax is designed to prevent you from saving on estate taxes by skipping over your children—who then, upon their death, would have estate taxes due—and leaving money directly to your grandchildren. The tax cost on this? Up to 60 percent per generation.

CRT—Charitable Remainder Trust

Considered to be for the asset-rich-but-income-poor, the *charitable remainder trust (CRT)* has been dubbed the "ultimate tax shelter" by some financial planners. The CRT starts with a contribution of assets (cash, stock, bonds, etc.) into an irrevocable trust. The trustee agrees to pay you an income each year, either for your the rest of your life or a term of years. If you choose a term instead of life payments, Uncle Sam says the maximum term can only be 20 years; the minimum payout you receive is five percent.

There are two kinds of CRTs: the *CRUT* (Charitable Remainder UniTrust) and the *CRAT* (Charitable Remainder Annuity Trust). CRUTs allow you to make additional contributions to the trust in the future; the CRAT allows you to make a one-time deposit. To understand how a CRUT might work, consider this example:

George and Betty decided to fund their CRUT initially with $250,000 worth of stock they purchased 20 years ago for $25,000. Because the CRUT is tax-exempt, the trustee (remember: an independent person!) sells George and Betty's stock *tax-free* and reinvests the proceeds into income-producing assets.

Here's where the fun begins. If George and Betty want to receive annual income—they're both retired and need additional monthly income (recall the senior money strategies in Chapter 21)—they can do so. So they decide they want monthly payments for 15 years and to have the CRUT pay out nine percent each year. That means their income would be in the ballpark of $23,000 a year. Plus there's a substantial tax deduction they can take on the income tax returns.

The benefits of a charitable remainder trust are that you can give the assets to your favorite charity at a future date, get current tax breaks, and still receive a stream of income from the gifted assets during your lifetime. In George and Betty's case, their tax break came when they didn't have to pay any capital gains taxes on the $225,000 profit they received from selling their stock. ($250,000 [current value] – $25,000 [initial purchase] = $225,000 [profit].)

Don't place all your assets in a charitable trust, however, especially if you have heirs to whom you want to leave something when you die. In addition, set up an irrevocable trust for your children. This way you're reducing your capital gains taxes *and* getting current tax benefits, reducing the size of your taxable estate, leaving some of your financial assets to your heirs, giving a contribution to your favorite charity, and still receiving income.

The Least You Need to Know

➤ By setting up a will, you can designate beneficiaries that your assets will go to and who will be in charge of wrapping up your financial affairs. If you don't make a will, the state you live in will make these decisions for you.

➤ Although it won't save you estate taxes, setting up a living trust will spare your heirs the pain of probate, and it will keep your financial affairs private.

➤ You can save on estate taxes by using the unlimited marital deduction, setting up an A-B trust, a family limited partnership, an irrevocable trust, or an irrevocable life insurance trust. Make sure you check with your lawyer or tax advisor before attempting to set these up.

➤ You can make sure your money goes to the beneficiaries you want it to go to—without getting tied up in taxes—by giving it to them when you're alive. Gifts under $10,000 are not susceptible to gift taxes.

Index

Symbols

PLUG YOURSELF INTO...

THE MACMILLAN INFORMATION SUPERLIBRARY™

Free information and vast computer resources from the world's leading computer book publisher—online!

FIND THE BOOKS THAT ARE RIGHT FOR YOU!

A complete online catalog, plus sample chapters and tables of contents give you an in-depth look at *all* of our books, including hard-to-find titles. It's the best way to find the books you need!

- **STAY INFORMED** with the latest computer industry news through our online newsletter, press releases, and customized Information SuperLibrary Reports.

- **GET FAST ANSWERS** to your questions about MCP books and software.

- **VISIT** our online bookstore for the latest information and editions!

- **COMMUNICATE** with our expert authors through e-mail and conferences.

- **DOWNLOAD SOFTWARE** from the immense MCP library:
    - Source code and files from MCP books
    - The best shareware, freeware, and demos

- **DISCOVER HOT SPOTS** on other parts of the Internet.

- **WIN BOOKS** in ongoing contests and giveaways!

TO PLUG INTO MCP: ➞

GOPHER: gopher.mcp.com

FTP: ftp.mcp.com

WORLD WIDE WEB: http://www.mcp.com